TWELVE INDIAN STATESMEN

TWELVE INDIAN STATESMEN

GEORGE SMITH

GYAN

Published by

Gyan Publishing House
5, Ansari Road
Daryaganj, New Delhi-110002
Phone: 011-47034999, 9811692060
E-mail: books@gyanbooks.com

Distribution Network
gyanbooks.com
India, USA, Canada, UK, Australia

ISBN: 978-93-6920-596-7 (PB)

First Published, 1897

2nd Impression 2025

Printed at: Gyan Press, Delhi.

TWELVE INDIAN STATESMEN
Author: GEORGE SMITH

TWELVE INDIAN STATESMEN

CHARLES GRANT

From the Portrait by Sir Henry Raeburn—in the Castle at Inverness.

TWELVE INDIAN STATESMEN

BY

GEORGE SMITH, C.I.E., LL.D.

FELLOW OF THE ROYAL GEOGRAPHICAL AND ROYAL STATISTICAL SOCIETIES

Οἱ διὰ πίστεως κατηγωνίσαντο βασιλείας, εἰργάσαντο δικαιοσύνην

LONDON

JOHN MURRAY, ALBEMARLE STREET

1897

DEDICATION[1]

"To all my Countrymen who care for India, and especially to the young whose lot is to be cast in it; to show how possible and good it is to unite the Statesman with the Soldier, the Philanthropist with the Patriot, and the Christian with all, in the Government of a Subject Race."

[1] Written by Sir Herbert Edwardes as the Dedication for his *Life of Sir Henry Lawrence*, which he did not live to complete.

PREFACE

The Twelve Statesmen sketched in this volume were chief among the Empire-builders of the nineteenth century. Eight of them were identified with the conflicting policies of the two Afghan and two Sikh wars of the last half-century, which have resulted in the Russo-Afghan peace and the present subjugation of the independent tribes of the Frontier. Except the first, I had the good fortune to know them all, and to count some of them as intimate friends. It is an accident, but all the more significant on that account, that the twelve unconsciously revealed that strain of Puritanism which has been said to mark the greatest and most zealous patriotism.

Charles Grant was the first to work out the ethical principles on which alone Great Britain could found its Indian Empire; he also had the chief influence in educating public opinion, and persuading Parliament to give these principles active authority. They were applied to the Princes and to the Army of India by Henry Lawrence; to its Peoples by John Lawrence. The brothers having become leaders of the two great schools of Anglo-Indian administration, Henry Lawrence had as his disciples James Outram, Herbert Edwardes, Henry Marion Durand, and Colin

MACKENZIE; John Lawrence was followed by HENRY RAMSAY and CHARLES AITCHISON. The Historian who recorded and the Journalist who continuously influenced much of the Imperial policy on Puritan lines was JOHN MARSHMAN. The Jurist who justified and applied these principles to the India of the Queen-Empress, embodying them in legislative forms so that they became fruitful for ever, was HENRY MAINE.

The only Governor-General among the twelve was John Lawrence. Hereafter, I hope to review, historically, the acts of the whole series, from the Marquess of Dalhousie to the Earl of Elgin II. Then also it may be possible to do justice to other workers with whom I have been associated, such as Sir Henry Yule and Sir Henry Daly, Sir George Campbell and Sir Bartle Frere, Dr. John Muir and Sir William Mackinnon. The missionary statesmen I have already sketched on a more elaborate scale. Sir Richard Temple has told his own story. Lord Roberts has written the narrative of his brilliant career in a book which must live as long as our Empire and Army of India. The other great Field-Marshal, Sir Donald Stewart, Mr. Meredith Townsend, Dr. William Miller, Sir William Muir, Sir Henry Norman, Sir Richard and Sir John Strachey, and others, are still happily spared to their country.

I thank William Canton, Esq., for his great courtesy.

G. S.

SERAMPORE HOUSE, MERCHISTON,
EDINBURGH, 24*th August* 1897.

CONTENTS

TWELVE INDIAN STATESMEN

I

CHARLES GRANT, 1746–1823

First and Greatest of Indian Philanthropists

The life of the purest and the ablest statesman whom Scotland, if not the United Kingdom, has ever sent to India, has yet to be written. In the seventy-seven years ending 1823 Charles Grant lived, a servant of the East India Company, in Bengal, and then Chairman of its Court of Directors; a Member of Parliament, and father of two statesmen as pure as himself and only less able—Lord Glenelg and Sir Robert Grant, Governor of Bombay. Charles Grant saw and mitigated the greatest famine on record, which swept off four millions of human beings in Bengal, Behar, and Orissa, a century and a quarter ago. He purged the Company's government of abuses at the worst period of its history. A friend of the great missionary, Schwartz, and succourer of Kiernander, the first Protestant missionary to Bengal, he helped William Carey to Serampore, he sent out the evangelical chaplains through Simeon, he founded

Haileybury College, he was the chief agent in the institution of the Church Missionary and Bible Societies, he fought for the freedom of the African slave as wisely as for the enlightenment of the caste-bound Hindu. He was the authority from whom Wilberforce derived at once the impulse and the knowledge which gained the first battles for toleration in the East India Company's charters of 1793 and 1813. Above all, Charles Grant wrote in 1792 the noblest treatise on the Asiatic subjects of Great Britain, and the means of improving their moral condition, which the English language has even yet seen. Printed by the House of Commons in 1813, that too is forgotten, like its author. But in both the historian of the civilisation of our Indian Empire will recognise the most remarkable factors of the progress and the happiness of a population amounting, a century after, to two hundred and eighty-six millions of human beings.

On the southern shore of Loch Ness, near the point where it narrows into the Caledonian Canal and the swift river Ness, stands Aldourie House embosomed in woods. Here was born Sir James Mackintosh. Near this, twenty years before him, on 16th April 1746, in Aldourie farmhouse, Charles Grant first saw the light. Not far off, at the very hour of his boy's birth, the father was fighting for Charles Edward Stuart on the field of Culloden, where he was severely wounded. Suffering incredible hardships, he remained in hiding for two years, while his little property was almost ruined from depredations. As a volunteer with the prospect of a commission, which he obtained, he joined one of two Highland regiments raised to reinforce the army in America, and at the siege of the Havana held a small fort through the extremes of famine till he was relieved. His solitary wife was helped to bring up her children by Grant of Shewglie, the head of the family, whose own father had died in prison a victim of the rebellion.

The father, Alexander Grant, in a deed of 1742 is described as tacksman, or tenant, of Easter Inchbrine, Glen Urquhart. He was descended from the Chiefs of Grant, as shown in the pedigrees at the end of Sir William Fraser's authoritative record of the great clan. He married Margaret Macbean, daughter of one of the Macbeans of Kinkyle, who held the Aldourie farm. On both sides the Grants and Macbeans were active supporters of the rebellion. When Alexander Grant left Glen Urquhart with two of Shewglie's sons for the Highland army, he seems to have taken his wife to her father's farm, where their boy was born, and was named after the Prince. Thence the mother and her family returned to Glen Urquhart.

In his accurate and delightful book, *Urquhart and Glen Moriston: Olden Times in a Highland Parish*,[1] Mr. William Mackay of Inverness pictures the surroundings of the valley, and the village, in which the future colleague of the Governor-General and chief ruler of India from Leadenhall Street was trained for his benevolent career. On the north side of Loch Ness,

[1] In 600 royal octavo pages, published in 1893 by the Northern Counties Publishing Company, Inverness.

in the heart of Urquhart, nestling at the foot of a hill and looking forth on the little strath formed by the Enerick stream, stood the village of Milntown. There the Scottish Society for the Propagation of Christian Knowledge had, in 1732, opened one of its free schools. To that Mrs. Grant sent her boy. There, on the classic Braes of Glen Urquhart, in scenery so lovely that it is called by Robert Chambers the Tempe of Scotland, the child grew in all the rudimentary knowledge and God-fearing life of a Scottish Highland parish, a scion of one of the greatest of the Jacobite families of the North. This ancestral home[1] was shut in by hills and forests, and could then be entered only by the rocky peninsula jutting out into Loch Ness, where from ancient days the "royal" castle of Urquhart had guarded the independence of the country. By roads and canal the land was long after opened up chiefly through Charles Grant.

From Milntown the lad was sent to the best school in the North, then in Elgin. Just when he left school there arrived in the town, on his yearly visit from Cromarty, the principal merchant and shipowner of the North, Mr. William Forsyth.[2] "Pleased with his appearance and the simple ingenuousness of his manners," Forsyth carried off Charles Grant to Cromarty,

[1] In 1737 Lord Lovat wrote thus of Charles Grant's father: "One Alexander Grant, a soldier in Captain Grant's company, and son to Robert Grant in Milntown, a cousin-german of Shewglie's." From being the son of Robert he was generally known as "MacRobert."

[2] His Life was the first book published, in 1839, by Hugh Miller. It appears in the tenth volume of his works under the title of *A True Story of the Life of a Scotch Merchant of the Eighteenth Century* (William P. Nimmo, 1883).

where the boy spent five years of his youth as a clerk under the very best conditions for the development of character. Books, friends, and the spiritual influence of his master, combined with business habits to make him the wise and upright statesman he became. When a Director of the East India Company he showed his gratitude alike to the Forsyths, and to the Urquharts who had helped his mother in his childhood, by sending several youths bearing these names to the Indian services.

From Cromarty Charles Grant moved to London, where he joined the office of Alexander Grant of Shewglie, one of the two brothers who had accompanied his father to Culloden, from which he fled to Bengal where he served under Clive. On the battlefield of Plassey he atoned for Culloden. Returning to London, he carried on business as an East India Merchant in Bedford Row. There, in April 1765, Charles Grant became one of his clerks. Having mastered the details in a few months, he set his face towards the East. In a letter dated London, 27th September 1766, to the Captain's brother (as the hero of Culloden and Plassey was always called), Patrick Grant of Lochletter, Charles writes: "I am in hopes of getting ready for India by next spring, of which I am the more impatient, as the good accounts which we have lately received inflame me more with the desire of being there." A youth of twenty-one, he landed at Calcutta in the year 1767. That was a time of attempted reform in Bengal. Clive had just bid a final farewell to India, having put down a mutiny of the

European officers, and checked the corruption of the underpaid civil servants. Richard Becher, an upright member of Council, was on the look-out for young administrators of his own stamp, and at once laid hold of the grave Highlander.

He might well be grave, for he had not been a year under Becher, at the court of Murshidabad, the Musalman capital of Bengal, when the great famine was upon the country. For two seasons not a drop of rain had fallen on the rice-fields of Bengal. The insufferable heat of 1769 burned up every kind of grain or pulse.

"Rice rose gradually to four, and at length to ten, times its usual price, but even at that rate was not to be had. If the people had seen that the calamities of that period proceeded from human hands, they would not have borne them; they would have helped themselves to grain, perhaps have risen upon their European masters. No, they well knew and acknowledged whence their distresses came; they foresaw them in the drought of successive seasons, a drought not confined to their provinces; and felt in them the dispensation of a superior Power. This was one of those severe inflictions of the Almighty, by which offending creatures, who forget their Maker, are reminded of His being and of His government of the universe. Those poor people sought by superstitious observances to propitiate their deities, but they were '*Gods that could not save*,' and their votaries remained without any moral change."

Such is a bit of the picture drawn by the young adventurer, as he and Becher worked night and day to save the people. Having secured what proved to be an insufficient store for the Sepoys, without whom society would have gone to pieces, they fed daily seven thousand in the city. All the cultivators fled who could, and the rest died as the months went on till September 1770, when Becher officially reported: "Certain it is that, in several parts, the living have fed on the dead, and the number that have perished is as six to sixteen of the whole inhabitants." Worn out, Charles Grant returned home to find his leader and the Company traduced all over Europe, by their French rivals, as having caused the famine. With the calm skill of an economist who had learned to know the people, he showed that two-thirds of the usual crops had failed, that monopoly had not existed, and that Becher was a man noted for his honesty and humanity, whose exertions to alleviate the miseries of that whole period ended in an illness that almost cost him his life.

Having married Jane, a daughter of the Frasers of Balnain, and obtained a writership, he returned to Bengal with his wife's mother and sister and Lieutenant Fergusson, a friend of the family. During the long voyage of the East Indiaman in those days duels, or the occasions of duelling, as we know from Clive's experience, were only too frequent. Provoked to fight at Cape Town, young Fergusson was killed by Captain Roche, under circumstances which led Charles Grant to demand justice from the Dutch authorities. Failing to obtain it, he afterwards applied to the India Government, which sent Roche home to stand his trial. The case became famous in the history and the ethics of duelling during the two subsequent years. Grant's action led to such discussion that public opinion began to set in against a practice which has long since been estimated at its true level of baseness.

At Madras another event occurred which suggested to Grant the advocacy of the only effectual means of raising the moral condition of the people of Asia and of the Company's servants—Christian missionaries and ministers. He and his family found an old friend there, the early Orientalist William Chambers, who was soon afterwards to follow them to Bengal as Master in Chancery in the court of which his brother was to be Chief-Justice, and to become Grant's brother-in-law. Chambers introduced Grant to Schwartz. The blessing of the already old missionary rested on the young civilian, who took with him as a faithful steward O'Beck, one of his disciples, and kept up a close correspondence with the apostle of South India till the end of the century. When Schwartz died it was Grant who induced the East India Company to erect in St. Mary's Church, Fort George, Madras, a marble monument in memory of the missionary whose political services to the British Government had proved second only to his life-long sacrifices for the people of South India.

Landing the second time at Calcutta, on the 23rd June 1773, Charles Grant found Warren Hastings, the first Governor-General, hard at work on the new administrative system, begun under the Act of the previous year. The youth of twenty-seven was just in time to do his part. First as Factor and then as Secretary to the Board of Trade, for eight years he won such a reputation that Hastings officially commended him to the Court of Directors as "a very deserving servant," and then gave him the prize of the service, sending him up-country to Malda as commercial Resident in charge of their great silk filature. Here he was virtually lord over a whole province, making advances to the peasantry for the breeding of silkworms and cultivation of the mulberry, buying the cocoons, reeling them off in a vast factory, and manufacturing the thread into the pure creamy yellow silk which then distanced the dragon fabrics of China in the markets of Europe. For this the salary was great, and the hospitality was correspondingly splendid. But this appointment supplied only a part of the Resident's income. Under definite rules he received a commission on all articles purchased as the Company's trading investment, and he was encouraged to carry out a private trade which should not interfere with the prosperity of the Company. Money flowed in on him so fast that his scrupulous conscience was quickened.

Careful examination showed him that he was acting with a strict regard to rule, but to avoid every appearance of evil he asked the Governor-General to have his private books examined along with his public accounts. Lord Cornwallis had just entered on the office, and was keen in reforming the abuse of perquisites to eke out salaries. He himself eagerly overhauled the Malda accounts, and returned them with the compliment of an official wish that all the servants of the Honourable Company were equally scrupulous. His Excellency at once promoted him further, in 1787, to the direct superintendence of the whole trade of the Company in Bengal. In that position Charles Grant exposed a series of systematic frauds, which would soon have proved fatal to the Company's chief staple. A few more years and he himself must have been made Governor-General instead of his friend and junior, Shore, afterwards Lord Teignmouth, when his wife's health hastened him home. Lord Cornwallis declared his services to be so essential to the interests of the Government that for any less urgent reason he would have insisted on his remaining in India.

Grant's "private trade" consisted of an indigo estate within the widespread ruins of Gaur, which he had placed under Mr. H. Creighton, one of the first Englishmen to care for the education of the natives of Bengal in their mother-tongue and in the vernacular Bible. Gaur had been, from prehistoric times, the capital of Bengal under its Hindu sovereigns, when it stood on the sacred Ganges. In 1204 the Musalmans conquered the country, and Gaur continued as the capital for three hundred years, when the Afghans stripped it to adorn their new and now ruined metropolis of Panduah. Covering at least twenty square miles of ruins still, Gaur must have contained a population of at least three-quarters of a million in its palmy days. For centuries the place has been a quarry for cities like Murshidabad and even Calcutta. When Charles Grant was there he was liberally interested in the building of St. John's Church, afterwards the cathedral of Middleton and Heber. The writer of that rare work, *Historical and Ecclesiastical Sketches of Bengal until the Virtual Conquest of that Country by the English in* 1757,[1] rescues for us a letter of Grant's, written on the laying of the foundation stone of the church by Warren Hastings in 1784.

"The most remarkable letter I find recorded on this occasion is that from Mr. Charles Grant, then residing at Malda, which, as it contains some observations respecting the ruins of the ancient and renowned city of Gaur, I will make such quotations from as may be acceptable to the speculative traveller and historian.

"'MALDA, *9th June* 1784.—I imagine a number of stones sufficient for the pavement of the New Church may be collected from the ruins of Gaur. The stones are of various sizes, many from a foot to two feet long, seven inches to fifteen broad, and seldom less than six inches deep. They are of a blue colour; those I have occasionally viewed have appeared to be hewn on three sides, but not polished. All the remains of Gaur are unquestionably the property of Government, which we may dispose of at pleasure, as was the custom of the Soubahdars.

"'It may not be amiss to add, that besides these stones, which are used in the buildings of Gaur, there are among the ruins a few huge masses, which appear to be of blue marble and have a fine polish. The most remarkable of these covered the tombs of the kings of Gaur, whence they were removed about fifteen years ago (1768-69) by a Major Adams, employed in surveying, who intended to send them to Calcutta, but not being able to weigh them into boats, they still remain on the banks of the river. Some time since I was desired to give my aid in procuring blocks

[1] Printed at Calcutta, 1831.

of marble from Gaur for a private use, but as I knew not how to comply, unless these masses which are real curiosities were broken in parts, I rather declined. The present occasion is, however, of a different nature. They are already removed from their original situations, and if any use can be made of them entire for the church, they would there be best preserved, as indeed they deserve to be. There are also some smaller stones, polished and ornamented with sculptures of flowers, fretwork, etc., and a few freestone of great length.'"

"Under deep concern about the state of my soul," as he long after told the Rev. Joseph Ivimey,[1] Charles Grant had landed the second time at Calcutta. "There was no person then living in Calcutta from whom I could obtain any information as to the way of a sinner's salvation." At last he betook himself to Kiernander, the Swedish evangelist trained under Francke at Halle, sent by the Christian Knowledge Society to Cuddalore, and thence invited to Calcutta by Clive when the French war extinguished the mission. With his wife's fortune he had just built the only church which then supplied the city after its sack by Suraj-ood-Dowlah, and through the Portuguese language conducted a mission to natives and Romanists. It must have been at the time when the pecuniary troubles brought upon him by his sons had begun to affect him that the young Grant called on him, and this incident took place. "I found him lying on his couch. My anxious inquiries as to what I should do to be saved appeared to embarrass and confuse him exceedingly; and when I left him the

[1] *Baptist Magazine* for 1828, p. 254.

perspiration was running from his face in consequence, as it appeared to me, of his mental distress. He could not answer my question, but he gave me some good instructive books." While pitying, Grant soon learned to appreciate the sincerity of the old man.

The twenty-one years of Charles Grant's residence in Bengal, from 1767 to 1790, with an interval at home, cover the time when Christianity was so dead among the baptized residents of Calcutta and North India that Dr. Thomas publicly advertised for a Christian to help him in "the more effectually spreading the knowledge of Jesus Christ, and His glorious Gospel, in and about Bengal," and found one in James Wittet, a shopkeeper, who told him of Mr. Charles Grant and the family at Malda. On their removal to Calcutta two years after, at the end of 1786, Grant found both David Brown, afterwards the first evangelical chaplain of the Church of England, and Dr. Thomas, the erratic Baptist surgeon of one of the East Indiamen. To both, as representing the Anglican and Nonconformist divisions of English Christendom, he submitted the first scheme for bringing out and supporting eight missionaries in North India, each on £350 a year. Meanwhile he proposed to maintain Thomas if he would reside at Malda, and there preach the Gospel. Practically this meant the formation in India itself of the first missionary society so early as the year 1786. Owing to the jealous temper and provoking debts of Thomas on the one hand, and the inability of Charles Simeon at Cambridge to find English clergymen willing to sacrifice themselves as missionaries on the other, the loving generosity and foresight of Grant were defeated. Thomas went home, and accompanied William Carey back to Bengal. The efforts of Grant in England, and of Brown and the godly chaplains in Bengal, resulted at a much later time in the formation of the Church Missionary Society.

Thus baulked for a time, like the Haldanes, who projected a similar plan later on and sold the estate of Airthrey to endow it, "Mr. and Mrs. Grant, with about eight or nine others, dependants, serving God," as Thomas then described them, gave themselves to the support and extension of all that was earnest and aggressive in practical religion in Calcutta. The chaplains then were hopeless, and even long afterwards they persecuted Henry Martyn while they made fortunes in trade. But Kiernander was doing his best to propagate the Gospel. In 1770 he raised money from Grant and others for what is still known and used as the Mission Church and property. When his failure brought it to the hammer, Grant prevented the outrage by at once paying down 10,000 Sicca Rupees, about £1250, and placing it under a trust, which secures it for ever to the Church Missionary Society. In all the then infant philanthropic institutions of Calcutta which he founded or fostered, Charles Grant, his family and friends, were foremost, while his sound judgment was ever in request in their management.

The winter of 1790-91 found Charles Grant and his wife happily settled near London, with a family of three sons and two daughters, of whom the eldest boy, the future Lord Glenelg, was then twelve years of age. He became one of the group of statesmen and philanthropists whom Sydney Smith, in the *Edinburgh Review*, dubbed "The Clapham Sect," a name which Sir James Stephen has immortalised in one of his charming "Essays in Ecclesiastical Biography." By Clapham Common, Battersea Rise, the good and the then great merchant and Member of Parliament for Southwark, Henry Thornton, had found a mansion, for which William Pitt planned an oval saloon. That lofty library became the council chamber of the men who, from 1792 to 1833, introduced the modern missionary era, abolished the slave trade, reformed the constitution of British India, and did much to liberalise the institutions of Great Britain itself. For Charles Grant Thornton built one house separated from his own by shrubberies, and another for the brother-in-law of Pitt, Eliot, who was there succeeded by Wilberforce. In this wainscotted hall, its walls covered with books save where it looked forth on forest glades and grassy lawns, these men met, with Babington and Zachary Macaulay, Granville Sharp and Clarkson, Lord Teignmouth and James Stephen, John Newton and Hannah More, Lord Muncaster and Charles Simeon, John Venn and Daniel Wilson, and, occasionally, stray visitors to London like Dr. Marshman from far Serampore and Dr. Chalmers from St. Andrews. In all the deliberations of such men that related to India Charles Grant was first, inspiring his friends to action not less by the soundness of his judgment and his lofty principles than by the ripeness of his past experience, and the influence derived from his daily duties in Leadenhall Street.

He had not settled down in the delightful ease of his new home, after the years of his busy exile in Bengal, when he was summoned to conflict by the discussions which ended in the renewal of the East India Company's charter in 1793. A loyal servant of the Company and one of its proprietors, he could not continue to tolerate its failure to play the part of a Christian or, at least, a moral ruler of the twenty-four millions of Asiatics whom Providence had put under its sway at that time. So in the quiet of his first summer in leafy Clapham, and with the independence of one who was for a brief time free from office, he wrote the first draft of the *Observations on the State of Society among the Asiatic Subjects of Great Britain, particularly with respect to Morals and on the Means of improving it.* With no more education of a literary kind than could be got by a boy in Elgin in the middle of last century, Charles Grant distrusted his writing powers, though the "minute" system which then and still takes the place in India of our Parliamentary chatter had given him a special training. So he kept his paper concealed even from the friends in the library which Pitt had designed for his neighbour, Henry Thornton. But when the conflict over the charter approached a climax in April 1793, and the General Court of Proprietors, of whom he was one, met to discuss "the pious clauses" of the Bill, which he seems to have drafted for Wilberforce, he resolved to seek election to a chair, and soon after he became a director of the East India Company in his forty-ninth year. When, in the next three years, he had established his influence with his colleagues, he revised his *Observations* and submitted the work to them as "One of those many 'Papers of Business' with which the records of your governments have been furnished by the observation and experience of men whose time and thought have been chiefly employed in the concerns of active life." The treatise was the guide of his own official action, and its influence constantly reappears in many of the noble despatches written to the Government at Calcutta by himself and by his son from the Board of Control. It was not published till the discussions on the next twenty years' charter of 1813 led the House of Commons to order that it be printed. The copy before me belonged to William Carey and afterwards to Dr. Marshman.

What Carey's *Enquiry,* written in 1786 at the shoemaker's stall, is to Foreign Missions, that, produced six years after, is the work of the retired Bengal Civilian to the whole history of India and its civilisation. For one thing, Grant lived for thirty years afterwards, with the power and the influence to apply his principles to practical legislation and administration. But this fact should not hide from us the truth, calmly stated, that his treatise anticipates, in principle and often in detail, all the great moral and not a few of the political reforms of the century in India. The work contains one hundred and twelve folio pages, and is divided into four chapters. In the first twenty pages we find an historical review of the British territorial administration for the thirty years after Clive's victory at Plassey, showing how, after superseding Portugal, Holland, and France, the fourth Power of Great Britain had become responsible for the weal of millions, so that "all the duties of rulers are incumbent on us." In the next twenty, in the spirit of the Master who had compassion on the Asiatics of His day being as sheep without a shepherd, Charles Grant tells the truth as to the low moral condition of the Hindu subjects of Great Britain. The picture he draws from their own literature, his own experience, and that of the few experts up to that time, is wonderfully correct still, even of the Zanana system, and he shows that from the government and intermixture of the Mohammedans the Hindus had certainly derived no improvement of character. His object is "to engage compassion, and to make it apparent that what speculation may have ascribed to physical and unchangeable causes, springs from moral sources capable of correction." In forty pages the writer traces the causes of the demoralisation to the Hindu religion and priests.

It is in the thirty-eight pages of what we may call the Remedies that the statesmanlike observation and foresight of Charles Grant appear most brightly. "The true cure of darkness is the introduction of light," and that he would give in the four forms of the English language and literature; western mechanical science; improved modes of agriculture, "the skilful application of fire, of water, and of steam"; "but undoubtedly the most important communication which the Hindus could receive through the medium of our language would be the knowledge of our religion." These are wonderful pages to have been written in the year 1792, the year in which modern missions were being begun by Carey's Society, thirty-seven years before Duff was chosen to go out, and more than forty years before he led Lord William Bentinck and Macaulay to introduce, legislatively, the "new era of the English language." Some of the sentences read like predictions: where, for instance, he forecasts what has happened in the colonisation of South Africa and Australasia, and estimates the relative advantages and results of the English and the vernacular languages. He anticipates the present transition period of the social system of India when, if the Christian Government failed to do its duty, the people "would be loosened from their own religious prejudices, not by the previous reception of another system in their stead, but by becoming indifferent to every system." He even pictures the political danger, the first symptoms of which we already lament, when the tendency to imitate that freedom in manners, that latitude as to religious opinions and observances, which they see in their European masters, may result in discontent and anarchy. "By planting our language, our knowledge, our opinions, and our religion in our Asiatic territories, we shall put a great work beyond the reach of contingencies; we shall probably have wedded the inhabitants of those territories to this country; but, at any rate, we shall have done an act of strict duty to them and a lasting service to mankind."

Although in 1793 Parliament remained satisfied with

voting, in mere resolutions which were not incorporated in the Act, the substance of Charles Grant's *Observations*, he got them carried out in the next charter of 1813. In 1793 he asked permission only that thirty missionaries, "if proper persons," should be allowed to settle in India at an annual charge to their supporters, including dwellings, of £14,000. Refused that, he outflanked the intolerant Company, of which he soon became Chairman, and the House of Commons in which he sat for nineteen years, by the happy device of recommending Marshman, Ward, and the others who went out to Carey at the end of the eighteenth century, to settle under the Danish Government at Serampore. Meanwhile, helped by Simeon, he took care that the only chaplains sent out to Bengal were men like the Scottish Buchanan, the Cornish Henry Martyn, and the English Corrie, Thomason, and Dealtry. For in 1813 he had triumphed in the charter, which not only organised a double establishment of bishops and chaplains for the British settlers in India, but practically allowed missionaries and teachers free access to the natives, and granted funds for the enlightened education of the people,—till now there are five millions of young people in the inspected schools of all kinds, and many of these are girls.

Next to the writing of his *Observations*, the greatest thing Charles Grant did was to influence Wilberforce, by information and inspiration. Living in adjoining houses, meeting in the same haunts daily during a whole generation, active members of the House of Commons, and communicants in the same parish church,

Wilberforce, Grant, and Thornton were inseparable, and the enlightened zeal and energy of their character gradually carried all those reforms which have marked the period as "the era of benevolence" in the history of modern evangelical Christianity.

As twice Deputy-Chairman and twice Chairman of the Court of Directors, Charles Grant identified himself with the conservative interests of the Company, a fact which gave the more authority to his conscientious advocacy of Christian principles. He was the friend of Cornwallis, Sir George Barlow, and Lord William Bentinck, rather than of Lord Wellesley. He founded Haileybury College for the education of the young civilians appointed by patronage. He was one of the Commission for erecting new churches on which a Parliamentary grant of a million sterling was spent. He was an active office-bearer of the British and Foreign Bible Society, the Anglican and the Highland Societies for Promoting Christian Knowledge, the African Institution in the interest of the slaves, and the South Sea Company. He was, of course, a director of the Church Missionary Society. He introduced Sunday Schools into Scotland, and for twenty years was himself a Sunday School teacher. His own ancestral Highlands, north of Inverness, and the good of the scattered Gaelic-speaking peasantry, were ever his care, notwithstanding his apparent absorption in the imperial philanthropies of the Indies, East and West. He was the principal promoter of the Caledonian Canal and the Highland Roads and Bridges Act. He purchased the estate of Waternish in Skye.

Charles Grant's was the joy of seeing his two sons follow in his footsteps, and rise to eminence alike as statesmen and Christian men. Young Charles and Robert Grant were distinguished students at the University of Cambridge. When a Fellow of Magdalene College, Charles, in 1805, won the prize offered by Dr. Claudius Buchanan for a poem on the Restoration of Learning in the East. Robert Grant printed from time to time these sacred poems,[1] which, as collected by his brother, and republished in successive editions down to 1868, have given him a high place among English Hymnologists.[2] His two Sketches of its History, and his companion volume on the Expediency of Maintaining its System, both published in 1813, are the most valuable contributions to the annals of the East India Company at that critical time, and practically shaped the Charter of 1813. The friend of John Wilson, as his father had been of Schwartz and Carey, Sir Robert Grant died when Governor of Bombay. The elder brother succeeded his father as Member of Parliament for Inverness-shire in 1819, till he was raised to the peerage as Lord Glenelg in 1836, after holding three Cabinet offices.

When President of the Board of Control he virtually governed India, as his father had done when at the head of the Court of Directors. When the Charter of 1833 was passed by Parliament, he chose Daniel Wilson, his father's friend when Vicar of Islington, to be the first Metropolitan of India, and Daniel Corrie to be the first

[1] *Sacred Poems*, by the late Right Hon. Sir Robert Grant. London (Longmans).

[2] Julian's *Dictionary* (John Murray).

Bishop of Madras. To him England owes the Despatch of 20th February 1833, thus removing for ever the scandal of the active patronage of idolatry in India by a Christian Empire, which, nevertheless, was intolerant to its own national and catholic faith. So his father had written and sent out the Court of Directors' Despatch of 25th May 1798, which, in dignified terms, forbids such systematic "profanations of the Sabbath" as Sunday racing and card-playing, and enjoins that divine service be regularly performed. Such a sentence as this, written in 1798, received a terrible commentary in the Mutiny of 1857, and was unconsciously reiterated by John Lawrence when too late: "To preserve the ascendency which our national character has acquired over the minds of the natives of India must ever be of importance to the maintenance of the political power we possess in the East; and we are well persuaded that this end is not to be served either by a disregard of the external observances of religion, or by any assimilation to Eastern manners and opinions, but rather by retaining all the distinctions of our national principles, character, and usages." Brougham pronounced Lord Glenelg "the purest statesman he had ever known."

On his retiring from Parliament, Charles Grant held the office of Chairman for the Issue of Exchequer Bills till his death. Leaving the leafy retreat of Clapham, he spent his last years in Russell Square, where he died suddenly on the 31st October 1823. In his parish church of St. George's, Bloomsbury, where the East India Company raised a memorial of his unique services and character, Daniel Wilson, who had so often co-operated with him in his good works, pronounced upon him this eulogy:—

"He had a vigorous understanding, a clear and sound judgment; a sagacity and penetration, particularly in the discernment of character, which were seldom deceived or eluded; a singular faculty of patient, impartial, and comprehensive investigation; an activity of spirit, and a power of continued and persevering application, which difficulties could not damp, nor labour exhaust. These qualities, united with quick sensibility of feeling, delicacy of sentiment, and a strong sense of moral rectitude, constituted, even independently of religion, that which is generally understood by the term *greatness of character*. It was not, however, the possession, but the direction and the improvement of these endowments and qualifications; it was the use which he made of his powers and faculties; it was the sincere and honest dedication of every talent and acquirement to the service and glory of God, which constituted him, in the proper sense of the term, a Christian. He did not indeed learn this lesson easily, or at a small cost. At an early stage of his Indian career, it pleased God to visit him with a succession of severe domestic afflictions, painfully illustrative of the vanity of human hopes, the precariousness of earthly enjoyments, and the awful nearness of the things which are unseen and eternal. He was in circumstances very unfavourable to religious improvement, heathenism and false religion prevailing all around; the partial intermixture of Christianity which existed, possessing little of that divine religion beyond the name, his situation ill allowing of seclusion from worldly occupation and society. Yet that season of heavy calamity was blessed to his mind. It led him to the only true source of felicity. He derived, on this occasion, much useful spiritual counsel from a friend, who afterwards became a near connection, and who was himself the disciple of the celebrated missionary Schwartz. Thus, in a soil prepared by the means of grief and trouble, it pleased God that the good seed should be sown; it was subsequently cherished amidst the silence and comparative solitude of one of the remoter stations in our Indian dominions; and it produced blessed fruit to the praise and glory of God. The deep persuasion of the importance of religion which now possessed itself of his whole soul, did not slacken his attention to his proper duties. On the contrary, he laboured, if possible, only the more abundantly. A new principle of action governed him, a profound and abiding sense of his obligation as a Christian, and grateful and affecting remembrance of the mercies of God in Jesus Christ, and a solemn anticipation of the awful account which he must one day give of the talents committed to his charge."

Almost the last act of Charles Grant was to send Dr. Carey a copy of the notorious work of the Roman missionary in Mysore, the Abbé Dubois, the *Letters on the State of Christianity in India, in which the Conversion of the Hindus is considered impracticable.* Urged to answer the book at once, Dr. Marshman devoted the two hundred pages of a complete number of the Quarterly *Friend of India*[1] to its exposure, in language hardly more scathing than that which, at the same time, Bishop Heber applied to the production in his primary charge in St. John's Cathedral.[2] Charles Grant's lifelong admiration and support of the Brother-

[1] *The Friend of India* (Quarterly Series), No. x. vol. iii. 1825.

[2] *Bishop Heber, Poet and Chief Missionary to the East*, pp. 183, 195, 305 (John Murray, 1895).

hood of Serampore did not cease even with his death, for he bequeathed to their Mission a legacy of £200, which was doubled by Lord Glenelg.

What his contemporaries called the "extraordinary endowments" of Charles Grant and his most reliable judgment were consecrated by the purest of all aims, and applied by the unflagging energies of half a century for the highest good of mankind. By nearly a century he anticipated men like the Lawrences and their school, making it possible for them to become what they were. From Clive to Lord William Bentinck, for nearly sixty years, this Highland Scot never ceased, in India and in English political life, through Cornwallis, Pitt, and Wilberforce, as well as by Carey and Schwartz, Claudius Buchanan and Henry Martyn, the Church Missionary and Bible Societies, to keep the English people to their duty of giving Christianity, and all that the teaching of Jesus Christ involves in time and in eternity, to the ever-increasing millions of our Indian Empire, and through them to all Southern and Eastern Asia. His lofty character and far-seeing statesmanship redeem the reputation of the East India Company at its worst, though his counsel was unheeded too long to save the Company from the extinction which followed the Mutiny of 1857. When India is Christian, its sons will place before the names of Clive and Hastings, Wellesley and Dalhousie, Lord William Bentinck and the Lawrences, that of Charles Grant.

Our portrait (frontispiece) is taken from the Raeburn which adorns the walls of the castle in Inverness. It was painted at the expense of the grateful County.

II

SIR HENRY LAWRENCE, K.C.B., 1806–1857

Provisional Governor-General of India

In the year 1855 Sir Henry Lawrence paid the last of his rare visits to Calcutta. Emphatically a man of action, whether as a soldier, a "political" in the Anglo-Indian sense, or an administrator, he had spent the thirty years of his brilliant career in the swamps of Arakan, the villages of the North-Western Provinces, the passes and forts of Afghanistan, the solitude of the valleys of Nepaul, the court and camps of the Punjab, and the arid wastes of Rajpootana, relieved only by a few weeks' rest in the cool heights of Mount Aboo. He was known personally to few of those in the great cities who, whether Englishmen or Natives, form the public opinion of India. But his name had for some time been in every mouth. Keen interest was felt in the man who, having helped Lord Hardinge to win the first Punjab War, and having prevented the second from being attended by disaster at Chilianwala, had converted the turbulent brotherhood of Sikh prætorians into sturdy peasants or contented landlords, and yet had given way to his younger brother John, as ruler of our new frontier province. The Marquess of Dalhousie was at the height of his well-deserved fame as Governor-General. But all the circumstances which a year before had led him to transfer Sir Henry Lawrence from Lahore to the inferior appointment of Agent for the States of Rajpootana, were not known, and especially throughout the Indian Army keen sympathy was felt with the officer who had been thus superseded. Not only they who thus sympathised, but all officials who had long admired Sir Henry for his own sake, united to do him honour in a banquet, public enough to be thoroughly representative, but not so public as to chill the flow of private friendship, or check the expression of frank admiration.

But Sir Henry Lawrence was something more and higher than a great soldier and administrator. He was remarkable in both capacities, because the root of his nature lay deep in Christ. While his brother officers and civilians crowded to recognise in him their professional ideal, there were some who knew his inner life and the true secret of that influence which radiated from him; there were many who saw in him chiefly the beneficent philanthropist, the friend of the poor, the helper of the needy, the pattern of self-denial. The day of the banquet given in his honour by the "Services" he spent with me in visiting the various charities and schools of Calcutta, happily abundant in both, to which he had been long a subscriber. He knew well that there is a wise as well as a foolish way of spending money in seeking to do good, and in all the cases on which he spent the bulk of his income he sought by personal knowledge, or by means of those friends whom he employed as his almoners, to secure the wise way. On this occasion he was chiefly interested in the children of poor European parents, and in that class of Eurasians, the descendants of English fathers and native mothers, who are often neglected. The same spirit which led him to establish for soldiers' children the noble Asylums that bear his name, prompted him all through his career to care for the class of adventurers, the runaway sons who used to enlist in the East India Company's armies before the Colonies offered a healthier outlet to adventurous spirits. Of this class, and of individuals whom he had secretly assisted ever since he had been a Revenue Surveyor, we talked much, and he expressed to me his intention to follow up his earliest production, *Adventures of an Officer in the Service of Runjeet Singh*,[1] by a work on European "blackguards" in India. He used the term humorously and kindly, including in it the soldiers of fortune, French as well as English, who had fought in the service of native chiefs, as well as those poor "loafers," vagabond sailors, soldiers, and Australian grooms, whose increasing num-

[1] Published by Colburn, in two volumes, in 1845, and dedicated to his mother. Under the character of Bellasis and his "imaginary autobiography," Henry Lawrence gives his own experience, and sketches the most realistic picture of the Maharaja Runjeet Singh and his government that we have. The book is one of the earliest, and it is as yet the wisest of Anglo-Indian romances. His wife thus described that and their other literary labours in the comparative rest of the Nepaul Residency, in a letter to a friend:—

"Henry for ten years led a life of such urgent *external* labour that he had little leisure for study or thought. He is now reading systematically,

bers soon after caused so much political difficulty and moral scandal as to necessitate the interference of the Legislature.

I had corresponded with Sir Henry Lawrence for some time, and had formed my own idea of the *personnel* of the man whose impetuous but shrewd benevolence, whose literary enthusiasm tempered by the grace of his noble wife, and whose eagerness as an Indian political reformer, I had good reason to know. But I was not prepared for the tall form, the gaunt features, the almost wasted face, and grizzly hair, which gave him the ascetic stamp of the old Puritan till the soul within spiritualised his expression. What the fever of Arakan began in the young Lieutenant, marring his features and to some extent his form, was intensified by hard work and occasional disappointment in a tropical climate. A few months before this his wife had been taken from him.

and writing a good deal. How I like to think of your reading our Bellasis, for it will give you many a sketch of our actual experience. I suppose the book has had no public success, or we should have heard of it. Colburn published it on his own responsibility, and we have never heard from him since its appearance. The friends to whom we sent copies speak of the work as interesting for the author's sake, but if any review or even newspaper has thought it worth criticising, we have never heard. It is not, therefore, for fame that Henry now keeps his pen busy. Last year a work was started in Calcutta, called the *Calcutta Review*. We liked its principles and style, and knew more or less of almost every contributor. Henry therefore has made an effort to help on the work, and, little interest as our local Indian literature excites at home, I think you may possibly have heard of this periodical, as it is in some degree the foster-child of the Indian Free Church. Dr. Duff's name you may probably know, and he and his colleagues write for the *Review*. Should you meet with the work, and have courage for our sakes to venture on an Indian publication, you will find much that I think will interest you. Our contributions treat of 'The Sikhs and their Country,' 'Kashmir,' etc., 'Military Defence,' 'Romance and Reality,' 'Oude,' 'Mahrattahs,' 'Carriage for the Sick and Wounded,' 'English Children in India,' and 'English Women in Hindustan.' Writing and reading are truly a resource here, where we have no society."

The time had even now come for that sick leave to England which the doctors had often pressed upon him, and which his appointment as Chief Commissioner of Oudh, the year after, prevented him from taking. The photograph taken of him when he first went to Oudh, and engraved in Rees's *Narrative of the Siege of Lucknow*, unfortunately remains the only published portrait of one who has justly been termed the greatest man England has ever sent to India. His *Life*, by his friend and disciple, Sir Herbert Edwardes, completed by Mr. Herman Merivale, does not contain a portrait. If a biography is valuable in proportion as it represents what its subject was, as well as what he did, then it is deeply to be regretted that Sir Herbert Edwardes did not live to complete his labour of love. Rarely has so valuable an addition been made to religious or to Anglo-Indian biography as the first volume of this work. It is unfortunate that the tale of Sir Henry Lawrence's administration of the Punjab and removal to Rajpootana, and the story of the Mutiny in Oudh crowned by that death-bed in the Baillie Guard of the Lucknow Residency, have not been told by the man who was, next to the brothers Lawrence, *facile princeps* among the statesmen of the Punjab, who kept the gate of India at Peshawar against all odds in 1857, and who belonged to the same school of catholic Evangelicals as his great master.

Henry Lawrence was an Irishman, but of the Scots-Protestant type. Those who are curious in such matters will observe that the three countries divide very fairly among them the distinguished men who have won and built up our Indian Empire. Clive and Warren Hastings were purely English, while Lord William Bentinck—like the later Governor-General, Lord Northbrook—was of Anglo-Dutch descent. Lord Minto, who has never received justice; the Marquess of Hastings, whose long administration was so brilliant; and the Marquess of Dalhousie, who excelled even that nobleman in his services to the Empire and to humanity, are claimed by Scotland. But it is to Ireland that we must give the honour of having sent to India the Marquess Wellesley, who, though overshadowed in the eyes of Europe by his younger brother, the Duke of Wellington, was the "glorious little man" of Indian contemporaries like Metcalfe and Malcolm. To Ireland also we owe the Lawrences—George, Henry, and John.

The first, less known than his younger brothers, won a solid reputation alike as a soldier, a "political" and a captive in the Afghan War, and as Henry's successor in the control of the eighteen principalities of Rajpootana. The story of Henry and of John seems even more romantic than that of the Westminster schoolboys, Warren Hastings, Chief-Justice Impey, Lord Chancellor Thurlow, and the poet Cowper; or that of the three Christ Church students, Lord Dalhousie, Lord Canning, and Lord Elgin, who succeeded each other as Governor-General of India. Henry Lawrence, the artillery officer, fevered by the swamps of Arakan, came home to find his younger brother, John, eager to go out to India as a soldier. Dissuaded from this by his brother, John landed in Calcutta in the Civil Service, and, other things being equal, by that one fact gained the start and distanced his elder brother in the honours of life. So important was it, so valuable is it still, to be a "covenanted" civilian rather than a soldier in the East. Henry found himself ousted from the Punjab by the brother whom he had as his colleague in the Board of Administration, and honourably enough so far as that brother was concerned. When the supreme crisis of the Mutiny came, John was Chief Commissioner of the Punjab, and Henry had been appointed by Lord Canning Chief Commissioner of Oudh. Henry was the one man in India to whom England looked as the successor of Lord Canning, and Lord Palmerston nominated him Provisional Governor-General. But death carried off the elder brother before he could fill the highest position, for good or evil, that a subject of the British Crown can hold; and on Lord Elgin's death the same Premier appointed John, who after a few years' term as Viceroy was raised to the peerage.

Alexander, the father of the Lawrences, was the youngest son of a mill-owner in Coleraine. He was worthy of such sons. When just seventeen he went off to India as a military volunteer. There he so served for a quarter of a century that he would have won his commission and a Victoria Cross, had there been such a reward, many times over but for the lack of interest. Forced at last to purchase, the veteran was soured, and when the time came for his sons to enter the Army he warned them against the Royal Service. Nor were the boys less fortunate in their mother, a Knox, and a collateral descendant of the Scottish Reformer, through Andrew Knox, Bishop of the Isles. In their long roamings over India and Ceylon, and during occasional visits to England, this couple were blessed with twelve children, of whom three of the five boys and their eldest sister, Letitia, concern us most. Henry Montgomery Lawrence was his mother's jewel, being described by her as her Matura diamond, in allusion to his birthplace, which is known for its precious stones. He was born on 28th June 1806. What with their father's grievance and his sometimes thoughtless generosity to his old comrades and their families, their mother had need of all that administrative ability for which her son Henry so fondly gives her credit. The family income was very narrow, and, on their return to England, Guernsey, and afterwards Clifton, was selected as their home.

But the boys were educated by their uncle, the Rev. James Knox, who was headmaster of the Foyle College, at Derry, a town ever since associated with the Lawrences, and justly proud of their reputation. There Henry was remarkable for his love of truth-telling even to his own hurt, and for the thoughtfulness of his character. Mrs. Lawrence was fortunate not only as a manager, but in her relation as cousin to Mr. Huddleston, who was both an East India Director and a Member of Parliament. This good man, who had been the intimate friend of the missionary Schwartz, in Tanjore, liberally provided cadetships and a writership for the Lawrence boys, the last falling to John. Henry chivalrously refused any appointment which did not involve an examination, and hence he passed for the Artillery, lest it should be said that no Lawrence could face an examination. He left behind him at Addiscombe the reputation of being "backward and slow." Both he and John were wont to confess that they were dull at scholarly studies, and that their education had been neglected. But Henry came out the first of his year. His so-called slowness seems to have been due to that habit which was the secret of his success. He was what the Germans call "gründlich," refusing to advance till he had thoroughly mastered every step, always seeking the causes of things. It is true, however, that competitive examinations, as now conducted, would have deprived India of Henry and John Lawrence, and of many of their great predecessors. There was at least one man who foresaw Henry's future. When Letitia, the beloved elder sister and companion, was so bewailing her brother's approaching departure that he proposed to take her with him, and set up a school or a shop in the Himalayas, Mr. Huddleston said, "You foolish thing, Henry will distinguish himself. All your brothers will do well, I think; but Henry has such steadiness and resolution that you'll see him come back a general. He will be Sir Henry Lawrence before he dies." So away from Clifton one September morning, leaving the young ones in bed, and parting with his sister on Brandon Hill!

His mother's counsel is characteristic of both, and tells of a life of struggling, not unmixed with happiness, "I know you don't like advice, so I will not give you much.

But, pray, recollect two things. Don't marry a woman who had not a *good* mother; and don't be too ready to speak your mind. It was the rock on which your father shipwrecked his prospects." In all this we have as yet hardly a glimpse of the higher life. But Sir Herbert Edwardes tells us that the mother had inherited no small share of John Knox's "strong, God-fearing character," and we know that Letitia, the sister, prayed much for her favourite brother, that he might be led into all truth. We learn afterwards, too, that the scarred old Colonel, the victim of many wrongs, and oft grumbling over his grievances, found before his death their true remedy in the love of Him who bears every burden, a fact which Henry joyfully records.

It was in 1823, towards the close of the cold season in February, that Henry Lawrence joined the head-quarters of the Bengal Artillery at Dum Dum, now almost a suburb of Calcutta. Two or three months later there landed with his regiment at the same place a young officer of the Royal Service, who on the soldier side of his character so resembled Lawrence—Henry Havelock. Both saw their first campaign in the first Burmese War, which was already brewing. Both came under spiritual influences at once, Havelock in the saintly circle of Baptists at Serampore, Lawrence among the Church of England evangelicals at Dum Dum and Calcutta. Both took part in the Afghan conflicts. And both, by very different paths, found a soldier's grave in '57, Lawrence in the hallowed ground of the beleaguered Residency of Lucknow, Havelock in the then fortified garden of Dilkooshah, from which he had advanced to the relief of that Residency. When Henry Lawrence had time to look from professional details to the society around him, he found that some of his most intimate companions at Addiscombe, who had landed a few weeks before him, had undergone a change. One especially, named Lewin, was a new man altogether. We find Henry writing again and again of this change to his sister. In a letter dated eight months after his arrival he recurs to it as something at once marvellous and worthy of his own imitation, but yet hardly attainable by himself. "Lewin has turned an excellent religious young fellow," writes the Lieutenant of seventeen. And again: "There is a play here to-night, but as I did not feel inclined to go, I took tea with Lewin, and am just returned home. It is really wonderful to me the conversion of Lewin, having known him as a worldly-minded lad. His whole thoughts seem now to be of what good he can do. I only wish I was like him."

The occasion of the change was this. The Rev. George Craufurd, who afterwards held the family baronetcy as Sir George William Craufurd, had gone out in the same ship with Lewin and the other cadets, as assistant chaplain to the Rev. Thomas Thomason. With the cadets was Lawrence's friend, James Thomason, soon to become the Lieutenant-Governor of the North-Western Provinces, whose admiring disciple in all things, Sir William Muir, afterwards ruled in his spirit over the thirty millions of Hindustan proper. Sir George

Craufurd's name is one henceforth to be remembered with those of the Simeonites, Brown, Buchanan, Corrie, Henry Martyn, Bishop Wilson, and Bishop Dealtry, who, with the Serampore and the Scots missionaries, have made India spiritually what it is, and what it promises to be. Not only as the father in Christ of Henry Lawrence and others, but as the man who first asserted religious liberty for the Sepoys, ought the name of Sir George Craufurd to be recorded. The story has a sad interest since the Mutiny.

When chaplain in Allahabad, in 1830, Craufurd was visited in his own house by some Sepoys curious about the Christian religion. Assisted by a Mirza, his catechist, Sir George finally accepted their written invitation to teach the Church catechism in the lines. The Major commanding, excited by the dread of insubordination, interfered. The General, much better disposed, laughingly permitted the chaplain to teach only such Sepoys as chose to visit him privately. The result was the application of several for baptism. Lord William Bentinck, the Governor-General, overborne by his advisers, it was thought, had ordered Archdeacon Corrie to forbid the visiting of the native soldiers in their lines. But when the question of baptism arose the matter seemed more serious. It is deeply to be lamented that two such men as Lord William Bentinck and Archdeacon Corrie went so far as to prevent the baptism of Sepoys; and the former issued that order prohibiting all chaplains from speaking to native soldiers on the subject of religion, which did so much to foster the ignorance that ended in the Mutiny. Even after the abolition of the East India Company, Lord Canning rebuked a civilian for attending the baptism of a Sepoy. The disgraceful and inexpedient order of Lord William Bentinck's government still remains in force, so far as I know.

The prayers of Lewin, his companion, and the labours of Craufurd were blessed in time to the conversion of Henry Lawrence. Very slowly does he seem to have opened his reserved and questioning heart to the influences of that circle. At last we find him reaching this point in his intercourse with the chaplain: "What I want to be assured of is that this Book is God's. Because when I know that, I have nothing left but to obey it." On the Christmas Day of 1823 we find this joyous entry in Lewin's journal: "Lawrence took the Sacrament; God bless him now and for evermore." On the subsequent 17th of April the words occur, "I have been greatly pleased to-day to see dear Lawrence reading his Bible considerably." The good seed was then sown.

The cold season of 1823-24 was passed amid preparations for war with Burma. The first half of the eighteenth century, or from the death of Aurangzeb, about the time of the union of Scotland and England, to Clive's victory of Plassey, was the period of anarchy in India. All, Musalman and Hindu, Maratha and Rajpoot, English and French, sought to keep what they had got, and more or less consciously, on our part at least, to obtain supremacy. The Musalman was effete. The Hindu had no power of recuperation, and sought only, as in Rajpootana, to be protected from his enemies. The Marathas, themselves Hindus, were the most formidable—a veritable scourge of God. Of the European Powers then trading in India the Portuguese were as hopeless as the Musalman, while the Dutch had only sought gain in the paradise of the Eastern Archipelago, which their culture system still oppresses. The peninsula lay open to the English and French. But the latter, in spite of great names like La Bourdonnais and Dupleix, were not supported, save by Colbert for a time, at home; and their designs were of the purely selfish military class. Whether deserving it or not, England was used to save society, and all who, like the princes of Rajpootana and the Nizam of Haidarabad, clung to the English were preserved, and have been fossilised to this hour. While India proper was thus seething, what the ancients called India beyond the Ganges was undergoing a similar revolution. The robber-chief Alompra founded in the valley of the Irawadi that house whose cruelties led eventually to its disappearance.

For years the dynasty of Alompra had, from Ava, their capital, insulted the Governor-General, who had sent envoys to the Golden Foot, but had otherwise been too busy to think of Burma. In an evil moment the Burmese not only claimed, but invaded Assam and Cachar. The Empire had enjoyed five years' peace, the treasury was full, and Lord Amherst, the weakest of Governors next to Lord Auckland, was in power. So a two years' war was waged and brought to a successful issue; thanks to Sir Thomas Munro, the great Governor of Madras. Henry Lawrence and his guns formed part of the Chittagong column which, under General Morrison, crossed the jungles and hills of Arakan and took its capital. Havelock, with the main army, seeing that there was no chaplain at all with the force, converted a cloister of the great Shwè Dagon pagoda of Rangoon into a church, and there, by the light of a lamp placed in the lap of the images of Gautama that lined the walls, he ministered to the soldiers of H.M.'s 13th. The hot weather of 1825 came, and even by May of that year the early rainy season of Burma was upon our troops. As Havelock, the historian of the war,[1] records, "In a month General Morrison had no longer an army." Of all the artillery officers, only Henry Lawrence and his Colonel were fit for duty, and the former received his first promotion as Adjutant. But there he too was struck down, and after being nursed in Calcutta by Mr. Craufurd, he was ordered to England. In May 1827 we find this noble testimony from a mother in her journal:—"Returned from Arakan after the Burmese War, my dearest beloved, Henry Montgomery, not twenty-one years old, but reduced by sickness and suffering to more than double that age. Self-denial and affection to his whole family were ever the prominent features of his character."

[1] *Memoir of the Three Campaigns of Major-General Sir Archibald Campbell's Army in Ava.* By Henry Havelock, Lieutenant in the 13th Light Infantry, and D.A.G. Serampore, 1828.

Who shall describe the joys of the first visit home of the Indian exile? Yet that is an easier task than the attempt to picture the other side of the poetry of Anglo-Indian life—the separation of husband and wife, of parents and children, of the friends of youth and of manhood, often for long years. That, and nothing else, is the price we pay for India, for death is less bitter. That Henry Lawrence was changed in other respects than in form was soon apparent. His first act was to consult his sister Letitia about family prayers. After some surprise on the part of the household, he brought out his Scott's Bible, and from that day there was an altar in the house. This holiday of two years and a half was memorable for some things. Notably, with his sister's companionship and the spiritual privileges, which he enjoyed alike at Clifton and when he visited the north of Ireland, he grew in grace. Hard by his father's house, Robert Hall's preaching was sounding forth, and drawing good men of all sects to listen. His younger brother John was grumbling that Mr. Huddleston had presented him with an appointment to the Bengal Civil Service, instead of giving him the chance of becoming a soldier, like his seniors. He admired the young hero of the Burmese War, and could not understand why that somewhat stern person should side with his father in the advice—"If you want to be independent, be a civilian." So to Haileybury the future Viceroy went, but not before he had often helped Henry to carry the delicate Letitia up the hills from Clifton, to be in time for the preaching of Robert Hall.

A picture worthy of a place in the Anglo-Indian historical gallery—the embryo soldier-statesman, one to have the Viceroy's throne in his gift, the other to fill it for five years, and both to save an empire, while acknowledging in all humility Him who had called them.

When, in one of those fits of home-sickness which so often recur in India, Henry had pined for the society of those he loved, he thought only of mother and sister. But now he had his wish fulfilled in an even higher form. He met his cousin, his sister's friend, Honoria Marshall, a fair Irish girl, once, twice, and again; and he made many inquiries as to her training, her tastes, the books she liked to read. The result was such an exalted opinion of her, and so humble an idea of himself in relation to her, that he returned to India without opening his heart to her. Aunt Angel, who figures much and lovingly in the early part of Sir Herbert Edwardes's volume, pronounced marriage at that time most imprudent—"they were little better than children." There was another reason for his silence: his dream was to create a pious fund for his father and mother. The old Colonel had steadily refused all assistance, even from his sons; but that could not always be. To marry now would be selfishly to neglect a sacred duty, and so, hating scenes, he parts with Honoria deliberately, "on the steps of a shilling show" in Regent Street. With the Arakan fever not quite extirpated, as it never was, he and John sail for India, and after a five months' voyage reach Calcutta in February 1830. Months passed on in the study of Persian and Hindustani at Karnal, varied by riding lessons, which fitted him for many a long journey in after-days. Soon John was appointed to Delhi, within a few hours' distance of both his elder brothers, and Henry was transferred to the Horse Artillery. A year or two passed; good appointments so came to him and his brothers, as the result of hard work, that the pious fund grew apace, and he begins to wonder if now he dare ask Honoria Marshall to be his wife. He dares, humbly, almost despairingly; and in 1837 she lands at Calcutta, only to find that there is no bridegroom. Illness had driven him to the hills, and her letters to him had miscarried. But when the news reached him at Simla, in August, the worst season, he soon made her his own.

Only those who have been privileged to witness their family life can tell all that Lady Lawrence proved to be to her husband. She was a woman of high culture and refined taste. Her literary productions were excellent; some of her letters, published by Edwardes for the first time, cannot be surpassed. The poetry of her prose articles in the *Calcutta Review*, especially on such subjects as the Englishwoman in India, married life in India, and the sick-room in India, is exquisite. Her influence on his intense earnest temper was purifying. A true soldier's wife, she ever strung up his nature to meet the call of duty, the claims of affection, and the appeals of neediness, while she gently turned away his spirit from dwelling too long on slights and wrongs.

In the one instance recorded by Sir Herbert Edwardes, in which the old temper burned so fiercely as to threaten a duel with an officer who had attacked his honour in its keenest part, she wrote him a letter, touching in its pathos and almost sublime in its appeals, and that only a fortnight after the birth of their first child. The sin was averted by the decision of his brother officers, that a challenge was quite unnecessary, the opinion of the Army being with him in the dispute. At a later period we find their positions changed to that which is more becoming, the husband determined on a deed of heroic self-sacrifice, and the distant wife, doubtful at first, but soon encouraging him to the venture.

When in 1842 Henry Lawrence was with Pollock's avenging force at Oosman Khan's Fort, fourteen miles in advance of Jelalabad, Akbar Khan sent a second message, offering to give up the English captives if Pollock would retire at once and release the Afghan prisoners. George Lawrence, a captive, was employed as one of the envoys, in the hope that he would influence his brother and the General to consent. The message was returned, that our force would advance, and the ladies must be sent in at once. With this George had to return to what seemed death at the hands of the murderer of Sir W. Macnaghten. Henry nevertheless volunteered to return in George's place, assured that his wife would approve. He had not mistaken her. Four letters, despatched to her husband on the 17th, 18th, 19th, and 20th of August, record an incident unmatched in the annals of heroism. The first and most doubting thus begins:—"And you offered to go in the stead of George, darling? I am glad you did it, and I am glad there was no time to ask me, lest my heart should have failed." The next is more assured:—"Yes, you see I *did* say you were right in offering to go, and furthermore I shall say you are right if you *do* go to Kabul." In the two next she rises to the full height of the self-sacrifice.

"*August* 19.—Last night I was a long time awake, and felt great delight thinking of your offer for your brother, and how pleasing it must be in the sight of our great Redeemer, who gave Himself in the stead of His enemies, that they might be made His friends, even His brothers. . . . The vivid feeling brought to my heart by your love and disinterestedness helped me more feelingly than I ever did before to thank Jesus Christ for what He did for our race, and for each individual of it."

"*August* 20.—And now, my husband, listen to what I say, for it is the steadfast purpose of my heart. You have more than my acquiescence in your changing places with George. Besides which, I cannot but feel that there is not an officer now in Afghanistan who may not be made a prisoner. Therefore, my Henry, if so it be your lot, your wife will be with you."

But George was worthy of such a brother, to whose wife he writes, "We return to-morrow Kabul-wards; Henry, as usual, volunteering to go for me, but this I could not allow."

Henry Lawrence's visit to England had been remarkable for more than the development of his higher nature, and winning the trust of such a wife. He had, as was his wont, gone to school again; this time, with the Royal Engineers. His Addiscombe training and artillery experience had given him scientific tastes, and he thought he could not spend his sick holiday better than in mastering the Trigonometrical Survey. In this he showed no little foresight. If our Indian administrative system lacked one thing above all in the fruitful period of Lord William Bentinck's government, it was a survey and righteous assessment of the land. In a country of which the Government is sole landlord, deriving half its gross revenue from the soil, the very root of economic prosperity and political contentment lies in a detailed settlement with the peasantry and the large landholders. About 1830, the experiments of half a century had resulted in the conviction that thirty years' leases, based on a careful survey, would alone prove fair at once to the public treasury and the agricultural classes. A Bengal civilian, still reverenced as Robert Mertins Bird, devised and applied this system to the North-Western Provinces, training a school of young civilians and soldiers, of whom Thomason and Henry and John Lawrence were the most distinguished. Henry Lawrence had just mastered the native languages, and got into the Horse Artillery, when, in 1832, his brother George, then on sick leave at Simla, obtained an interview with Lord William Bentinck, which is thus described: "Well, what have you come for?" asked the Governor-General. "Nothing for myself."—"What then? I can tell you, you are the first man I have met in

India who wanted nothing." The request was that Henry should be appointed to the Revenue Survey. It was done, and the Artillery Lieutenant became the ablest subordinate of Bird, showing him how to triple the out-turn of work every year, and training many who still fondly look back on him as the man who not only taught them their profession, but gave them for ever a high ideal of both work and belief. For five years Lawrence and his wife lived in camp, surveying almost every field in the Districts—each larger than Yorkshire—of Moradabad, Futtehgarh, Goruckpoor, and Allahabad. Arakan had taught him war, and to understand the British soldier. At home he had learned to sound the depths of his own nature and to educate himself. On his return he had mastered the native languages and the technicalities of his profession. And now he knows the people and how to govern them, as he lives in their midst. He is at last equipped to be a ruler of men, though he is only thirty-two. And he is wanted, for the Army of the Indus is assembling.

In August 1838, when completing the season's survey of the fields and villages of Allahabad, he was officially informed that the 2nd Brigade of Horse Artillery, to which he belonged, was under orders for active service. After he had joined his battery, it was determined that his brigade should remain behind with the army of observation at Ferozepoor. This made him only the more eager for political employment. The famous Bengal civilian, George Clerk (since known as Sir George Clerk, Governor of Bombay, and member of the Council of India), was political agent at Lodiana, and required an Assistant to administer the little barony of Ferozepoor, which had lapsed to us four years previously. Lawrence was delighted to receive the appointment on a smaller salary than he had previously enjoyed. His wife's first act was to propose to the American Presbyterian Mission at Lodiana the establishment of a branch in the new station. In reply to her offer of aid, the Rev. John Newton—the same venerable missionary whose invitation to united prayer, twenty-one years afterwards, was so generally welcomed—concluded his letter to Captain Lawrence with these words: "I should say that Mrs. Lawrence's sentiments about differences of denomination have my cordial sympathy." On this, the equally catholic and evangelical Edwardes remarks: "Yes; there is nothing like a heathen land for drawing Christians together. Differences about bishops look very small under the shadow of an idol with twelve heads." In Ferozepoor, thus consecrated, Henry Lawrence worked for three years, doing with all his might on a small scale what he was so soon to be called on to effect for the whole of the Punjab.

For, six months after his appointment, Runjeet Singh died at Lahore, and he virtually became Runjeet's successor. When the old Lion of the Punjab passed away we lost a faithful ally, and the kingdom was given up to anarchy. But before we could respond to the call for our interference, ending ultimately in conquest which we had not sought, and in annexation which we had honestly deprecated, we had to atone for our iniquitous policy and military incapacity in Afghanistan. It was due to Lawrence's ceaseless toils in Ferozepoor, through which the Bengal troops passed, and to his after-labours at Peshawar and in Afghanistan itself, that the atonement was not more difficult.

Our vacillating policy for the third of a century, our sacrifice of Persia contrary to treaty and to our own interests, the weakness of the weakest Governor-General ever sent to India, the headstrong selfishness of his counsellors both in England and in India, and the senility of inexperienced generals, all culminated in the disasters of the Kabul War. When the great Napoleon—first by himself, and again in alliance with Russia—sought to wound Great Britain through its Indian Empire, by encouraging Zemân Shah, the Suddozai ruler of Afghanistan, to invade India, we formed a counter-alliance with Persia in the year 1800. Our policy then was precisely that which in later times public opinion forced on Lord Lawrence, and which was so heartily adopted by Lord Mayo. It was the "buffer" policy; that of so supporting the strong *de facto* Powers all along our border as to enable them to keep back invaders from the north without our direct interference. Afghanistan was against us at the end of last century; but Persia, far more powerful than she is now, was only too eager to work with us. The danger from Napoleon passed away, and the Afghan Suddozai, Zemân Shah, became a pensioner in our own territories. The mayors of the palace in Afghanistan, the Barukzai family, had turned out the royal Suddozais, and were represented by Dost

Mahomed, the ablest ruler Asia had seen since Timour. With France and the Suddozais thus removed, it was clearly our policy to maintain our alliance with Persia, so as to prevent Russian aggression, and to be friendly with Dost Mahomed, who had overturned our Afghan enemy. We followed the opposite course. We allowed Persia to be swallowed up bit by bit by Russia, contrary to our treaty, and for failure of duty we submitted to the humiliation of paying Persia heavy compensation. This was the act of George Canning, who, like all English statesmen except Pitt and Palmerston, was indifferent to our interests in the East, though at one time about to go out as Governor-General. In Afghanistan, we rejected all the advances of Dost Mahomed, and adopted the cause of the Suddozai *rois fainéants*, to whom we had given an asylum at Lodiana. This was the act of Lord Broughton, when President of the Board of Control, and of Lord Auckland. Thus Persia and Afghanistan alike were thrown at the feet of Russia. The "buffer" policy, adopted in 1868, has preserved at least Afghanistan.

By the tripartite treaty which the English, Runjeet Singh, and the Suddozai king, Shah Shooja, signed at Lahore on 20th June 1838, and by the mad proclamation of war which Lord Auckland issued from Simla on the 1st of October thereafter, the die was cast. The Bengal and Bombay forces slowly made their way through the passes, Ghuzni fell to young Durand's powder-bag, and the puppet king was enthroned in the Bala Hissar of Kabul. Dost Mahomed was captured and sent to Calcutta, where he drove with the Governor-General's family on the course, and astonished the public by daily at sunset getting out of his carriage to pray towards Mecca. But now incompetent generals were used to avenge an evil policy, and an inevitable attempt to retrench the enormous expenditure in a foreign country, which we were forced to occupy indefinitely, resulted in the assassination of our leaders and the massacre of our forces. Yet, apart from these leaders, never had a country been served by a nobler set of officers, who became the victims of a war which in their hearts they condemned. Such were Lieut.-General Colin Mackenzie, C.B., and Colonel Haughton, C.B. To his hardships in Afghanistan, of the captivity in which he is the historian, Sir Vincent Eyre added his triumphs in the Mutiny campaigns. Such were Generals Macgregor and Troup, in whose career the youth of our country may see of what stuff the men were made who have built up our Indian Empire. All the Afghan heroes are now with the mighty dead!

Henry Lawrence struggled hard to be in the thick of the disaster; but Providence, as we now see, kept him back to train him for the founding of a later school of officials—that of the Punjab, and for the toils of the Oudh rebellion. Poor Lord Auckland was superseded by the impetuous and sometimes fickle Lord Ellenborough, whom Durand, the young soldier that had blown in the gate of Ghuzni, tried to keep straight when his secretary. It was then that Durand first learned to admire the kindred spirit of Henry Lawrence, and, with all the influence of a Governor-General's private secretary, helped to push him on. The troubles in Afghanistan made it necessary to send Lawrence to Peshawar. Supports had to be pushed up to relieve Sale and the illustrious garrison of Jelalabad. The resolute Nott, with Sir Henry Rawlinson, had refused to evacuate Kandahar. But the first relieving brigade was placed under another incompetent leader, who was told to ask the demoralised Sikh government of Maharaja Shere Singh for guns and auxiliaries. The result may be imagined. Only George Clerk's influence at Lahore obtained the orders for this Sikh force, and it was many months before even Lawrence's tact and energy at Peshawar could atone for the General's inefficiency, or induce the Sikhs to assist. The tide of disaster turned when the Government selected General Pollock to lead the avenging army to Kabul from the Bengal side, while Nott advanced from Kandahar.

That General—who died full of years and honour a Field-Marshal—was fain to take Lawrence on with him from Peshawar. The Khaibar Pass was forced on 5th April 1842, Lawrence playing his guns from the heights to the admiration of beholders. Slowly did Pollock advance up the dreadful eight-and-twenty miles, only to find, when, on the 16th, he reached Jelalabad, Sale's garrison coming out to meet them with the band playing "Oh, but ye've been lang o' comin'." Sale's 1800 men of all arms had driven off the 6000 Afghans who besieged them. Now Pollock from Jelalabad and Nott from Kandahar, in spite of contradictory orders from Lord

Ellenborough, made a race for Kabul, rescued the captive officers, ladies, and children, and returned in triumph.

The mutinous conduct of the Sikhs at Jelalabad had rendered it necessary for Lawrence to be sent for. There he met Havelock, who showed him round the fields of battle and took him to his chapel in the town, where some forty soldiers and twelve officers joined in the extempore prayers and listened to the read sermon of the Captain, who had so recently led to victory one of the columns that had routed Akbar Khan and his Afghans. Lawrence led his Sikhs into action at Tezeen, and, ever true to "the Blues," his own loved Artillery, helped his brother officers to lay the guns, which his Sikh cavalry had dragged along. Lord Ellenborough, more just to him than to the noble captives whom he had helped to rescue, rewarded him with the appointment of Superintendent of Dehra Doon, that paradise which the low range of the Sewalik hills shuts in between Mussoorie and the plains of Hindustan. But it was found that only a covenanted civilian could hold that office, in which already the soldier-administrator had begun to plan all sorts of improvements. So Lawrence was transferred to Umballa, with the title of Assistant to the Envoy at Lahore. Thereafter he gained new experience in the settlement of the lapsed territory of Khytul. Finally, promotion came to him in his appointment as Resident at the protected Court of Nepaul. In almost as many months he had, to his own disappointment, been moved about four times on the official chess-board. These changes, so evil in ordinary cases, inasmuch as they prevent the individual influence of the English officer flowing forth to a people whom he knows, and who become loyal for his sake, were beneficial in this instance. And now it was rest that he really wanted, though his active spirit chafed at such promotion. The years 1844 and 1845 were fruitful, however, in other forms of action. His essays in the *Calcutta Review* revealed him as a thoughtful reformer, skilful alike in the highest quality of statesmanship—foresight, and in that which is its basis—the ability to gather the fruits of experience in the study of men and of events. And to these years India owes the Lawrence Asylums.

Only twelve per cent of the seventy-five thousand men who form the British garrison of India are allowed to be married. This, though a higher proportion than is the rule in Great Britain, is a frightful fact, as all know who are acquainted with barrack life in the tropics. The two military arguments against a married army—that is, an army in which only half the men would probably avail themselves of the permission to marry—are these, the mortality of the women and children in time of peace, and the difficulty created by such impediments in war. The expense need not be noticed, for that is really greater under the present system, if all the effects of that system be considered. Now, in the Indian Army, even under improved sanitary conditions, at least one woman dies annually out of every twenty, and one child out of every ten, to say nothing of ever-prevalent sickness. Such mortality, however, is less to be lamented than the effect of barrack life, on the girls especially. The deduction is not that our Indian Army should live in the vilest concubinage by being unmarried, but that the children should be reared on the hills from an early age, away alike from moral contamination and the effects of a hostile climate. No English parents, who can afford to send their children home, keep them in the tropics after they are five or six years of age. If a policy of military colonies on the hills, so modified as to fit into a sound strategical system in the plains, cannot be carried out on a fair scale, at least the children of soldiers may be educated in the sanitaria of the Himalaya and the Nilgiri ranges.

Henry Lawrence saw this at an early period. During the month that he had charge of Dehra Doon, and Mussoorie, its hill station, he resolved that his first task would be the establishment of what he then called a European charity-school. Again, at Umballa, having Simla in his jurisdiction, he proposed the endowment of such a school at Kussowli, and Sir George Clerk approved. No sooner was he at rest in Nepaul than he elaborated his plan, and on 22nd July 1845 formally submitted it to the Government of India. He said, "My proposal is no sudden freak of wild enthusiasm, but the sober result of long acquaintance with the condition of barrack children, and of the especial degradation of girls." He offered £500 at once and £100 a year, sums which he afterwards far exceeded. He had already failed in inducing the managers of the military orphan schools in Calcutta to remove them to the hills, although he offered £500 for the purpose. After some unwillingness on the part of even Mr. Thomason, Lieutenant-Governor, and of Lord Hardinge, the Governor-General who superseded Lord Ellenborough, the scheme was sanctioned amid the smoke of the first Sikh War.

The traveller, who, panting from the hot winds of the plains, climbs slowly the great wall of the Himalayas where it towers up 4000 feet into the table-land of Kussowli, rests a little on his way to Simla to gaze at the Hill of Sunâwur, which he passes on the road to the next stage of Subathu, or Dugshai. There stands the first Henry Lawrence Asylum, a happy colony of soldiers' children, girls and boys, saved from moral and physical death on the plains to feed the educated labour-market of India. Begun in March 1847, by Mrs. George Lawrence, the Sunâwur Asylum now reckons as its offspring similar institutions at Murree, in the Punjab; at Mount Aboo, in Rajpootana; and on the Nilgiris, in Madras. The Bible without sectarian comment is the corner-stone of the whole system of education, which is industrial as well as ordinary, a principle practically objected to only by Roman Catholic priests, but not by Roman Catholic parents. The children of each sect may receive religious instruction from their own pastors. How near the soldiers' children were to the heart of this great philanthropist, not only the large sums which he spent on them every year, but his last words testify. When dying amid the shot and shell of the siege of Lucknow, he faintly murmured, "Remember the Asylum; do not let them forget the Asylum." And in addition to his expenditure on the Asylum, this Indian officer, without a private fortune and with a family to provide for, spent £400 a year on other charities through one of his almoners, and more through others.

From the solitude of Nepaul Lawrence sent his wife to England, while he himself was summoned to that very position on the Punjab frontier in which he had before been Assistant. Lord Hardinge had early discovered his ability, alike as a soldier and an administrator, and leaned upon the soldier-statesman all through his term of office. The murder of Runjeet Singh's successor, Shere Singh, was followed by a succession of similar crimes, and finally by the march of the Sikh army across the Sutlej. The battles of Moodki, Ferozeshuhr, Aliwal, and Sobraon were the result. In all it was seen that our Sepoy army and our military system were only just a match for the levies trained by the European officers of Runjeet Singh. Henry Lawrence was by the side of the Governor-General, who had so chivalrously placed himself under the inferior commander-in-chief at the final victory of Sobraon, and he confirmed Lord Hardinge in his desire not to annex the Punjab. The hopeless task of reconstructing the Sikh Government was tried, and if it could have succeeded, Henry Lawrence was the one man in India to secure success. As it was, the almost fascination which radiated from him kept the kingdom quiet, so as to allow some civilising progress to be made for a time. But it was at the expense of such expedients as the sale of Kashmir and its people to a man like Gulab Singh, a transaction fruitful in bitter consequences. And even he came to be rather less unfavourable to annexation. But sickness forced him home with Lord Hardinge to receive at last his K.C.B. The inevitable catastrophe came, in the second Sikh War. That converted Lord Hardinge, but not Sir Henry Lawrence, to the necessity of annexation. Lawrence hurried out with his wife at the end of 1848. He saw Mooltan fall. He was in time to convert the drawn battle of Chilianwala into a seeming victory, by prevailing with Lord Gough to remain on the field. He learned from Sir Colin Campbell our success in the last battle at Goojrat when he was again taking charge of his office as Resident at Lahore. Lord Dalhousie was Governor-General.

We now come to what Lawrence himself considered the turning-point in his career. The former Governor-General had consulted him on all great occasions, and had followed his advice. That advice had seemed to be justified by success so long as he ruled the Punjab. The second war he looked on as partly due to his absence. He had carried his point, too, in the sale of Kashmir to Gulab Singh, a chief whom even Edwardes had described as base beyond conception. What he did not see was that it was only his personal influence which had prevented failure at an earlier period, and that the time was past even for that influence. John Lawrence agreed in the inevitable; and on the 29th of March 1849 the Punjab was proclaimed British territory. Yet such was Lord Dalhousie's regard for Henry Lawrence, that he had delayed this proclamation, and he refused to accept his resignation of the Residentship. The government of the Punjab was entrusted to a Board, of which Henry, with special charge of political matters, was President. The other members were John, with revenue and finance as his department, and Mr. Mansel in charge of the judicial administration. For a time this worked well. Accepting annexation, Henry could not but feel a little bitterness, even though he had been kept in office to make the change as easy as possible for the demoralised Khalsa or Sikh brotherhood. The moment that our comparatively rigid, because equal and just, system of administration came to be applied to a chaos in which might had been right, and riot had wasted a noble peasantry, John could not help seeing that the period of a sentimental regard for the spawn of Runjeet Singh's court must not be indefinitely extended. On this point the brothers divided, and Lord Dalhousie sided with John, as he could not help doing. There was, in truth, no alternative between a return to Henry's favourite plan of a protected Sikh government on the purely Asiatic system, and a financially sound administration in that elastic form of the Anglo-Indian system known as "non-regulation."

The result has justified Lord Dalhousie alike in the loyal support given by the Punjabis to the Empire in 1857, and in the annually growing prosperity of the people and their chiefs. Much as I admire the *sentiment* of Henry Lawrence's policy, which only he could have worked, I marvel still more at the delicacy with which Lord Dalhousie conducted his part of the relations, which ended in the breaking up of the Board and the honourable transfer of Sir Henry to Rajpootana. Lord Dalhousie's reputation can afford to wait for justice; Henry Lawrence's can suffer no abatement even in the eyes of those who differ from him on this point.

When, in such circumstances, Henry Lawrence closed his four years' administration of the Punjab, he wrote a letter to John showing undiminished affection. The secret of his chivalrous self-abnegation, combined with impetuous zeal for what he believed to be right, will be found in the following passage from a journal, written amid the bustle of administrative work as he sailed down the Ravi, and at a time, the 2nd of October 1852, when his official differences with his brother and the Governor-General had reached their height.

> "O Lord, give me grace and strength to do Thy will, to begin the day and end it with prayer and searching of my own heart, with reading of Thy word. Make me to understand it, to understand Thee: to bring home to my heart the reality of Thy perfect Godhead and perfect humanity, and above all of my entire need of a Saviour, of my utter inability to do aught that is right in my own strength. Make me humble, reasonable, contented, thankful, just, and considerate. Restrain my tongue and my thoughts; may I act as ever in Thy sight, as if I may die this day. May I not fear man or man's opinions, but remember that Thou knowest my motives and my thoughts, and that Thou wilt be my Judge. It is not in me to be regular: let me be so as much as I can. Let me do to-day's work to-day, not postponing, clear up and finish daily; so living in humility, thankfulness, contentment."

The removal to Rajpootana, like the promotion to Nepaul years before, had at least the attraction for Lady Lawrence of possible rest. But Mount Aboo, the hill sanitarium, was rarely visited by Sir Henry. He spent even the hottest months in camp, for the Anglo-Indian disease, the crave for work as a refuge from the climate and disappointment, was on him. Soon the necessity for sending their second boy to England wrung the strong woman's heart. Her last letter was to her boys at home. To her loving exhortations the father added this postscript:—"Remember how much your mother's happiness—indeed her very life—is in your hands." In a few weeks she departed, looking out for those letters from her boys which arrived two hours after she breathed her last, and repeating her daily prayer for them, that they might live to be good men, honest and straightforward in word and deed, kind and affectionate, and considerate to all around, thoughtful and pitiful for the poor and the weak, and those who have no friends.[1] Such is the tragedy of many an Anglo-Indian household. May each be irradiated as Henry Lawrence's was with the presence of the spirit of Christ! The memory of Honoria Lawrence is fitly enshrined in the little chapel of the Asylum at Sunâwur by a stained-glass window and an inscription on a monumental slab.

[1] The elder, Alexander, who succeeded to the Baronetcy, which never reached his father, was a Bengal civil servant, and was dashed to pieces, with his horse, when riding along the Tibet road fastened into the side of a precipitous hill some miles from Simla. His son, born in 1864, is Sir Henry Hayes Lawrence, Bart.

The stricken husband plunged still more deeply into work. In one of his letters he states that Lord Dalhousie offered him the newly-created Chief Commissionership of Oudh, which was annexed by orders from England in 1855. Sorrow and sickness probably led him to decline a position which he eagerly accepted from Lord Canning eighteen months after, although the doctors had ordered him home. It was unfortunate for the new province, and for himself, that he was not its ruler from the first. Had he organised the administration as sole governor, there would have been no rebellion in Oudh, probably, and its great barons might have been used, like the Punjab chiefs, to help us actively in crushing a purely military rising. But the North-West civilians, entrusted with the administration, mismanaged the land settlement, and quarrelled among themselves. Even General Outram's military and political arrangements were condemned by Sir Henry Lawrence as worse, for that noble soldier would enlist no Sepoys or policemen who had not been in the ex-king's service, while the troops, the unprotected magazine, and the treasury were scattered over a wide area. When, at the end of March 1857, Sir Henry reached Lucknow, he found discontent in the city and throughout the country. His European force was hardly 700 strong, and the military arrangements were thus defective. This was the result of the neglect of Lord Dalhousie's orders, due to the interval between the departure of a strong Governor-General and the time when his successor could govern for himself. Such was the magic of

Henry Lawrence's name, such the effect of his firm but loving rule, that "in ten days" the mass of the difficulties disappeared.

But side by side with the local discontent there was, throughout all Northern and Central India, the mutinous spirit of the native soldiery. At Berhampoor and Barrackpoor, in Lower Bengal, and then at Meerut and Delhi in Upper India, the storm had burst. From the beginning of the cartridge excitement, Lawrence saw the extent of the danger, and the best way of meeting it.[1] "He told me," says the ablest of his staff,

[1] Sir Henry Lawrence was the one man in all the Empire who anticipated the Sepoy Mutiny. In the articles which he wrote when I edited the *Calcutta Review*, and some of which I reprinted (Serampore, *Friend of India* Press, 1859), he proved himself an able military critic and reformer. But his warnings were unheeded by Lord Canning's Government, and it needed the Sepoy campaigns with all their horrors to make the Indian Army what it now is, after the sanitary reforms of his brother John, when Viceroy, and successive Commanders-in-Chief, like Lord Strathnairn, Sir Donald Stewart, and Lord Roberts. Mr. Herman Merivale thus correctly estimates the foresight of Henry Lawrence :—

"I select from his publications of March 1856 a passage which is now of importance only as showing the views entertained by one so capable of judging as himself, of the probabilities of that terrible catastrophe which was then imminent. The organisation of the Indian military system, its defects and excellences, and the measures required for its improvement, had constituted the engrossing subject of his meditation for many long years. He had written incessantly respecting it, and had, in his own person, done still more. Nevertheless, in what may be called his controversy, though posthumous, with Sir Charles Napier, Lawrence did not share the former's views as to the mutinous disposition of the native army; he leaned, perhaps, to the side of favourable prediction the more naturally, because Napier's utterances had been so decidedly the other way. But there was no such by-reason for the language in which he weighs the same probabilities in a much later article (*Calcutta Review*, 'Indian Army,' March 1856). He is complaining of the slowness of native promotion and scantiness of native reward, which would, in his opinion, finally sap the loyalty of the Sepoy army, on which we yet entirely relied. 'Ninety in a hundred Sepoys have every reason to be

"that nearly the whole army would go, that he did not think the Sikhs would go." His policy was to segregate the Sikhs and selected men from the mutinous mass. He placed the artillery with the European infantry, he distributed the discontented irregulars, he garrisoned the fort called Muchi Bhawn, he prepared the Residency. In directions and personal intercourse with the native officials and troops he attached to himself many who afterwards helped us, and neutralised the hostility of others. By the 17th of May, one week after the fatal 10th at Meerut, his military reorganisation was complete, and he awaited the storm in calm confidence. Ever thoughtful of others, he encouraged General Wheeler at Cawnpoor, and so comforted Lord Canning, that he looked on him as "a tower of strength." The English Government quietly nominated him Provisional Governor-General. When, on the night of 30th May, the outbreak came, it was fitful; it had been discounted. But in the out-stations of the province the Sepoys

delighted with the service. Several of the remaining ten are satisfied. One, two, or three are dangerously discontented. The reason is plain. They feel they have that in them which would elsewhere raise them to distinction. Our system presses them down." . . . He urged, therefore, the needful measures of encouragement as desirable, but not pressing, still less as too late. "We must not wait," he said, "until, in a voice somewhat louder than that of the European officers in the days of Clive, the 'excellent drills' and the 'tight pantalooned' combine to assert their claims. What the European officers have repeatedly done may surely be expected of natives. We shall be unwise to wait for such occasion. Come it will, unless anticipated. A Clive may not be then at hand." Questions of pay, he observes, have been the most prominent cause of murmurs and mutinies. "The other chief cause of mutiny is religion—fanaticism. Hitherto, it has been restricted to Mohammedanism. Hindoos are contented to be let alone." Such, and no greater, was the real extent of Sir Henry's prevision in March 1856. Within little more than twelve months the army of Northern India was in general rebellion.

were triumphant; the great landholders, while occasionally giving refuge to the English fugitives, were acquiescent. At Cawnpoor Nana Dhoondopunt had shut in Wheeler, and had already butchered several. On 31st May the mutineers had been driven northwards from the city of Lucknow. On 29th June, worn out by constant toil and vigilance, and overruled, it is believed, by rash advisers, Sir Henry Lawrence marched out of Lucknow to reconnoitre the insurgents at Chinhut, some little distance from the city. He had only 336 white troops and 11 guns; his 220 natives went over to their brethren. The reconnaissance became an attack, the attack a rout, and Sir Henry Lawrence and the garrison were shut up in the enclosure of the Residency which he had prepared for the worst contingency.

On 1st July an eight-inch shell burst in Sir Henry's small room without injury. When urged to leave it for a safer, he laughingly replied that the enemy had not an artilleryman good enough to send another after it. Round shot followed later in the day. The 2nd of July he spent in withdrawing the garrison of Muchi Bhawn to the Residency amid the dreadful heat of that season, and at 8 P.M. he lay down in his clothes exhausted. He was again urged to go to a lower room. His nephew lay on a bed parallel with his. As he was directing alterations to be made in a memorandum which was being read to him by Colonel Wilson of his staff, the fatal shot came: "a sheet of flame, a terrific report and shock, and dense darkness." Colonel Wilson fell stunned, and on recovering consciousness could see neither Sir Henry nor his nephew amidst the smoke and dust. In great alarm, he twice cried out, "Sir Henry, are you hurt?" The third time there came the low response, "I am killed." Some soldiers of the 32nd rushed in and bore him to a safe room. Then, Dr. (now Sir Joseph) Fayrer, telling him he had only forty-eight hours to live, had him removed to his own house beside the Baillie Guard Gate.

These hours he spent first in duty—in giving instructions to those who were to take his place. That done, he did not even then think of himself, but called to his bedside those officers whom he knew in private life, that he might tell them the one lesson of his life. "Earnestly he entreated them to consider the vanity of earthly things, and the importance of living unto Christ while life and time were granted to them. He exhorted them not to set their hearts on the transitory pleasures, or honours, or riches of the world. . . . He spoke most humbly of himself as having failed to do what he ought, though he had tried; spoke of himself as unworthy, and died, I hope and trust, a humble, good Christian, none the worse for being a soldier of the centurion's stamp, who did not deem himself worthy that our Lord should come under his roof." These words were written by Sir Henry Durand as he took them down from the lips of Dr. Fayrer, the Christian physician, soon after the relief of the garrison. They have new interest now, since Sir Henry Durand was himself, when Lieutenant-Governor of the Punjab, struck down by a still more terrible death when passing under the low gateway of the frontier tower of Tânk. Of all the great men it has been my privilege to meet, these two Christian soldier-statesmen are the greatest. Of both we may ask, with Durand himself, when commenting on that death-bed, "Will God prosper the soldier's sermon?"

The Residency of Lucknow, like the area around the massacre-house and well of Cawnpoor, is now a sweet garden-cemetery, amid the foliage of which the long, beleaguered ruins look like some old cathedral. There lies all that is mortal of Henry Lawrence under a simply massive tomb, which speaks of him only as one "who tried to do his duty." When last I visited the hallowed spot his brother John, standing as Viceroy of India on the terrace of the Residency, which overlooks the plain of the Goomti, was receiving homage from all the chivalry of Oudh! The national memorial of Henry Lawrence, a marble statue, has its fitting place in St. Paul's. With Durand we may best apply to him his own favourite lines from George Herbert:—

"If soldier,
Chase base employments with a naked sword
Throughout the world. Fool not; for all may have,
If they dare try, a glorious life or grave."

III

JOHN, LORD LAWRENCE OF THE PUNJAB, G.C.B., 1811–1879

Saviour of India in the Great Revolt

In all the century only one man of the people has been made Viceroy of India. Warren Hastings was the first Governor-General; his pupil, John Shore, became the third, after Lord Cornwallis, because he knew the people and the country at the critical time of the permanent settlement of the land-tax of Bengal. The East India Company's jealousy of its own great servants led it to forbid the appointment of Sir Charles Metcalfe, whom the Crown afterwards sent to Jamaica and Canada as governor. The Crown's constitutional relation to political parties, the exclusiveness of the Whig and the *esprit de corps* of the Tory governing families, operated practically in confining the selection of a Viceroy to themselves. George Canning was, indeed, appointed to the office afterwards filled by his son, and both Crown and Company twice urged its acceptance on the Hon. Mountstuart Elphinstone. But John Lawrence, whom the English and Indian peoples still mourn, was the only man who, from Warren

Hastings to the present hour, sat for the usual term of five years in the Viceroy's seat, and yet was not a peer. Shore became Lord Teignmouth and Hardinge viscount while yet in the high office; Lawrence was no more than a baronet until, in 1869, he had retired from its responsibilities and its splendours.

In administrative genius and as a ruler of men John Lawrence comes only second to Warren Hastings. But the sixteenth towers far above the first Governor-General in unsullied purity of life and lofty nobility of purpose. Warren Hastings consolidated the empire which Clive had created; John Lawrence saved the empire which Dalhousie had developed in peace and in war. Sent out as Viceroy in the panic caused by the Umbeyla campaign and the death of Lord Elgin, John Lawrence was selected for a task which no inexperienced peer could undertake, for three reasons: he had civilised the Punjab; he had created a school of administrators able to govern in his spirit; he had saved the empire of British India in the Mutiny of 1857. These, followed by his five years' work as Viceroy, and adorned because rendered possible by his righteous and kindly personality, constitute his title to a grave in the Abbey, to a brilliant page in the annals of his country, to a foremost place among the statesmen and warriors who have made the British Empire what it is.

It was while his father was enlisting recruits in Yorkshire, in 1811, that John Lawrence first saw the light at Richmond. Born on English soil, of an Irish father and a mother who used to boast that she was a descendant of John Knox, the boy seemed to inherit all the national virtues which went to make him the future Viceroy. But, above all, he was a soldier. His mother's faith was in him directed by the veteran's military spirit. His father, Colonel Alexander Lawrence, had won his company when storming Seringapatam in the force led by Arthur Wellesley. When they were together again in the Waterloo campaign, and he applied to be allowed to take to the front a body of picked men from the garrison of Ostend, which he commanded, the Duke of Wellington replied that he believed Lawrence to be too good a soldier to wish for any other post than that which had been assigned to him. The anecdote, often told in the family, marks precisely the line where John Lawrence differed from his impulsive Irish father. "We derived most of our metal from our father," he afterwards said. But the soldier's ardour he at once restrained and directed by the civilian's sense of duty. His elder brother, Henry, had an equal devotion to duty, derived from the same faith, but in his generous impulses and keen affections the nature of the father and of his countrymen was more evident. John was the more Scottish as Henry was the more Irish of the two. The contrast became almost conflict when they were associated in the government of the Punjab, and Henry had to give way to the more cool and practical younger brother. But both were selected by Lord Palmerston, who had denied their father a slight increase of pension, to be Viceroy —Henry, had he lived, as Lord Canning's successor, in the Mutiny of 1857; John as Lord Elgin's, in the Sitana War of 1864.

It was a bitter time for John Lawrence when the boy was told that, instead of going to Addiscombe, like Henry, to be a soldier, he must study at Haileybury for the richer position of a Bengal civil servant. But here, too, duty was his guide. He passed through Haileybury with more than the average reputation of his fellows. Long after, in the height of his fame, he said to Sir Herbert Edwardes, his most trusted assistant, "Henry and I were both bad in languages, and always continued so; we were not good in anything which required a technical memory, but we were good in anything which required thought and judgment. We were good, for instance, in history." And so they became great in making history. After two seasons of hard work in the old Company's College—like its army, too rashly abolished—John Lawrence went out to Calcutta in the same year, 1829, as Dr. Duff and Sir Henry Durand. It is curious to reflect that while, in 1830, the young civilian was completing his mastery of Persian and Hindi in Calcutta, the first missionary of the Church of Scotland, Alexander Duff, five years his senior, was, almost in the next street, laying the foundation of his great Christianising agency. In the old college of Fort William he gave himself to Persian, of which he was ever afterwards the colloquial master; and the moment he had passed his examination there he demanded to be sent to Delhi. There young Charles Trevelyan was earning his spurs; but the city and its county were not popular with the young civil servants.

The place was full of work and full of risk. The shadow of power rested on the throne of the Great Moghul, the son of Shah Aalum, whose titles and letters of honour were eagerly coveted by our other tributary chiefs. The city was turbulent with the rabble of a titular court and the sensuality of a sullen aristocracy. The surrounding district was almost as bad as the worst Turkish province at the present day. But that was precisely why the young civilian chose it. There he was ever in the saddle, when he was not administering rough-and-ready justice in the city court or in the leafy tope of trees. He learned to know every man of mark in the capital, every village over an area as large as his native county. He was a born detective. Who that has heard him tell it can forget the story of his discovery of the assassin of his superior officer, William Fraser, in 1835? The ominous intelligence reached him when about to enter the bath after his forenoon's work. His first thought was to consult a certain Nawab, whose professions of loyalty the English authorities had always trusted. On reaching his palace Lawrence was informed he must wait, for the great man was in the hareem. The young civilian, being a lover of horses, resolved to look at the stables meanwhile, and there he saw the Nawab's favourite Arab still covered with foam. The fact, thus accidentally stumbled upon, led to the discovery that the chief was himself the murderer.

This unpublished anecdote of him may be added.

When he had risen to be Collector, or terrestrial providence to the half-million, a lawless chief in the desert-tract of the country refused to pay his land-tax. Attended only by his orderly, "Jan Larren" rode out from Delhi for many miles in the early morning. He found the walled village closed to him, and himself defied. There were no troops within thirty miles. It was the fierce time of tropical May, and no shelter was visible, save a meagre babool tree. Was he to ride back *re infecta,* trailing with him the prestige of his Government, and so inviting all the country to go and do likewise? He retired to the scanty shade of the tree, pencilled a note to an officer in Delhi ordering out a battery, and took up his position in sight of the principal gateway. High rose the sun, more thirsty and wearied became the Collector, but he must take the village, even as he was long after to take Delhi. Still no troops appeared. As he scanned the horizon for them, he observed a solitary native approaching. "Sahib," said the Oriental, "why do you sit there? If you wish to humble these traitors to their salt, I will help you before the guns come." The speaker was the chief of a neighbouring fort, who had no objection to take this opportunity of at once avenging his private wrongs, and gaining the favour of the dread Collector. The result was the submission of the recusant village, the payment of the land-tax with a fine superadded, and the return of the resolute civilian to Delhi. Years passed on, the Mutiny came and ceased, and when "Jan Larren" was the Lieutenant-

Governor of the whole Punjab, a list of the names of rebels sentenced to death was put before him for his signature. The first name caught his attention, he remembered it was that of the Goojur who had assisted him on the burning May day, and he spared his life.

But John Lawrence's study of human nature and love of the people found another field than that of the swashbucklers and nobles of the Moghul's court. The land-tax of the whole Lieutenant-Governorship then ruled from Agra, as now from Allahabad, was being settled for thirty years on principles benevolent in intention at least, though, from the continued want of permanence, still dangerous to the social and political well-being of the people. With Thomason and W. Muir, John Lawrence came under the spell of Mertins Bird, the author of the settlement. Thus he found, or he thought he found, on the plains of Hindustan, the same question of tenant-right with which in Ulster he had become familiar, and which Mr. Gladstone was the first to settle there. As against the oppressive but not always unjust barons of India, known as Talookdars in the Upper, and Zemindars in the Lower Provinces, he set the claims to proprietorship or beneficial occupancy of the mass of the cultivators. "Whose is the sweat, his is the soil," was practically the sentiment which guided him towards the creation of whole races of peasant proprietors. Thus he gradually learned to become the Stein of the Punjab, and he tried to work the same revolution in Oudh, and even in Bengal, where the action of his predecessors had made the attempt come too late. In the Punjab, at least, he was right, for the Province was almost such a *tabula rasa* as Lord Canning afterwards legally made Oudh, and there were few large landlords to be ejected or converted into indebted annuitants on estates which they claimed as their own. His great heart yearned over the millions who had been for centuries the sport of invading hosts and pampered chiefs, and he longed to make them physically happy if Providence denied them political freedom. Hence he used to burst forth into this ideal, as reported by Dr. R. N. Cust when one of his subordinates—"I would see this country thickly cultivated by a fat, contented yeomanry, each man riding his own horse, sitting under his own fig-tree, and enjoying his rude family comforts."

The time soon came when he was given the power of doing as much to realise that ideal as human nature rendered possible in a quarter of a century. The help which he gave as Collector of Delhi made possible the victory at Sobraon, and led Lord Hardinge to appoint him, in 1846, when only thirty-five years of age, Commissioner of the ceded territory of the Jalandhar Doab, or the mountain land from the Sutlej to the Indus. The second Sikh War soon after ended in the conquest of the whole Punjab, which Lord Dalhousie placed under Henry and John Lawrence and Sir Robert Montgomery as a Board. Henry's generous impulse was to continue to the usurpers of the Sikh brotherhood the large revenues, sucked from the people, which, on Runjeet Singh's death, they had alienated to themselves.

His policy, like Lord Canning's after him, was aristocratic—to govern the dumb millions through their natural leaders. John's practical experience as a civilian convinced him that thus the Punjab would never pay its expenses, while his sympathy with the people made him resolute to withstand his brother's sentimental though pure policy. The new Government came to a deadlock, and a Governor-General like Dalhousie decided in favour of John. It was well, even for the military chiefs. What Henry's Irish heart would have made of the whole Punjab is seen in the iniquitous misrule, for years, of Kashmir, which was sold to Gulab Singh. How John saved the chiefs from their own vices, while protecting the people and the public revenue spent upon both, was seen when every man of them came forward in the Mutiny of 1857 and helped him to hold the Province and take Delhi.

In spite of Sir Richard Temple's reports, justice has not yet been done in official or English literature to the English pacification and civilisation of the Punjab by the two brothers Lawrence, but chiefly by John. He solved the problem which defied Imperial Rome, Spain, and Portugal in all their glory, France in its attempts from Algeria to Anam, and Turkey and Russia all through their history of lawless gloom. An autocrat, a military dictator, a revenue collector, an aggressive Christian, he yet was not a provincial proprætor, nor a fanatical inquisitor, nor a mere marshal, nor a "reforming" pasha, nor an "orthodox" exterminator of the Warsaw type. He was a righteous democratic Will, the terrestrial providence of nineteen millions of people, warlike and yet dumb, whom he understood because he loved them, and whose natural leaders he controlled because he knew them. On the one side he poured into their lap material prosperity, by creating property in land and produce and trade, which the anarchy of the previous centuries had made impossible. On the other side, to trade and roads, railways and telegraphs he added schools and colleges, vernacular and English, for girls and boys. And while, in the freedom of Anglo-Indian life, all the world might see him at his own devotions in his tent, he helped Christian missionaries, he invited them to help him, always within the limits of a careful toleration. Long before the Queen was led, in the Proclamation of 1858, to tell her Indian subjects that, even as she relied on the Christian religion for herself, she had no design to impose it on others, John Lawrence had carried out, all over the Punjab, the policy which saved India, and which he thus formulated :—"Sir John Lawrence does entertain the earnest belief that all those measures which are really and truly Christian can be carried out in India, not only without danger to British rule, but, on the contrary, with every advantage to its stability."

But he could never have done a tithe of all this had he, however great in himself, lacked that other indispensable qualification of a ruler of men—the ability to select, to train, to trust subordinates of like mind. The same God-given power which enabled him at once to fascinate and to master the natives of all classes, for their own good, made him first feared and then for ever loyally supported by his coadjutors. Hence his creation of the Punjab school of officials. Even when he was still a young man at Delhi, Thomason used to send to him from Agra the most promising assistants to be trained. So, too, it was with Henry. The two gathered around them a band of some sixty administrators in all, half of them civilians and half military men, but all for civil duty yet all masters of the military art in turn. Let me recall some of them.

Robert Napier, first Lord of Magdala, was the engineer officer who gave the Punjab its first necessity after peace—roads so good that railways run on them now, but so costly that they were said to be paved with silver. To go on with the professional soldiers there was Herbert Edwardes, the young lieutenant who, having taken Mooltan, was to save Peshawar and live long enough to write only the first volume of his master Henry's *Life*. There was General Lake, the gentle and the brave, equally good in the field, on the bench, and at the missionary committee's table. There was Reynell Taylor, who civilised one mountain band and then another wild frontier. And there was John Nicholson, who, when worshipped as a god by the warlike tribe he first defeated and then flogged for their adoring superstition, led the movable column to Delhi, where, as he fell, John Lawrence wept. There were the other brother Sir George Lawrence and Sir Henry Lumsden.

First among the civilians comes Sir Donald M'Leod, the scholar, as well as the ruler who succeeded his chief, great in the simplicity of a renewed nature which ever led him to sacrifice himself for others, whether natives or his own countrymen. An earlier successor, the wise and gentle Sir Robert Montgomery, disarmed the Sepoys. Edward Thornton, too, was one of the elder men. As to the younger, they reached everywhere high positions in the East. Sir Charles Aitchison was their leader, and his is the best *Life* of John Lawrence. Sir Richard Temple, their historian, has filled every ordinary high office in India. When the old regulation system collapsed in 1857, the Punjab men, derided before by their ignorant brethren as too self-assertive, were found by the tardy Lord Canning to be the ablest in the service. From Bengal to Bombay and Mysore, and then from Burma to Lahore, they almost monopolised the well-paid offices, which demand a knowledge of men and a prudent fearlessness in ruling them. John Lawrence, in this sense, has never ceased to govern the Empire he saved.

When the hot season of 1857 came he had won his pension. His health was failing, and he dreamed of well-won rest at home. He was at Rawal Pindi when, on the 11th of May, the Delhi signallers remained just long enough at their post to telegraph: "The Sepoys have come in from Meerut, and are burning everything. Mr. Todd is dead and, we hear, several Europeans. We must shut up." The old Collector of Delhi knew all that this implied. Unequal to the strain, the Commander-in-Chief of that day, then at Simla, allowed the rebels to pour into Delhi in such strength that a protracted and long doubtful siege became inevitable. John Lawrence could not give him the political and military genius required; but none the less he accepted the task of undoing the mistake. He had to pacify his own Province and take Delhi, all on his own responsibility, for communication with the rest of India was cut off. Happily for him, and for the Empire, or the Punjab might have had its Cawnpore! His whole plan and action may be summarised in two lines—"Disarm the Hindustani regiments at once; raise loyal Punjabi levies to take their place." Not only in his own subordinates, but in Queen's officers like Corbett and Cotton, he found noble support. Nor there alone. As if to prove that justice to the people does not mean wrong to the chiefs who, uncontrolled, would oppress them, the princes and nobles of the Punjab, with their feudal armies, flocked to his standard. The civilisation of all Southern Asia, the prestige of all England, trembled in the balance. John Lawrence stamped his foot and every village sent forth the warriors of Runjeet Singh whom he had converted into grateful peasants. John Lawrence waved his hand, and from every native castle there came streaming the chivalry of Putiala and Nabha, Jhind and others. Forgetting the inexperience and the slow intellect which misled Lord Canning at the first, men have praised him for his clemency as they reproached him then with equal wisdom. It was John Lawrence who, truly merciful, at once disarming to prevent striking, or smiting only to anticipate worse evil, needed no penal acts like the bloody statutes of Lord Canning's council, and arrested the sword of judgment the moment it had done the work, while others were still wildly wielding it at the dictation of panic or revenge.

It was said—said in the House of Lords, by Lord Granville, in his eagerness to apologise for Lord Canning's early inactivity—that Lawrence had recommended the Governor-General to treat with the rebels. Again, the councillors around Lord Canning further sought to shield their own impotence by asserting that "Iron John," as he used to be called, was ready to abandon the Peshawar valley! Sir John Kaye has done this subject so little justice, that I here state the actual facts, which I ascertained soon after the events, from the very highest authority on such charges.

In the first week of July, when our position was gloomiest, the King of Delhi proposed to turn traitor, and promised the General besieging the city to admit the British troops into the palace if he were forgiven. Such a service might atone for treason, but it could not wipe out the stain of murder, and the reply was returned, that the offer would be worthy of consideration if the king were innocent of the murder of Christians. In command of the palace-citadel, we would have crushed the mutineers who afterwards escaped to feed the rebellion in Oudh, and the campaign might have ended a year sooner than it did and at one tithe of the expense of blood and treasure. So in the case of Peshawar. When Delhi still defied us, when the last man had been sent to the Ridge, when Musalmans and Sikhs alike began to doubt our power to recover our position, and Sir John Lawrence began to make arrangements with friendly chiefs for the protection of wives and children, then surely came the question, What is to be done if Delhi stands? In that event, Sir John Lawrence was *prepared* to give up Peshawar before the end came, that he might utilise its garrison for the safety of the English in the Province. The question was one of the possible end of the British Empire in the East, and before that came Peshawar must go.

On the other hand, what did the Chief Commissioner do? what would he have done had Anson been under his orders? Finding that Montgomery, Corbett, and Macpherson had proved themselves equal to the strain at Lahore, he placed himself at Rawal Pindi, in the most central position between the frontier and the capital. Except the disarming of Sepoys when he was in the hills at Murree, all the policy was his. We find Sir R. Montgomery, in the Mutiny Report, expressing, on the part of "every officer in the Province," "sincerest admiration of the intrepid policy he *originated* and so nobly carried out—even to complete success." His first act had been to urge General Anson to make an immediate advance on Delhi, at a time when every officer consulted by His Excellency was adverse to that course. Had Anson been a soldier, Delhi would have fallen a week after it declared for rebellion, and long before its scanty Sepoy garrison had been reinforced by the crowds of mutineers whom the rebel flag induced to desert. To John Lawrence, and to him alone, is due even its long-delayed fall. Just, too, as Lord Canning to the last was advised not to disarm the troops at Dinapoor, which delayed the march of all British reinforcements, and led to the massacre of Cawnpore, General Anson would not disarm the Umballa Sepoys, although pressed to do so by the Chief Commissioner. The result he tells us in the despatch of 25th May 1858, which reviews the events of the Mutiny, "the advance of our troops towards Delhi, and the victory at Badli-ka-Serai near that city on the 8th June, which proved to the country that there was vitality in our cause and power on our side." "Thus it was that, through mistaken leniency and blind confidence in native soldiers, an opportunity was missed, whereby, at the outset of the disturbances, a whole brigade might have been successfully dealt with in a vigorous and exemplary manner." How the 4th Light Cavalry, the 5th N.I., and the 60th N.I., the soldiers referred to, deserted or mutinied, fired on their officers at Rohtak, and swelled finally the Delhi garrison, history tells. Living through these events, and studying them now as recorded in cold blood, I have failed to find one flaw in the action or the policy of John Lawrence in these days, and at the very darkest hour England showed its appreciation by sending him the Grand Cross of the Bath.

When the triumph came, how did he bear it? The despatch thus concludes, "In causing this narrative to be recorded, Sir John Lawrence has not been actuated by any motive of self-laudation. Throughout the crisis he could not but feel that human means and human precautions were utterly impotent, that everything which was done or could be done to surmount such dangers and difficulties was as nothing, and that trust could be placed in Divine Providence alone. . . . His mercy vouchsafed a happy issue to our measures, and confounded the devices of our enemies. Human aid could avail us nothing in that crisis, and it is owing to an overruling Providence, and that alone, that a single Englishman was left alive in the Punjab." I have reason to believe that this passage expresses more than the public, or historical, or providential conviction of the writer as to God's working. There he speaks of his country, his Government, his administration. But the Mutiny crisis and deliverance brought, if not a new, certainly a vitally intensified spiritual experience to himself. I remember well a conversation with him, when he was Governor-General, at Peterhof, Simla, in September 1866, when he reverently alluded to his solitary musings at the darkest time, having arranged for the protection of his wife and family by a faithful chief if the worst should come. Few could pass through that fire untouched, and he came out of the hottest of the furnace, like many men and women in humbler life, seven times refined.

Hence the most famous of all his Minutes, to which I now come, that of 21st April 1858. Sir H. Edwardes had officially sent him a somewhat extreme memorandum on "the elimination of all unchristian principle from the

Government of India." Sir Donald M'Leod passed on the communication with a letter which Sir John pronounced "more moderate in its tone and marked by an enlightened and excellent spirit." Lawrence was willing to teach the Bible in State schools, and in voluntary classes wherever there were Christian teachers, "in order that our views of Christian duty might be patent to the native public." Edwardes would have resumed idol endowments, Lawrence declared that "the judgments of Providence would become manifest in the political disaffection which might ensue," and such a step would retard the progress of Christianity while it is condemned by the whole tenor of its teachings. On the subject of caste Sir John pointed out that Government had not recognised it except in the Sepoy army, urged the raising of sweeper regiments as he himself had done, and of corps from the non-Aryan tribes, and anticipated the "happy time" when regiments of native Christians could be raised. But while encouraging Sepoys to consult missionaries, he condemned preaching to the native soldiers in a body, unless they were of the aboriginal tribes destitute of a faith. He refused to disallow native holidays; earnestly desired to see the law altered in reference to polygamy and early betrothals; would prohibit religious processions in public as he did in the case of the Mohuram at Delhi, and would interdict obscenities in temples; would restrict prostitutes to their houses; would increase the number of married soldiers and improve the condition of their wives and widows; condemned the opium monopoly, accepting the existing system; but did not agree as to the evil tendency of the liquor excise in the Punjab, where it has diminished the drunkenness encouraged in the Sikh *régime.* And the despatch concludes with a passage which is worthy of being made the keynote of our policy in India, as it was of his own administration:—

"Sir J. Lawrence has been led, in common with others since the occurrence of the awful events of 1857, to ponder deeply on what may be the faults and shortcomings of the British as a Christian nation in India. In considering topics such as those treated of in this despatch, he would solely endeavour to ascertain what is our Christian duty. Having ascertained that according to our erring lights and conscience, he would follow it out to the uttermost, undeterred by any consideration. If we address ourselves to this task, it may, with the blessing of Providence, not prove too difficult for us. Measures have, indeed, been proposed as essential to be adopted by a Christian Government which would be truly difficult or impossible of execution. But on closer consideration it will be found that such measures are not enjoined by Christianity, but are contrary to its spirit. Sir John Lawrence does entertain the earnest belief that all those measures which are really and truly Christian can be carried out in India, not only without danger to British rule, but, on the contrary, with every advantage to its stability. Christian things done in a Christian way will never, the Chief Commissioner is convinced, alienate the heathen. About such things there are qualities which do not provoke nor excite distrust, nor harden to resistance. It is when unchristian things are done in the name of Christianity, or when Christian things are done in an unchristian way, that mischief and danger are occasioned. The difficulty is, amid the political complications, the conflicting social considerations, the fears and hopes of self-interest which are so apt to mislead human judgment, to discern clearly what is imposed upon us by Christian duty and what is not. Having discerned this, we have but to put it into practice. Sir John Lawrence is satisfied that, within the territories committed to his charge, he can carry out all those measures which are really matters of Christian duty on the part of the Government. And, further, he believes that such measures will arouse no danger; will conciliate instead of provoking, and will subserve to the ultimate diffusion of the truth among the people.

"Finally, the Chief Commissioner would recommend, that such measures and policy, having been deliberately determined on by the Supreme Government, be openly avowed and universally acted upon throughout the Empire; so that there may be no diversities of practice, no isolated tentative, or conflicting efforts, which are, indeed, the surest means of exciting distrust; so that the people may see that we have no sudden or sinister designs; and so that we may exhibit that harmony and uniformity of conduct which befits a Christian nation striving to do its duty."

The triumphant statesman and soldier who wrote thus was made only a baronet by the Crown on his retirement from India. But the expiring East India Company voted him a life-pension of £2000 a year.

The beginning of 1859 saw profound peace all over India. Delhi was made over to the Punjab, converted into a Lieutenant-Governorship. Save in its battered walls and new-made graves, I then saw no traces of the death-struggle through which the Province had passed. It was more prosperous than ever. The man who had done his work, as he thought, retired to rest in the slumberous shades of the new-made Council of the Secretary of State for India. There he was sitting in 1863, when Sir Charles Wood looked into his room and said, "You are to go to India; wait till I come back from Windsor." So the seat of Warren Hastings was once more filled from the Bengal Civil Service. In Calcutta and at Simla, Sir John Lawrence had to work a very different system from the splendid "non-regulation" autocracy of Delhi and Lahore. Councillors and Secretaries, Governors and Lieutenant-Governors, a Secretary of State and Parliament had all to be consulted or considered. The more was the pity, for both him and the Empire. But men like him come only once in a century, and centralised systems must be created for ordinary mortals. Of all that was Christian, philanthropic, and enlightened Lord and Lady Lawrence were the leaders. Boldly carrying out his Punjab Christian policy, he did not hesitate to preside at the examination of Dr. Duff's College, going there in all the state of the Viceroy, as both he and his predecessors had gone to secular colleges. In all that concerned the education of the people, the good of the British soldier, his wife and children, the sanitary condition of the country and the towns, and the reasonable progress of railways and canals, he distanced every preceding Governor-General. A born financier as to instinct, he would have developed the wise and too-soon-forgotten policy of James Wilson, if he had been allowed to do his own work. His reign is identified with two still disputed military and political schools—those who advocate the irregular system, with few officers, for the whole army in India; and those who were content with the old Peshawar frontier, whether Russia intrigued and advanced south or not. His feudatory policy was as gentle as his brother Henry's would have been. He was the first Viceroy who could address the assembled nobles of the Empire, in Durbar, in their own tongue.

The time was the 20th day of November 1866. The place was Agra, the capital of Akbar, the greatest of all the Asiatic rulers of India. Let me recall the scene as I witnessed it in all its splendours, and its political significance for the good of the seventy millions of India who are directly ruled by their own feudatory sovereigns.

The great Durbar tent, with its accessories, covers a space equal to rather more than half of Exeter Hall, and stands in front of the Viceroy's private tents, with which it communicates. Before it is a richly-adorned canvas canopy, called a "shamiana," which acts as a portico for the reception of chiefs and the guard of honour, while in front of that is the Royal Standard of England, and the wide centre street, with its rows of snowy palaces, to which all the other streets behind and around run parallel. The street is lined with English cavalry, and all the numerous salutes are fired from the fort, two miles off, except that of the Viceroy.

In the centre of the long side of the Durbar tent stands the throne, covered with richly embroidered cloth of gold. Taking up our position at the foot of the dais we behold stretching away to right and left lines of Hindu and Musalman nobles decked in jewels and rich stuffs, such as no other country or nobility in the world could produce. We feel that this is the land of the Koh-i-noor, of Punna and Golconda, of the diamond, ruby, and pearl. The Courts of Europe, even during their most gorgeous ceremonials, can present no such sight as this. Nor is it so barbaric as Milton's well-known descriptions would lead us to suppose. If we except the peculiar crinoline-like petticoats in which from the earliest ages the sovereigns of Rajpootana have hidden their legs, there is an amount of taste and art evident in the array which befits a people whose architectural triumphs far exceed those of Christendom.

The only point in which our European pageants seem superior to this is in the abundance of drapery, with its rounded outlines and flowing expanse. Except the Grand Master of the Order of the Star of India, the Secretary of the Order, and the Jeypoor Maharaja, who ordered it by telegraph from England, none of the Knights already made, or chiefs, wear the blue robe or mantle of the Order. This is especially marked in the Begum of Bhopal, a noble old lady, ever loyal to us, whose tights require some covering. But this absence of drapery is to some extent compensated for by the wild military character of the dress of the chiefs of Bundelkhand and the Punjab, and by the flowing beards of many a stalwart hero and aged Wuzeer. All the princes of the first and second ranks have their antique swords with jewelled handles, some even two, but the Boondela carries also his shield, with its silver bosses, and in some cases his massive mace or battle-axe. Behind the front ranks to right and left, forming a semicircle, within which the ceremony of investiture is to go on, sit the attendants of the chiefs in number and position according to the rank of their lords. Interspersed among them are the various English political officers who reside at the Courts of our feudatories, and strive to guide them aright in the management of their tenantry. Closing in the whole, at the far back on either side, and raised on a platform, are the favoured few ladies for whom accommodation could be provided —a novel sight in a Durbar, and justified by the fact of the English character of the investiture. The more brilliant throng to the left consists of Knights of the Order and those about to be invested; that to the right of all other chiefs. As the right is the seat of honour, Sindia was for a time much offended that he was placed on the left, nor was he altogether willing to understand that precedence that day was regulated by the rules of the Order, and not by the customs of India. Similarly Jeypoor and Jodhpoor were offended that the Begum of Bhopal should sit above them, because she received the Order before them, though she is next in rank to them. The trumpets sound, the Rifles, who form the guard of honour, present arms, the thunder of a royal salute is heard, and the Grand Master enters, preceded by his aides-de-camp, and followed by his secretaries, his long robe flowing behind him. Bowing to right and left, he takes his seat on the throne; Sir William Muir, the Foreign Secretary and Secretary to the Order, reads the Queen's letters of appointment in Hindustani and English. Along with Sir W. Mansfield, as junior Knight Grand Commander, he leads in successively the Maharaja of Jodhpoor and the Maharaja of Kerowli, the Grand Master addresses them, and puts the collar around their neck and the star on their breast, and they are conducted to their seats among the other Knights. Then follow eleven Knights Commanders and twenty-five Companions, and the Viceroy, in Hindustani, addresses the whole assembly.

Let us look more particularly at some of the nobles who compose it. That burly form, with scowling face, in the post of honour is Alijah Jyaji Rao Sindia, feudal lord of territories which yield him £930,910 a year, and of tenantry who number two and a half millions. He is the only one present of the four great Chiefs who rose to power during the anarchy of Maratha rule and the degeneracy of the descendants of Sivaji. Holkar, jealous of his rank, feigns sickness that he may be excused from obeying the Viceroy's summons. The Guicowar is too far off, and belongs more to the Bombay Presidency. The Bhonslas of Nagpoor have ceased to rule, and are represented by a distant relative to whom we gave estates in Bombay. Sindia's family is very recent in its origin. He cannot trace it further back than to that menial Ranaji, the slipper-bearer, whose fidelity in his humble office attracted the notice of Balajee Rao, the Peishwa. His son, stripped of many of his estates after the Maratha rout at Paniput, recovered and added to them, with the aid of French officers, to such an extent that in the latter half of last century he was master of Hindustan, and had seized the Emperor of Delhi. The quiet growth of our power relieved the country from Maratha rapine, Sindia entered into engagements with us, and the ruler who died in 1827 refused to adopt a son. We, however, placed Jankoji Rao on the throne under the regency of that Lucrezia Borgia of the Marathas, Baiza Bai.

The evil policy of non-interference, which prevailed almost from Lord Cornwallis to Lord Ellenborough, led to the brief war in which that Governor-General was forced to engage during the minority of the present chief. He assumed the management of his vast estates not long before the Mutiny, and no State in all India promised to be so satisfactorily managed as Gwalior, so long as he relied on the advice of the Raja, Sir Dinkar Rao. But, although this statesman saved him in the mad days of 1857, he could no more tolerate him than Victor Emmanuel could tolerate Ricasoli, and even went so far as to deprive his trusty servant of estates he had conferred on him in perpetuity. Not the least interesting incident in the Durbar was the knighting of Dinkar Rao, after which he magnanimously went up to Sindia and gracefully said, "I owe this honour to you, my master." For ability and veracity there was no native in India equal to Dinkar Rao. Next to

Sindia, that little figure is the Sekander Begum of Bhopal. The Bhopal family traces its origin to Dost Mahomed, an Afghan soldier of fortune, who served Aurangzeb, and carved out a principality for himself on the death of that Emperor.

The most attractive sight at the Durbar was the arrival of the chiefs on elephants, and the presentation to them of those rich *khilluts,* or dresses and jewels of honour, which are given by the Viceroy according to a fixed scale. The Maharaja Sindia receives a *khillut* of the value of £5000. The gifts are brought in on trays by long files of liveried attendants, from the Toshakana, or repository of State presents. Here all is Oriental, as in the pictures in which the old masters have represented Joseph at Pharaoh's Court, and the visit of the Queen of Sheba to Solomon. The tribute presented by the chiefs is periodically sold by auction. Many a rare sword and costly gem were purchased by the late Lord and Lady Canning privately from the Toshakana. Of late years the gifts have been more and more of a useful character—clocks, watches, scientific instruments, silver plate, and the Chiefs who choose to do so are allowed previously to select the articles they prefer up to the value allowed to their rank. As befits a Viceroy, they receive more valuable presents than they offer. A new feature at the general Durbar was the presence of nine native gentlemen, summoned to receive rewards for special services to the State, in education, literature, or loyal acts. Baba Khem Singh Bedi, for instance, has done much to extend female education in the Punjab.

Baboo Shivapersad was the great scholar of Benares, who had written many works, in which he communicates to his learned but superstitious countrymen the results of European science. Syud Ahmed Bahadoor is the remarkable subordinate civil Judge of Bareilly—a Musalman, who established an important literary society, translated many English books, and especially was the author of a translation of and commentary on the Bible on a gigantic scale, in the course of which, as a Musalman, he attacks Colenso and establishes the authenticity of the Pentateuch.

Sir John Lawrence's address is thus translated:—

"O MAHARAJAS, RAJAS, AND SIRDARS—It is with great satisfaction that I can see you all assembled before me this day. I bid you all a hearty welcome to this famous city, renowned for its splendid Taj, and, above all, in having been in former days the seat of the Government of the great Emperor, from whom it derives its name of Akbarabad.

"It is good for us thus to meet together; it is advantageous for me, as the Viceroy of the illustrious Queen of England and India, to see and become acquainted with so many chiefs of rank and reputation; and for you all, it is right that you should be able to speak face to face with me, and hear my views and wishes regarding the management of your respective territories.

"The art of governing wisely and well is a difficult one, which is only to be attained by much thought and care and labour. Few kings and chiefs in Hindustan have possessed the necessary qualifications, because they have not taken the precaution in their youth to learn to study and act for themselves; nor did they care to have their sons, those who were to succeed them, well instructed and carefully trained. Hence it has so often happened that after a chief has passed away he has not been remembered as a good and wise ruler. Great men when living often receive praise from their friends and adherents for virtues which they do not possess; but it is only after this life is ended that the real truth is told. Of all fame that such men can acquire, that alone is worth having which is accorded to a great and beneficent ruler. The names of conquerors and heroes are forgotten, but those of wise and virtuous chiefs live for ever.

"The days of war and rapine, it is to be hoped, have passed away from Hindustan never to return; but, perhaps, some of the chiefs now present can recollect the time in India, and all must have heard of the time, when neither the palace of the ruler, nor the cottage of the peasant, nor the most sacred edifices of Hindu and Mohammedan were safe from the hands of the plunderer and destroyer. In those days whole provinces were one scene of devastation and misery; for vast tracts of country scarcely the light of a lamp was to be seen in a single village. English rule in India has put all this down. No longer is the country a waste and a wilderness, the abode of savage animals. Now it is to a great extent covered with populous villages and rich with cultivation, and all the inhabitants are living in comparative safety under the shade of English power.

"But while such, no doubt, to a great extent is a true picture of the state of India, still, when we inquire closely into the condition of the different parts of the country, we cannot but perceive that much tyranny and oppression are still practised, that much individual suffering still exists, and that much crime escapes unpunished. That peace and that security from outward violence which the British Government confers on your territories you must extend to your people. None but the rulers of their own lands can accomplish this, and they only can do it by constant care and supervision. They have plenty of time to do all that is necessary if they have only the will. Chiefs have abundant time for their own pleasures and amusements; indeed, many of them have more leisure than they can employ, and are often weary from want of something to interest them. Others, again, waste their time in disputes with their neighbours, in quarrels with their feudatories, and even in still less satisfactory ways.

"If a chief will neglect his own proper duty, the care of his State, how can he expect that a deputy will perform it properly for him? Good laws and well-selected officials, carefully supervised, are necessary to ensure good government. An efficient police and a well-managed revenue are equally desirable, so that people may live in safety and enjoy the fruits of their industry. Schools for the education of the young and hospitals for the cure of the sick should also be established. Some chiefs are perhaps in debt, and would find it difficult to do much in the way I have sketched. But other chiefs have abundant revenues, and all I ask is that every ruler should act according to his means. Some among you vie with each other for precedence, and feel aggrieved at the position which they occupy. How much more to the purpose would it be if all would try which can govern his country in the wisest manner; in this way there is abundance of scope for all. The British Government will honour that chief most who excels in the good management of his people, who does most to put down crime and improve the condition of his country. There are chiefs in this Durbar who have acquired a reputation in this way. I may mention Maharaja Sindia and the Begum of Bhopal. The death of the late Nawab of Jowrah was a cause of grief to me, for I have heard that he was a wise and beneficent ruler. The Raja of Sitamow, in Malwa, is now ninety years old, and yet it is said that he manages his country very well. The Raja of Ketra, in Jeypoor, has been publicly honoured for the wise arrangements he has made in his lands. It is to me a very great pleasure when I hear of the meritorious conduct of any chief; and I try to make this known, so as to encourage other rulers to follow his example.

"Kings and chiefs in former times had no idea of opening out their countries. They often lived in difficult and almost inaccessible positions, surrounding their palaces with all kinds of fortifications, out of which they seldom ventured to any distance, and then only when attended by as many soldiers as they could muster. As to travelling to see the wonders of other countries, such an idea never entered their minds, or if it did it was dismissed as utterly impracticable. Now the princes of Hindustan have little hesitation in moving from one place to another at a distance from their own territories, and some chiefs have become so enlightened and far-seeing as to be willing to have roads made through the length and breadth of their lands, and some have contributed annually considerable sums for this purpose. I hope that others will follow their example, and do all they can to construct roads, canals, and wells in their country, thus enriching themselves and their people.

"I will now conclude by wishing you all again a welcome to Agra, and trust that what you have seen and heard, and the general reception you have met with, may make you long remember this Durbar. I have but one object—that you should govern your people well, and thus conduce to your own name and their happiness."

The Review and Durbars were but the serious events amid a succession of fêtes, which exhausted even the Governor-General. There were two fêtes in the Taj

Mahal gardens never to be forgotten. The first was given to the Viceroy and all Agra by the municipal authorities. Then the solemnly beautiful concave of the dome was lighted up, as at noon, with magnesium wire, and all its hidden glories of carving and ornamentation displayed as they have never been before. Finer than even this was the illumination of the Jumna, as only Hindus can light up a river. On a slight wicker framework thousands of lights were floated down its sluggish stream. For miles, as far as the eye could reach, the Jumna seemed a river of molten gold, combining with the purity of the Taj and its decorative designs in jasper, cornelian, and a hundred other stones, to form no unworthy realisation of the vision of St. John when he saw the new Jerusalem descending out of heaven adorned as a bride for her husband. The lighting-up of this queen of buildings in the fête given by Sindia to the Viceroy surpassed the efforts of the municipality. All who have seen continental gardens lighted up can realise what those of the Taj were. But to see the exquisitely proportioned outlines of the vast gateway,—itself a wonder,—the colonnaded approach, the two great mosques, and the graceful kiosks, all brought out in splendid relief by millions of Oriental "chirags," while the Taj itself—too pure to be defiled by one light placed *upon* it—was illumined by the electric light from its four minars and the mosques on either side,—to see this as it was seen for the first time in our rule that Saturday night, is to have witnessed a spectacle that the wealthiest capitals of Europe could not match, and a poet alone could fitly describe. On the sandy ridge thrown up by the Jumna, on the opposite side, where can still be seen the foundations of the tomb Shah Jehan meant to erect for himself, gorgeous fireworks were exhibited, reflected in the water, with a taste and an art the pyrotechnists of Europe have yet to learn. The Viceroy and Sindia, hand in hand, walked through the gardens and witnessed the spectacle.

When, in 1869, John Lawrence came home, leaving these as his last words in Calcutta—"Be kind to the natives"; and when, at last, he who had made and unmade many a Baron was himself created Baron Lawrence of the Punjab and of Grately, did the veteran of sixty go to sleep? He was elected the first Chairman of the London School Board, and there he toiled till failing eyesight forbade. In his place in Parliament, and in correspondence in the press, he did not cease to warn the country against a course which, he believed, would create insolvency and political discontent in India and disaster on the border. John Lawrence was ever, from boyhood to old age, the true, the righteous, the wise Christian, feared by the idle and the dishonest, loved by all right-hearted men; and with a strain of humour in his nature, which lightened public burdens to himself and official relations to others. In family and friends, few were so happy as he. Ever honouring God, he was honoured by God. To the last day of his life he worked for and along with such philanthropic agencies as the Christian Literature Society for India and the Church Missionary Society. He was Chairman of its Committee on the Uganda Mission in British East Africa as it now is. His last public effort was made for the people of India during the Budget debate in the House of Lords, on the 19th June 1879. "I am so weary," were the last murmured words of the hero who, during more than half a century, had done more than any other one man to make our Indian Empire what it is.

Dean Stanley, who had invited the family to lay the honoured remains in Westminster Abbey, declared, as he stood near the grave's mouth, that the Joshua of his country had fallen—"the great Proconsul of our English Christian Empire," who had saved "the India of Clive, of Hastings, and the illustrious statesman Bentinck, the civilisation which is sanctified by the missionary zeal of Martyn, of Duff, and Wilson, by the enlightened wisdom of prelates like Heber and Cotton." And the Nonconformist statesman, Mr. Forster, told the people of the manufacturing and labouring districts that one of England's greatest men, throughout her history, had passed away. "When our children's children, and the men of our race all the world over, in future times, shall read the wonderful story of our rule in India, there is no man to whose career they will look back with more justifiable pride than to that of Lord Lawrence. . . . You only know of him by repute; it has been my privilege to have had his personal friendship for the last few years."

Mr. R. Bosworth Smith, his biographer, quotes[1] these words written in 1869, when John Lawrence said fare-

[1] *Life of Lord Lawrence*, in two volumes (Smith, Elder, and Co.), 1883, vol. ii. p. 589.

well to India. "'He is great,' said the Editor of the *Friend of India*, a man who had watched his career carefully and had criticised some of his measures unsparingly—'he is great in the work which he has done as Governor-General; he is great in the moral spirit in which he has done every act; in the lofty principle which has guided him; in the noble private character which towers above that of any of his predecessors.'" Yes, it was mine to watch every step of his progress since he made the Punjab what it became when he used it to save the whole of India from anarchy and barbarism. It was mine to publicly chronicle and criticise every act of John Lawrence from the day that he took Delhi to the time when Anglo-Indians welcomed him back as Viceroy and Governor-General, and again speeded him home after five years in the highest office a British subject can fill, next to the Premier's. And when he exchanged the cares of Empire for the duties of the philanthropist and the peer in London—coming occasionally to Edinburgh, where, indeed, he discharged almost his last official act—I learned to know him as a man, even better than as one of the two greatest statesmen ever sent by our country to the East, his brother Henry being the other.

It is fitting that a sketch of what John Lawrence did, and of what he was, should reveal somewhat prominently what all other contemporary biographies and estimates of him have strangely omitted,—his views upon, his services to, Christian Missions. Beside the organisation of the Punjab Government and the capture of Delhi, we must place a third though forgotten achievement—the Minute of the 21st April 1858, in which he reviewed the principles of our government of India in the light of Christian duty. It is significant that Ward selected his true face and righteous bearing as the model, in the famous fresco, for the Baron who is represented as securing our liberties at Runnymede. But the first Baron Lawrence was more than that. He was a Puritan as well as a soldier-statesman, whom the fire of conflict and of victory had purged into the gentleness and the charity of a saint as he approached within two years of the allotted threescore-and-ten.

Although we remember how the younger brother was put in the place of the elder in Lahore, we do not marvel that the newly-made peer lovingly chose Henry's arms and crest as his own. On the right stands an officer of the famous Guide Irregulars, a Pathan of Peshawar; on the left is an officer of the Sikh Irregular Cavalry. The motto of Baron Lawrence of the Punjab is *Be Ready*, as his brother's was *Never Give In*. We think of both as we muse in the nave of the Abbey, where lie together Outram, Colin Campbell, and Livingstone, but no hero greater than John Lawrence.

IV

SIR JAMES OUTRAM, G.C.B., 1803–1863

The Bayard of India

When Dr. Bisset was Moderator of the General Assembly of the Established Church of Scotland, he asked the eleventh Earl of Dalhousie, an elder of the Free Church of Scotland, for a note of introduction for a friend, to Lord Elgin, at that time Viceroy and Governor-General of India. "I think your strongest claim on the Indian Government," wrote the Earl, who was then Secretary for War, "is that you have trained such a general and statesman as Outram for the public service, and this I have mentioned to Lord Elgin." When eleven years of age, in 1814, James Outram had been sent to Dr. Bisset's school at Udny, near Aberdeen, where, like the young Clive at Drayton, but without his fierceness, he became famous for deeds of daring and high moral courage. If we except Sir Henry Durand, who outlived him by a few years, James Outram was the last of the great soldier-statesmen of the East India Company, as John Lawrence was of its civilians. He comes next to Henry Lawrence, and second only to him who has been described as probably the greatest Englishman ever sent to India. It is because he showed, with these three, the enduring distinction of being a Christian under all and above all his earthly honours and natural virtues, that it is right to commend to the study of the new generation the biography, *James Outram,* written, with a soldier's dash and a "political's" experience, by Sir F. J. Goldsmid.[1]

We do so all the more because the inner Christian life of James Outram found very different modes of expression from theirs. Durand was an officer of such culture that he knew theology, which he used to discuss with his friend Judson, and he made Leighton's writings his constant companion. Henry Lawrence gave himself to Christ when a young lieutenant, and was ever, till he died, as ardent and open an evangelical as Charles Simeon himself. John Lawrence, after the Mutiny had anew revealed him to himself, never hesitated to put Christianity in the front in his most formal official documents. But Outram's hidden life found expression chiefly in truly Christian deeds, to Protestant and Romanist, to Christian and non-Christian alike. The shyness of reserve, combined with unfamiliarity with the phraseology of religious writings, never allowed him to speak or write publicly like Henry Lawrence, whom, nevertheless, he equalled in the good deeds that he did. At the last only, and when pleading for the highest interests of the private soldier, his wife and children, did the hero's big heart burst forth through his formal

[1] *James Outram*: a Biography. By Major-Gen. Sir F. J. Goldsmid, C.B., K.C.S.I. Two volumes. London: Smith, Elder, and Co., 1880.

Minutes, as we shall see, into counsels that a professional chaplain might have given. The most daring of all Anglo-Indian heroes was at once the most cautious of generals and most reserved of Christians. He acted, he lived, as Christ taught, in spite of the temptations of the camp, and the contradiction of meaner souls who often roused his indignation. Had he warred in Pagan times, he would have had the apotheosis of Hercules, whom on his physical side he most closely resembled throughout his career. Had he energised in early Christian times, he would have come down to us as a greater King Arthur. As it is, under the not dissimilar conditions of British Indian history, from 1820 to 1860, James Outram won for himself, and that in the mouth of his bitterest enemy, the title of The Bayard of India, which Dean Stanley adopted, and caused to be cut on the marble slab that covers his dust in the centre of the nave of Westminster Abbey. General Goldsmid writes:—

"We learn from the journals of the day that on 5th November a public dinner was given to Major Outram by the Military Society at Sakhar, on the occasion of his departure from Sind. At this, nearly one hundred officers of the three Presidencies were present; among them Sir Charles Napier, who, as chairman, spoke as follows:—

GENTLEMEN—I have told you that there are to be only two toasts drunk this evening; one, that of a lady (the Queen), you have already responded to, the other shall be for a gentleman. But before I proceed any further, I must tell you a story. In the fourteenth century there was in the French army a knight renowned for deeds of gallantry in war, and wisdom in council; indeed, so deservedly famous was he, that by general acclamation he was called the knight *sans peur et sans reproche.* The name of this knight, you may all know, was the Chevalier Bayard. Gentlemen, I give you the 'Bayard of India, *sans peur et sans reproche,* Major James Outram, of the Bombay Army.'"

Outram combined in himself the advantages of English birth and Scottish training. Born at Butterley Hall in Derbyshire, in 1803, he was deprived of his father, a famous civil engineer, two years after. His mother made him what he became. The daughter of the well-known James Anderson, LL.D., a *savant* to whom Lord Melville was much indebted in his administration of Scottish affairs, she continued to be all her life, which was spent chiefly at Aberdeen and Edinburgh, remarkable for her high spirit, ability, and conversation. Her modest *salon* in Edinburgh was frequented by the ablest men of the generation; when dying, the Marquess of Dalhousie said, "If I ever reach Edinburgh again, my first visit shall be to Mrs. Outram." For her eldest son, Francis, the widow had obtained an Indian cadetship, but as to James she consulted an Archdeacon brother-in-law about the Church. When the boy heard of it, he said to his sister, "You see that window; rather than be a parson, I'm out of it; and I'll 'list for a common soldier!" So he, too, passed through Addiscombe into the Bombay Army, where he soon became adjutant of his regiment; and his name began to be known all over Western India as the most reckless and successful tiger-hunter. The youth, who would have made a bad parson, was to display on a wider arena the virtues of the Christian soldier and philanthropist. This he did as civiliser of the shy and savage Bheels; tamer of the still wilder Dangchis; conqueror but friend of the Ameers of Sind; denouncer, to his own cost, of the evil policy of both the Afghan and Sind wars; guardian and reformer of the native States of Baroda and Satara; leader in the Persian War; hero of the Alumbagh; twice Chief Commissioner of Oudh, and protector of its barons from the confiscation threatened by Lord Canning; military member of that Viceroy's Cabinet, and counsellor of reforms which have saved and will yet bless more lives in the British Army in India than have been sacrificed in all its wars. For sixty years James Outram lived; for forty-three he thus toiled for the good of vast populations and of his own soldier-countrymen here and hereafter.

The story of Outram's civilising the savage Bheels forms the romance of Christian philanthropy. It is not surpassed by anything done by the Lawrences and Abbotts, by Nicholson, Edwardes, and Lake, and the other Christian officers of the Punjab school on the north-west frontier. His object was the same—to convert the most ignorant brigands, who had been the prey of successive Mohammedan rulers, and had fled to the fastnesses of their malarious hills, not only into peaceable subjects, but into loyal soldiers, and their children into decent Christians. The labours of Hercules were nothing to his—nothing to those of the British officers who, during the century from the days of Cleveland, under Warren Hastings, in the Kol and Santal hills, to the present time, when we are converting wild Afghans into faithful Sepoys, have carried on the God-given mission of Christianity in the East. The typical hero of Hellas represents conquests over only material or brute nature; those of Outram and his fellows in our own time have been won over the degradation of man, and through the power of a divine sympathy which Christ was the first to teach. For, like all successful man-tamers and Christianisers, Outram loved the dark races.

The splendid fascination of his character, which drew to him his own countrymen till it made the rawest subaltern a miniature of himself, revelled unchecked among tribes and races like those of Western and Northern India. True, alike in the taming of the Bheels and in the dispersion of the mutineers of 1857, he was first, what Mountstuart Elphinstone used to call him, "his sword," as Colonel Ovans was "his plough" to train to agriculture the wild men when reduced to obedience. But, in the interests of the tribes themselves, no less than of the whole Empire, the sword had to do its work first, in order that the plough, and the school, and the Church might have a chance at all. And if Outram was resistless in his courage and strategy as a general, he was even more powerful and successful as the administrator who made war only the handmaid of peace with all its blessings. Even in the darkest hour of the Mutiny, when he was seeking to relieve Lucknow, his pity, his mercy, went forth to the mutinous Sepoys ; he cared for the poorest camp-follower as particularly as for every white soldier on whom individually, in those days, the fate of the Empire seemed to hang.

It was in the ten years ending with 1838 that Outram gave his life for the Bheels and Dangchis of Khandesh, and the little-known land between Goozarat and Rajpootana, with what results, military and social, the wars and the progress of the next ten years testified. Let the following suffice regarding the social, written to himself by one of his assistants, Colonel C. M. Grant, in 1853:—"Did I once tell you that, in 1849, we visited Dharangáon? I went to the Bheel lines, saw the regiment on parade, with their band playing 'Love not,' or some civilised air, and then went to the schoolroom, where I saw at least fifty children of these *wild* (!) Bheels busy reading and writing. I do not know when I have been so interested in anything; and if, my dear Outram, the reclaiming of these wild creatures had been the one sole act of your life, it would have been sufficient to ensure you a pleasant retrospect as long as you live—had not your subsequent career been one long act of singleness of purpose and devotedness to your country, through rough disappointments and vexations enough to have tried the firmest resolve. This Bheel episode must, I am sure, form one of the most agreeable and satisfactory retrospects of your active and honourable career."

General Goldsmid remarks in his Biography:—

"No wonder that we hear of his memory still lingering in Khandesh, shrouded by a semi-divine halo. We are told that, a few years ago, some of his old *sipahis* happened to light upon an ugly little image. Tracing in it a fancied resemblance to their old commandant, they forthwith set it up and worshipped it as 'Outram Sahib.' Reminiscences of Khandesh life abound in anecdotes regarding these exploits in the *jangal* which formed an effective link in the chain of influence the young soldier made it the business of life to draw around his Bheels. He loved *dangerous* sport for its own sake, but rightly considered it a duty, though it happened to be a congenial one, to follow his own instincts in outdaring the brave little hunters whose hearts he sought to win.

"In May 1825, news having been brought in that a tiger had been seen on the side of the hill under the Musalman temple, among some prickly pear shrubs, Lieutenant Outram and another sportsman proceeded to the spot. Outram went on foot, and his companion on horseback. Searching through the bushes, when close on the animal, Outram's friend fired and missed, on which the tiger sprang forward roaring, seized Outram, and they rolled down the side of the hill together. Being released from the claws of the ferocious beast for a moment, Outram with great presence of mind drew a pistol he had with him and shot the tiger dead. The Bheels, on seeing that he had been injured, were one and all loud in their grief and expressions of regret; but Outram quieted them with the remark, 'What do I care for the clawing of a cat!' This speech was rife among the Bheels for many years afterwards, and may be so until this day.

"In 1827, it was reported to Outram that a tiger was lurking in the densely wooded ravine of 'Mahi Burda' in the Saigaon *jangal*. He proceeded thither, with his rifle, on foot. When near the spot indicated, it suddenly occurred to him that, by commanding the narrow end of the ravine, and placing the beaters at the other, the tiger must make his exit through the gorge, and he would get the opportunity of a close shot; but to find on the bank a place from which to fire was impossible, as the *jangal* grew close up to the sides, and the bottom of the ravine was not visible from the top. Outram's mind was one not to be baffled by trifles. He and some followers climbed a tree, a branch of which overhung the ravine. Securely posted on that branch, the Bheels tied their *pagris* (turbans) and waistbands together, passed a band round their commandant's chest and under his arms, and let him down dangling in the air. He now saw clearly all that was taking place beneath. The tiger, driven down by the shouts of the beaters, came within easy range of his rifle, and from his wonderful position he got the desired shot and killed the animal dead. Instantly drawn up into the tree again, he turned round laughingly to the Bheels, and said, 'You have suspended me like a thief from a tree, but I killed the tiger.'

"In 1833, when encamped at Sirpur, the villagers gave Outram information of a tiger that had been marked down in the thorny *jangal* to the north of the village. This part of the country was plain, and there was no hill or ravine near. Outram started on foot, spear in hand, a follower carrying a rifle, and some six others bows and arrows. The tiger broke ground on their approach; Outram followed him up on foot for three miles, and eventually speared him to death. This act, it is affirmed, has never been equalled, before or since, in Khandesh. During ten years, from 1825 to 1834 inclusive, he himself and associates in the chase killed no fewer than 235 tigers, wounding 22 others; 25 bears, wounding 14; 12 buffaloes, wounding 5; and killed also 16 panthers or leopards."

The highest work of the most renowned soldiers and statesmen of the British Indian Empire may often prove to be, it is evident, missionary work. But Outram, moreover, resembled almost all these military administrators in this, that he appreciated the missionaries, and drew to those of like spirit with himself. I have not found any evidence that he and Dr. John Wilson met, although the latter passed through the Bheel and the Dang districts more than once, and was full of projects for the Christianisation of the tribes, which the United Presbyterian and Free Churches of Scotland have since partially carried out. It is significant that, when driven to seek health in Egypt, he at once sought out the godly Lieder, who long represented evangelical Christianity at Cairo, and he there began the study of Arabic. But it was in Dr. Duff that he found, most delightedly, a brother soldier, a man of like fiery impetuosity and intense self-devotion to his work, with similar opinions on public events, and a burning affection for the natives. The first time I saw Sir James Outram was when he came to Calcutta to make the personal acquaintance of the Marquess of Dalhousie, who admired him, and when he gave up a Saturday to a careful inspection of the Free Church of Scotland's Institution. I had heard of him as brave even to madness, and was amused when, on the way to the college, he nervously stipulated that he should not be asked to make a speech. And yet he spoke better than many an experienced orator, whenever he was carried away by one of his own subjects, especially when called on to eulogise a regiment, or a brother officer, or a private soldier. He and Duff had come somewhat closely into contact, through the *Calcutta Review*, when that was made by the missionary the most influential literary organ in the East. But it was the iniquity of the Sind War, and the necessity of turning to good account the "Sind blood-money," as Outram called it, that first brought them together.

The share of Sir Charles Napier in that "useful and humane piece of rascality," as he cynically described his own unrighteousness in seizing Sind, was £6000 in prize-money. The amount allotted to Sir James Outram, who had protested against the whole policy which he was not allowed to prevent, was half that sum. What was he to do with it? When dying, the chief of all the Ameers, whom Outram had drawn to his heart, had entrusted his son to him as a ward, and nobly did the British officer discharge the unusual responsibility. To that ward, after consulting Duff, did he resolve to give the money as some atonement for the wrong. But there were insuperable difficulties in the way of such a course, as Duff reported after a confidential reference to the Government in Calcutta. So it ended in a division of the money among Henry Lawrence's Asylums for the children of British soldiers, the charities in Bombay, and a new mission school of the Free Church of Scotland at Bansbaria, on the Hoogli. Sir F. J. Goldsmid tells us that this grant, through Dr. Duff, "laid the foundation of an exceptionally warm mutual regard and esteem between these two large-hearted men, drawn together by human sympathies, yet outwardly walking in very different paths of life. An extract from one of his first letters (1846) to this chivalrous soldier of the Gospel—whose sympathy in his righteous cause had been warmly expressed—gives a fair sample of the tone and substance of Outram's extensive private correspondence during these days of trial." Outram wrote: "I do think that in your hands much may be done, while advocating the cause of the Ameers, or, rather, disapproving of the course of violence and injustice pursued towards them and their country, to forward the interests of philanthropy, and to deter future rulers from so recklessly trampling on the rights of their equals in the eyes of the Almighty. I rejoice in the forbearing course which our present Governor-General has pursued towards even wanton transgressors against us (though there is some excuse even for them, afforded by our previous acts to others). What a contrast to *our* wanton attack on the Ameers, and greedy appropriation of Sind! Sir H. Hardinge's measures will be a salutary example to future Governors-General, who will, I hope, turn the resources of this vast Empire to better purpose than forming costly armaments to subjugate our neighbours, and expend the resources placed at their disposal in great works calculated to ameliorate the condition of the wretched lower classes of our subjects, and to promote the welfare of the interior of neglected India ere further attempts are made to extend our dominions." We may add to these wise words,—well heeded until Lord Northbrook resigned the seat of the Viceroy rather than depart from them,—that all Sir James Outram wrote of the first Afghan war might be cited in condemnation of the second.

Never was man more scrupulously obedient to conscience than Outram. For this he suffered half his life through; for this his country and Christendom value him now. This, too, was the source of that fine chivalrous sense of honour which marked him from the time of his attendance at Dr. Bisset's school till the day he was astonished by the applause of Europe for waiving his right as commander, and allowing Havelock the renown of relieving the immortal Lucknow garrison, while he served as a volunteer. When shut up with it for a time, before the final relief, "he was no less particular in his attendance at family prayers than in his daily round of the defences, visits to the hospitals, and other military duties." In many of the able Minutes which he wrote when military member of the Governor-General's Council—for he had naturally a facile pen—we meet with personal allusions and spiritual references to which such documents are usually strangers. He was much occupied with the health of the Indian Army, after the Mutiny campaigns—health of soul as well as body. Here is a passage, of which Major Malan, in *A Soldier's Experience of God's Love*, tells us that it was handed to him for guidance, on board ship, by the Brigade-Major of Calcutta, adding, "How I thanked God for putting it into Sir James Outram's heart to write these instructions." "I trust," officially wrote Outram, "I shall not be deemed unreasonable if I express a very decided opinion that daily (before breakfast) the troops should be assembled for the public worship of God. I do not ask for a long service." Then follow details.

Very precious is the paragraph of "Auld Jamie"—

as his favourite 78th Highlanders always lovingly called the East India Company's commander—on the way in which officers should treat the women and children of their regiment. "It's not every officer, sir," said a private to one who had been kind to them in the Lucknow Residency, "as brings presents to our babies, and lifts his hat to our wives, and calls them Ma'am. She's gone, sir; she's gone, but she minded you to the last, and the time the colonel and you stopped your carriage to give her a lift, poor lass, from the railway on that hot afternoon." And after urging the formation of Ladies' Associations at each station, something like the Institute which he himself created at Dum Dum, Sir James Outram wrote: "Besides being the means of saving the immortal souls of some of our own countrywomen, these associations might tend to the spread of the Gospel in this land, prompting the heathen to moderate the rancour and contempt they bear our holy faith. . . . Whether at present we exert ourselves in behalf of our soldiers' wives as becomes those who realise the truth of the creed they profess, and feel in their hearts what they so glibly utter in their prayers, each man must answer to his own conscience. Mine, I confess, refuses a comforting response." Then he went on to "the subject of the spiritual instruction of our soldiers and their families," expressing a fervent hope "that the day is not far distant when each corps will have its own regimental chaplain, whose entire energies shall be exclusively devoted to the spiritual guidance and moral development of its members; when daily shall our soldiers be invited (not compelled) to meet together for the public worship of their God." Do we marvel any longer that the general and the statesman, who did not hesitate to write such words in formal Minutes and Blue-books, was, of all his contemporaries, the most unselfish, the most modest, the most jealous of the honour of others as of his own, the most lovable, and—next to Henry Lawrence—the best beloved? His pupil, Lord Napier of Magdala, represented the military side of his character, as his son, Sir Francis, has developed its Christian promise.

The East India Company, with all its faults, was the nurse not only of heroes but of Christians. If the Directors at home too generally fought against the light, the men they sent out often learned to walk in the light, and to hold it forth in the dark places. Outram died at Pau, in 1863, without a struggle. His last words were for others—especially for the Indian Medical Service, for which he had long made representations in vain. He bought a repeater, that he might not disturb his servant by asking the time in the weary hours of the night. He ever thought of his attendants—one a gentle Indo-Portuguese, another a poor band-boy, who had been found chained up in prison in Lucknow. In death, as in life, his country covered him with honours. In front of the clubs, Foley's fine equestrian statue reminds Calcutta what he was. On the Thames Embankment, London learns his form and face from Noble's statue. But Westminster Abbey is his memorial, beside Clyde, Pollock, Dundonald, Livingstone, John Lawrence. A

Bheel and a Balooch are represented as his mourners on the monument erected there by the Secretary of State for India, while the relief below represents the meeting of Clyde, Havelock, and himself at Lucknow.

Yes, the great and the good men of the East India Company's time have gone fast since 1863. Durand and John Lawrence, Edwardes and Lake, John Wilson and Alexander Duff, Colin Mackenzie and Donald M'Leod, Reynell Taylor and Henry Ramsay, to mention no others, have passed to their reward. There were giants in those days, and we are responsible for their heritage.

V

SIR DONALD M'LEOD, K.C.S.I., C.B., 1810–1872

Lover of the People of India

None of its rulers was so beloved by its manly races, Sikh and Mohammedan, as the third Lieutenant-Governor of the Punjab. The people were wont to say, "There are two *Ferishtas* (angels) among the English, Donald M'Leod and Reynell Taylor." His friend John Lawrence, who used to call him "The Cunctator," wrote thus of him to Herbert Edwardes in 1853: "Morally and intellectually he has no superior in the Punjab, perhaps no equal. But . . . he is too fond of polishing." As an administrator and judicial commissioner his refined culture, his keen sense of right and wrong, and his determination to do justly, led him to delay his decisions, to the even greater hurt of the public service and the interests involved. That was the one fault of his spotless career.

Donald Friell M'Leod, of the M'Leods of Assynt held by charter from David II., son of Robert the Bruce, was born at Calcutta of a Huguenot mother when his father was adding lustre to the Bengal Engineers. When four years old, he was sent with his sister and elder brother to the family home at Geanies, and there trained by "Aunt Kitty," who survived him. In October 1819 he became an Edinburgh High School boy under Samuel Lindsay, and afterwards at Putney he had Durand, Henry Carre Tucker, and Lord Canning as his schoolfellows. At Haileybury he was senior to John Lawrence. The year 1828 saw him back in Calcutta, a lad of eighteen. There he carried on those studies in Sanskrit as well as the Vernaculars which brought him into intellectual sympathy with the people whom he was to rule, of every class. The spiritual side of his unceasing devotion to their welfare was soon to follow, changing all his life and filling it with the purest happiness.

His first appointment was as assistant magistrate at Monghyr, on the Ganges, an upper district of Bengal. There he found a great preacher of the Scots school, trained at Edinburgh, the Rev. Andrew Leslie, Baptist missionary. The man who influenced Henry Havelock produced an impression on Donald M'Leod thus described in a letter dated 9th March 1831:—

"For about the last six months—that is, since I commenced attendance at your chapel—I have felt a change to have been effected in my spirit, towards which I have been gradually inclining for the last three years—that is, since my leaving England. This change I have for a long time had a strange conviction must at some time take place in my nature, as I felt it to be necessary to complete the being that God intended me to be. Of this unaccountable feeling I can tell you no more than its existence; and I have, in consequence, often thanked the Almighty that He formed me with weaknesses greater than the most of mankind, which forcibly led me to an unbounded reliance on Him, and led me to suppose that He had intended me to be a vessel formed to honour.

"My reasons for feeling this change to have passed over me are these: the whole tenor of my tastes and inclinations is changed. Attendance at church, which I formerly disliked, and never performed but as a duty, has become to me a pleasure, the anticipation of which presents itself to me during the whole week. My wish to partake of the Sacrament is also of this nature; but, of course, in every way more forcible. I have attained a confidence and tranquillity in regard to my worldly duties, from which the weaknesses of my character formerly debarred me; and I have now been freed from despondency and gloominess of spirits, to which for the five previous years I was continually a martyr.

"*P.S.*—In reading my letter, I think it may convey the idea of self-importance. I will only add, in the words of Pascal, that religion has 'abased me infinitely more than unassisted reason, yet without producing despair; and exalted me infinitely more than pride, yet without puffing up.'"

Though hitherto a Presbyterian, he determined to be again baptized, but beyond that he never ceased to be most catholic in his views and actions, supporting most evangelical missionary movements in India, especially that of Alexander Duff. The root of all his future life, official and private, for forty-one years, is seen in this letter to a friend, written at the same time:—

"I wish you to know my opinion, that I see no presumption

in feeling a certainty of going to heaven. The Bible in all parts abounds with declarations that they who love God and place their whole trust in Him shall have no cause to fear. You would smile at the person who should tell you you did not love your best friend; and why should a Christian be more ignorant of the state of his feelings towards God? . . . Be assured that this conviction which I have stated can never make me uncharitable in act. However false and unkind you may deem the sentiment, Christians have in all ages been eager in urging the necessity of regeneration. Our Saviour repeated it three times to Nicodemus almost in a breath, 'Marvel not that I said unto thee, ye must be born again.' It is only to be lamented that in urging this, much—very much—of indiscretion, and not a little of impropriety, has been used. Pray remember, however, that no confidence is placed in the merits of our own actions; the conviction arises solely from having placed entire trust in our Saviour, though this trust cannot truly exist unaccompanied by propriety of conduct. I cannot allow that imagination has the slightest part in the matter; it rests in the heart solely. Neither can I perceive how it tends to ambition. As regards my own particular change—as you say you more than doubt that any has taken place—I would say a few words. Prayer, which you recommend to me, and which was formerly an irksome duty seldom performed, has now become, I may say, almost the only pure pleasure I enjoy. I resort to it in the morning, not only as the most delightful, but as the most necessary act of the day; for without it I should have no peace, no power; and during the remainder of the day, whatever of difficulty or of annoyance presents itself, my mind flies up to its Creator, and is at rest—fully convincing me of the truth of that 'communion of saints' which the Apostles, and the Church of England after them, require us to believe, and which it yet appears that few do believe. The result of this is that I am never harassed for any length of time by anticipations of evil, nor fear of consequences, and am able (which formerly I was not) to obey the direction of our Saviour, 'Not to fear what man can do unto me.' My aspect now is consequently always more or less cheerful, which is certainly a visible change."

Sent by Lord William Bentinck to Jabalpoor to assist Sleeman in putting down the fraternity of Thug stranglers, and afterwards to Seoni, he explored the glorious highlands of the Satpoora range, and soon came to know their simple and untutored Gonds. He at once resolved to organise a Christian mission among them. Like Carey and Heber, not long before, he saw in the evangelisation of the casteless aborigines of India the means of securing centres round which the weaker Hindu proselytes, who have to sacrifice so much, might gather, as the foundations of the one Church in India are being laid. After three years at Seoni he was sent to Saugor, and in the interval visited Calcutta to interest the religious world there in his project, to carry out which he had refused a higher appointment elsewhere. Such words as these, written in 1838 by a young man still under thirty, mark the policy which, twenty years after, was to save our Indian Empire through the Punjab.

"Insulated as we are among Native States, it is surely the more incumbent on us to kindle that spark which may shine forth as 'a light to lighten the Gentiles.' Besides the interesting fact that in the heart of these territories we possess a numerous hill population, who (not being Hindus, but wild idolaters), from their freedom from prejudice and the trammels of a crafty priesthood, appear, in common with similar aboriginal tribes scattered all over the continent of India, to offer us an opportunity, too long overlooked, of planting the germs of India's evangelisation with (under God) the most cheering prospect of success.

"I am in hopes that I have in some degree succeeded, having almost got a promise that two or more German missionaries sent out by the Basel Society, and whom the Russians have compelled to quit Tabriz, will be sent here after the rains. And assuredly a greater blessing, humanly speaking, could not be conferred on this region. For, to give you an idea of the darkness which universally prevails, I may mention that at my last station of Seoni, where there were only three Europeans besides myself, I found that the natives were ignorant even that there is one day in the week which we are enjoined to hallow.

"When I look back upon our career in this country, and on our present irreligious state, I cannot believe that our deeds can be viewed otherwise at the throne of God than as deserving of Almighty vengeance. Never has a nation been so singularly marshalled on by the finger of God Himself, yet I doubt whether there has ever been one so utterly unmindful of the source whence its blessings flow. I often feel an awful hesitation in contemplating the purpose of our being sent here—whether we are destined to prove a blessing to this people, or to consummate our own shame; to confer on them the treasures of the Gospel, or to exhibit to them the awful fate of those who make a mock at the long-suffering of the Almighty. The nations we have come to rule over, in spite of their idolatrous darkness, acknowledge no truth more universally and habitually than that we are in all things at the immediate disposal of the Almighty.

And they possess also the salutary belief that the welfare of nations depends more on the virtue than the ability of their rulers."

At Jabalpoor, knowing the Kols as well as the Gonds, Donald M'Leod further developed his views in the *Calcutta Christian Observer* (1840). The year after the famous Gossner of Berlin sent him a missionary band of five evangelists, artisans, and agriculturists, with an apothecary. These he settled under Loesch, an experienced Basel missionary, at Karanjia, sixteen miles west of Amarkantak Hill, now in the State of Rewa, a centre of Gond reverence and Hindu pilgrimage. Cholera reduced their numbers, and the survivors joined the mission of Stephen Hislop at Nagpoor. Thence and from Jabalpoor the Free Church of Scotland and the Church Missionary Society, besides Swedish evangelists, are realising more than even M'Leod dared to anticipate.

Besides supporting his own Gond Mission, as we may call it, and the saintly Ziemann, whom I knew well, at Ghazipoor, Donald M'Leod's example had a most persuasive power over his native subordinates and friends. At the Liverpool Missionary Conference in 1860 the Rev. Behari Lal Singh told how, when a Rajpoot clerk, M'Leod sent him and his brother to be educated by Dr. Duff in Calcutta. The father also was influenced, his last objection to leaving caste being this, that the morality of the Bible was too high for a man to follow. "We all made up our minds to embrace Christianity. The pious example of Mr. M'Leod, his integrity, his honesty, his disinterestedness, his active benevolence, made me think that Christianity was something living—that there was a living power in Christ. Here is a man in the receipt of 2000 or 3000 rupees a month; he spends little on himself, and gives away the surplus of his money for education, the temporal and spiritual welfare of my countrymen. This was the turning-point of my religious history, and led to my conversion." Another native gentleman observed, "If all Christians were like Sir Donald M'Leod, there would be no Hindus or Mohammedans." When about the same time the Maharaja of Kapurthala resolved to impart Christian truth to his subjects, Donald M'Leod said, in the Punjab Missionary Conference, "I have watched his progress with exceeding interest. When he visited me with his brother at Dharmsala they refused to march on Sunday, or to make offerings at the Hindu shrines; even then he desired to attend divine service. He has set up an altar of family devotion in his own household, at which I and others have been privileged to kneel with him." [1]

Donald M'Leod's administrative rise was rapid. The young Writer who came to India in the good old days when a journey thither was a matter of six months, arrived so long ago as the year 1828, when the memory of Jonathan Duncan and his settlements had not been overlaid by that revival of the system of Akbar which was so minutely wrought out by Robert

[1] His descendant, Prince Harnam Singh Ahluwalia, C.I.E., has long been—with his wife, a missionary's daughter—a consistent member of the Punjab Native Christian community.

M. Bird and James Thomason. He came when the roar of Lord Lake's artillery was a sound still remembered by millions—when the Roi Fainéant still held his mock court in Delhi, and still had power to commit with a smooth face and secure mind cruelties which caused the sun of his dynasty to go down in a sea of blood and horror in 1857—when the British officer still clung to his silver stick-in-waiting as a necessary emblem of dominion, and still held it dignified to stalk in the midst of a herd of parasitical hirelings—when Suttee was rampant—when Simla was not—when Runjeet Singh was yet consolidating his power—when the wages of a day labourer were five shillings a month—when the native army was officered by those who knew and personally loved their men—when Christianity was among Christians almost a reproach, and the missionary was feared by his countrymen—when the race of mixed blood was springing up through the unhallowed associations that distance from England induced—when no furlough was of any use unless it was for three years—when the English mail was carried by any chance ship, and one might not arrive for six or eight weeks after the last—when there was no telegraph or railway in England much less in India. To men like Sir Donald who could recall this past, it must have been matter of pride that they had been instrumental in bringing about the changes which we now see.

His kindliness of disposition and success in controlling the uncivilised and isolated beings in the wild and almost unknown district of Jabalpoor, marked him out in time as a fit person for the highly important charge of the district and city of Benares, then almost a metropolis. Successful and vigorous administration there again recommended him to Lord Dalhousie as the man to rule the newly-conquered Jalandhar Doab. Thither he went as Commissioner in 1849, when John Lawrence, his old friend and contemporary, was called to take his seat at the Board of Administration then newly formed at Lahore. Here the elements from which order was to be educed were chaotic. It is true that John Lawrence had ruled the land for three years, but that had been in a rough-and-ready way, effective enough yet scarcely civilised. It was M'Leod's duty to introduce law and order; to suppress with a strong hand the violent crimes to which the disbandment of the Khalsa army gave rise; to settle the terms on which the native aristocracy were to retain their revenue-free grants—especially those troublesome tenures which the Sikh Government had freely given on condition of feudal service. In all these and other intricate and delicate affairs of State he was seconded by three able district officers, Herbert Edwardes [1] at Jalandhar, Robert Cust at

[1] Edwardes thus wrote of him:—

"We shall be together under the roof of Mr. M'Leod. He is a rare and excellent character—one whose whole life is one even career of duty to God and man, and whose mind and heart do not apparently contain one selfish thought or feeling. He is by nature blessed with at once the best of intellects and the kindest of dispositions; and an industry of study, stimulated by the desire to be useful, has given him a range of knowledge on all subjects bearing on the welfare of the people of India, such as I do not know that I ever saw equalled; yet few people hear of him; and in the noisy world the ripple of his gentle stream of goodness is altogether drowned—but it fertilises nevertheless; and when I come to compare my own brawling fame with the secluded usefulness of this good man, I quite

Hoshiarpoor, and E. C. Bayley at Kangra. They could all say of him, "Nil desperandum Teucro duce, et auspice Teucro." In the four years which elapsed before he was called to succeed George Edmonstone, as Financial Commissioner for the Punjab, his name had become a household word to gentle and simple throughout his fair domain. Whenever it was known that he was to pass by that way, the road was thronged with those whom his mild but firm rule had blessed and defended, longing to see but his face. This was perhaps the most useful part of Sir Donald M'Leod's life. Promoted to the higher rank of Financial Commissioner, the cast of his mind, which was to fetter itself unnecessarily with details, began to exercise a detrimental effect on his work. Had he been raised at this time, or even later, to a seat in the Government of India, the provincial character of his training would have been corrected. A ruler should have a genius rather synthetical than analytical. Able to analyse, he should be habitually versed in synthesis, should place side by side the circumstances of various races, climes, and orders of mind, should compare and collate, and surveying his charge from a high standpoint should not descend to the toil of minute inquiry. This, Sir Robert Montgomery, with intellectual abilities below Sir Donald's, did. The State was ofttimes deprived of his wise advice and calm judgment on matters of grave import, while he was busied over figured statements of revenue

shrink with shame, and positively rejoice that there will be a light in which the true value of things will stand revealed."

and expenditure which should have been drawn up by others.

While holding this appointment, there came on Sir Donald the Mutiny. Of all the brave spirits who rose to the wave none rode it more gallantly than he. Oppressed by serious ill-health and more crushing private grief, his mind was the calmest, his judgment the coolest of all at Lahore. No important strategical or political measure was discussed or resolved on at those anxious early morning meetings under his portico but was indebted to his sagacity and supported by his moral force. Of all Sir John Lawrence's counsellors he was the most trusty and most abundantly used, and well earned was the C.B. which he received. In 1859-60 a short visit to England recruited his much broken health. In 1865 he succeeded his very dear friend and relative Sir Robert Montgomery as Lieutenant-Governor of the Punjab, and was shortly after decorated as K.C.S.I.

He entered on the high office in the spirit of this letter, dated 21st January 1865:—

"Truly, when I look back on the past and the present, how can I but feel amazed, and, I may add, penetrated with conflicting feelings, in which humiliation bears a large part, that one so full of weaknesses and failings should have been elevated to such a post—the post in which the strong and vigorous Sir Henry and Sir John Lawrence won their first renown—the post which Sir Robert Montgomery has graced during the past six years by virtues rarely combined in one individual, and which has been filled by all of these with an ability, energy, and success which render the task of their successor doubly onerous and responsible? In my consciousness of weakness, and the prayers of many good men, lies my only strength; and well do I know, deeply do I feel, that if I should ever cease to look above for guidance and for strength, I must fail. God grant that it may never be so. I have felt much more solemnised than gratified by the position in which I find myself. But one source of unmixed gratification has been the hearty manner in which my accession to the post of Lieutenant-Governor has been hailed by a host of kind friends throughout the Province, European and native. The nomination has been made, I doubt not, in a prayerful spirit by Lord Lawrence, who is a God-fearing man. It has been accepted, I trust, in the same spirit; and I will not allow myself to doubt that it has been brought about in the decrees of an all-wise Ruler, for the welfare of this very interesting Province."

Five years of peace and prosperity followed, even on the Afghan and Baloochistan frontiers so often turbulent. The Ameer, Shere Ali, visited Lord Mayo at Umballa, where I witnessed the Lieutenant-Governor's political tact and personal influence for the best ends. He promoted agricultural improvements and public works at a time when each Province was not, as now, allowed to manage its own financial resources. He anticipated Lord Ripon's extension of municipal self-government, but after a far wiser and more permanent fashion. He sought to train the masses to what he well described as "habits of vigorous thought and self-reliance," and to imbue them with the enlightened views of the West. To educational reform and extension he lent all his influence for this end. In 1855 the Court of Directors had specially thanked him, with others, for the promotion of public instruction, anticipating from their efforts "that the Punjab will present to the world a signal example of the benefits which the British rule confers upon the natives of India." To him first of all, and then to Sir Charles Aitchison, we owe the recognition of the principle for which the Serampore missionaries and Brian Hodgson fought in vain till the Punjab University was created by legislative charter,—the recognition, side by side with English education (otherwise imitative chiefly in its effects), of the vernacular and classical languages, or education of a national character and Oriental tone. Alike in the Senate of the Calcutta University and in the *Friend of India* was this sound policy advocated, and it triumphed in the Punjab at last. Apart from its educational soundness, Sir Donald pressed the reform as likely to conciliate the learned classes of natives, Mohammedan and Hindu, whom the exclusively English system tends to alienate from progress and from their rulers.

Amid the unusually sincere regrets of natives of every class, and the eulogies of Lord Mayo, Lord Napier of Magdala, and his successor (Sir Henry Durand), at a banquet in Lahore, Sir Donald M'Leod left India. He had spent his all on the people. For eighteen months only did life allow him to work for them, and for the poor, in London. This was the burden of his public addresses:—

"The great question of the day, in truth, is—What direction is the intellectual development of India to take? It is one we cannot evade; and, seeing what an important and responsible charge devolves upon England in respect to her dependency of India, it is most incumbent on all our countrymen, but especially on all Christ's followers, to lend every assistance in their power towards guiding this development into healthy channels. The English in India, however, are but a handful. They can do comparatively little themselves, and it is to this great country, with all her wealth, knowledge, learning, and appliances, that India must look for adequate aid. I venture to hope that a large increase may be made in the amount of contributions to missionary work in that vast country.

"I must add, at the same time, my belief that if we have any regard to the security of our dominion in India, it is indispensable that we do our utmost to make it a Christian country. We are raising up a large number of highly intellectual youths, and if these youths are not imbued with Christianity, they will prove, I believe, to be the most dangerous part of the population. They see our newspapers; they travel about on our railways; they communicate freely with all classes, and they know well what is going on throughout the world. We cannot check this progress, and if we allow them to remain (as they are rapidly becoming) an infidel class, they will be more likely than any other to excite mischief. For this reason the prayers and exertions of a Christian people are required to press on the Government the necessity of doing everything a Government legitimately can do to promote the progress of Christianity and a sound morality throughout India, whether they can take a direct part in spreading the former or not. Above all, they should be urged to send out Christian rulers—men who are faithful, and are not ashamed of the Gospel."

Donald M'Leod died as he had lived. On the 28th November 1872, when attempting to enter a train on his way to advocate the cause of the Christian Literature Society for India, he was so severely crushed that he died four hours after. When his mangled body was laid in the accident ward of St. George's Hospital, his last words were, as he repeated after a friend the cry—"Come, Lord Jesus, come quickly"—"I shall then be free from sin and sorrow, and for ever with the Lord. Praised be His holy name for ever and ever."

Soon after his friend, Major-General Lake, C.S.I., sent me a copy of the *Record of his Forty-two Years' Service in India*,[1] with this remark, "My object is mainly to bring into prominence his earnest loving Christian spirit, his unceasing efforts to ameliorate the condition of the people of India, and his devotion to public duties. In all these he may be held up as a model for the rising generation of civilians who, for good or evil, must greatly influence the future destinies of India." Now, what was it that Donald M'Leod did for India? He was above all things a lover of the people, and one who made all natives love him and respect British rule for his sake. To him India owes the originating as well as the most perfect applying of these three great principles—the duty of caring for the aboriginal and non-Aryan peoples; the justice of the grant-in-aid system of public instruction leading to independent effort; the gradual training of the people to social reform and moral self-government.

[1] Religious Tract Society, London, 1874.

He was the purest of that brilliant and successful, because high-principled, Punjab School, which the Marquess of Dalhousie called into existence, which Henry Lawrence inspired and John Lawrence consolidated. His gentle spirit and sympathetic intellect linked it on to the princes and the people of the greatest Province of our Indian Empire.

VI

SIR HENRY MARION DURAND, K.C.S.I., C.B., 1812–1871

The Soldier-Statesman

Sir Henry Durand may be considered the last of that long roll of soldier-statesmen who first won and then governed India for England under the East India Company. It is difficult to say whether he was greater as a military officer and organiser, as a writer of no little scientific ability and literary power, or as a civil ruler concerned with those political and economic questions on the right settlement of which the happiness of millions of our fellow-subjects in the East depends. He was always known throughout India as an officer of surpassing ability, whose counsel was superior to that of all others, if it could be obtained; whose character was brave from its resolute independence, and fearless from its marked uprightness; but who had suffered injustice on account of that very righteousness, and ever seemed to be battling against disappointment and sorrow. Wrong-doers feared him, intriguers tried to escape him, and self-seekers shunned his withering scorn. In the last ten years of his life he was, by common consent, the foremost man in India, as an influence for good alike to his colleagues in the Government, to the army, and to the people.

Public life in India, with its secret despatches and minutes, does not afford the same materials for learning of what stuff a Governor-General's advisers are made as the parliamentary and platform discussions of a constitutional country like Great Britain. But a strong man cannot be hidden in India. His work declares him sooner or later, while the formal conversations in the Legislative Council, which are reported, give frequent glimpses of the capacity of the executive members. Moreover, in what has been called the "club" of Anglo-Indians, who know each other, and gauge the ability of their prominent men with considerable accuracy, scanning appointments and motives in a way impossible on the broader platform of English political life, every high official finds in time his just position in public opinion. All through the four administrations of Lord Canning, Lord Elgin, Lord Lawrence, and Lord Mayo, it thus came about that Colonel Durand, as he was generally known, was felt to be a power for good, valuable at all times, but supremely so should any crisis occur, whether political or military. When he was appointed Lieutenant-Governor of the Punjab by Lord Mayo our whole Eastern Empire rejoiced, Natives as well as Europeans. When, after a few months, a terrible accident suddenly laid the strong man low on the 1st day of 1871, all India mourned.

My intimate acquaintance with Sir Henry Durand covered these ten years. There is no great Indian question that we have not frequently discussed, and the memory of these valued conversations, especially during the leisure of some months at Simla in 1866, will ever abide. There are few such questions regarding which he did not correspond with me at other times, or his Minutes upon which—published by his son twelve years after his death—he did not permit me to read. As the last great example since his friend Sir Henry Lawrence, of the grand old Indian school of Metcalfe and Malcolm, and especially as the only instance of one of that school intimately connected with almost every detail of the Queen's as distinguished from the Company's government of India, the life and the opinions of Sir Henry Durand are of permanent value. In 1857-61 we entered on a new era of government in the East, and it is important that the life of the statesman who has most completely bridged the passage from the old to the new should be held up at once as a guide and a mirror to those who follow. We are forgetting the principles by which the Company's men gained the affection of the people, so far as to secure their co-operation in raising them to a higher level, and it is doubtful if we are substituting for these principles methods of procedure equally satisfactory. The opinions of an accomplished Anglo-Indian thinker and administrator like Sir Henry Durand ought to be placed in the hands of every young Englishman who gives the best part of his life to India, in whatever capacity, that he may direct his zeal and regulate his action by the ripe experience of a man all of whose policy, from Kabul in 1838 to Calcutta in 1870, events have so strikingly justified.

I know that it was Sir Henry Durand's intention to write an autobiography, had he been spared to enjoy the ease of retirement after forty-five years' service. That duty, with all his papers, was bequeathed to his second son, when a member of the Bengal Civil Service. Sir Henry Mortimer Durand, K.C.I.E., now British Minister at Teheran, has well discharged the sacred trust. He published[1] *The First Afghan War and its Causes,* written by Captain Durand, Bengal Engineers, and left incomplete in MS. That volume is the only accurate history of the dark event, and is the necessary corrective of Kaye's romantic narrative. After some years' experience of administrative work in a distinguished position in India, Sir Mortimer published[2] his father's *Life,* with his Essays and Minutes. The Memoir and opinions form the most valuable manual of state-craft for the administrators and soldiers of India which has appeared since Sir John Malcolm's *Memoir of Central India* in 1824, with its golden, but now unhappily forgotten, "Instructions to Assistants and Officers."

Born on the 6th of November 1812, son of a cavalry officer distinguished in the wars with Napoleon, Henry Marion Durand was first educated at Putney, where Lord Canning and his predecessor in the Punjab, Sir

[1] London: Longmans, Green, and Co., 1879.
[2] London: W. H. Allen and Co., 1883, in two volumes.

Donald M'Leod, were his schoolfellows. He was then sent to Addiscombe, preferring to Haileybury and the Civil Service the soldier's career. There, as he once amused his grave colleagues in council by recalling the fact, he had for a fellow-student Lord Napier of Magdala, who commanded the corps of gentleman cadets to which he belonged, and who on one occasion severely punished him. When little more than sixteen he passed his examination for the Bengal Engineers, and embarked for India in the *Lady Holland.* Amid the varied passengers proceeding by the Cape in those days, he and the young Scots missionary, Alexander Duff, soon found out each other, and began a warm friendship which was broken only by death. Dr. Duff tells how the young cadet was marked out from his fellows by certain grave and studious habits, which ripened into an earnestness of disposition that never proved incompatible with the pleasant joke or the merry laugh. The long five months' voyage of these days was devoted by both to a study of the country to which they had consecrated their lives. Had the tedium been felt, it would have been rudely broken by shipwreck on Dassan Island. Obtaining another vessel at the Cape, the party came on destitute of books, papers, and baggage. Young Durand and Dr. Duff landed at Calcutta in the heat of May 1830—that year from which we date so much that is now remarkable, and all that will probably prove abiding in the social and intellectual progress of Bengal. When the former took up the quarters to which he had been invited in the Bishop's palace, he was fain to clothe himself in episcopal garments until a new outfit could be procured. It is characteristic of Durand that to the last he ever looked on the missionary's career as far nobler than his own. When congratulated on the tardy honour of Lieutenant-Governor of the Punjab, he pronounced his life a flash in the pan compared with that of Dr. Duff. Lieutenant Durand joined his station up-country in the company of the short-lived Bishop Turner and of the better-known Bishop Corrie, who was then archdeacon.

As an engineer officer his first work was to complete the depôt for invalid soldiers in the Himalayan sanitarium of Landour. He was also called to report on other sites for military hill settlements, and it is an instance of the sound judgment and foresight for which he was always so remarkable, that one which he recommended, Chakrata, was adopted forty years after. His work done there, he was set to canals, and then it was that he was thrown into intimate intercourse with those three distinguished members of the corps of Bengal Engineers, Sir Proby Cautley, Lord Napier of Magdala, and Sir W. Baker. The Jumna, where it issues from the hills, was to supply the water, and this rendered necessary a careful geological examination of the whole lower and outer ranges of the Himalayas thence to the Sutlej. The young lieutenant found himself on familiar scientific ground, for he had supplemented his early reading by a careful study of the then rising science of Geology. Dr. Falconer, too, was pursuing in these very regions those investigations which resulted in the determination of the age of the Sewalik hills. Lieutenant Durand revelled in their rich fossil remains, which first led to the discussions on the antiquity of the human race that long since reached a point beyond which his cautious spirit refused to go. He wrote several palæontological papers in 1835, which are to be found in the *Bengal Asiatic Society's Journal.* Coming farther south, his survey of the country around Delhi brought him into personal contact with Lord Auckland and his secretaries, Thomason and Colvin, who afterwards became Lieutenant-Governors of the North-Western Provinces. Then it was that he obtained that economic and practical knowledge of the land and the people which he used with good effect in subsequent controversies, when he was a member of the Governor-General's Council. So thoroughly, like Sir Henry Lawrence in somewhat similar circumstances, does he seem to have mastered the land question, always the greatest in India since the Permanent Settlement of 1793 in Bengal, that this almost beardless soldier was asked to become Secretary to the Agra Board of Revenue. But the news of an advance into Afghanistan summoned him, like so many rising officers, to the front. Having prepared the engineer park in Delhi for the campaign, he found himself in orders as topographical surveyor to the Army of the Indus.

Durand's name first became known to India by that exploit of his which opened the Kabul gate of Ghuzni to the besieging force. Since his death there has been some discussion as to the part which he took—whether he acted independently or under orders. We may content ourselves with the eulogy of Lord Napier, who, at the dinner given to Sir Henry Durand by his brother officers at Simla in 1870, declared that it was he who, when the powder had been laid down at the Kabul gate of the city under a strong fire, and when failure was announced, "with a keener observation saw that no failure had taken place, and arrested the bugle which would have sounded a retreat." On this occasion Durand scraped the hose with his nails, when he found that the powder would not at once ignite. The fearlessness and promptitude of resource shown on that occasion marked all his career. When Kabul was reached, he, as engineer to Shah Shooja's force, saw at once that, unless our troops were securely lodged in a defensible and sheltered place, disaster would be the result. He frequently urged the envoy, Sir William Macnaghten, to allow him to fortify the citadel known as the Bala Hissar. But the barracks that he constructed were made over by our vacillating commanders to the king's hareem, and the result we all know. There even a smaller force than we sent to Kabul might have maintained their position against all Afghanistan, and our history might have been spared many pages of black disaster. But Durand was one of several officers —prominent among them the old hero, Lieut.-General Colin Mackenzie, C.B.—whose words of wisdom were unheeded. Unlike them, however, he did not become a victim to the policy which he so ably exposed in the

Calcutta Review, for he returned to India along with Sir J. Keane. After a short furlough, he became Private Secretary to the new Governor-General, Lord Ellenborough.

Though, like most Anglo-Indians then, of no political party, Durand was of the school which, in India most emphatically, sees the political danger and evil of all changes not absolutely necessary or justified by the highest reasons. He was a wise Conservative, though many of his principles were very radical, notably all the reforms which he suggested in the constitution and working of the East India Company, and which he lived to see fully adopted. Perhaps his warmest political friend, next to Lord Ellenborough, was the 15th Earl of Derby, whom intellectually he so closely resembled, except in the coldness of that nobleman's political nature. What Durand believed he had arrived at slowly, he held passionately, and he expressed in the most trenchant style. The position of Private Secretary to the Governor-General is unlike any other office in any country, save Russia, or perhaps Prussia under the old *régime*. To a man of ability and tact the power is vast, alike in patronage and in influence upon the ruler's policy. No Governor-General can do half his work as it ought to be done without trusting others, and the man he most trusts is his secretary, whom for that very reason he has carefully selected. With only one exception, all the private secretaries I have known, from the time of Lord Ellenborough to the present, have been in their way able men. The late Earl of Ellenborough's papers[1] show traces of Durand's influence. Brilliantly able, that Governor-General was often annoyingly crotchety and painfully unjust. The solid and judicious counsels of the Private Secretary, his stern uprightness, and his perfect knowledge of men of both the civil and military services, were invaluable to such a Governor-General, even though, while approving the better course, he sometimes followed the worse. In one point, however, Durand must have encouraged his master—in breaking up the old clique of Bengal civilians who had led Lord Auckland to ruin, and had opposed as interlopers all who desired progress and fair play. The Private Secretary was present with his chief at the battle of Maharajpore, and there made himself for the first time personally acquainted with the Native States of Central India, of which he proved himself subsequently so successful a Political Agent.

When Lord Ellenborough was recalled he might, according to custom, have obtained one of those high offices to which a private secretary in either of the services is always appointed. But it was left to the next Governor-General, Lord Hardinge, to send Captain Durand to Moulmein as Commissioner of the Tenasserim Provinces. The office had been filled by a civilian of the lazy order, under whom abuses had grown up and corruption had fattened. The new Commissioner knew what he was sent to do, and he knew also the penalty

[1] In the *History of the Indian Administration of Lord Ellenborough* (Bentley 1874), consisting of his letters to the Queen and correspondence with the Duke of Wellington, the Duke writes, "Let me see Lieutenant Durand's papers!"

of doing it; but he felt that he would be supported by the Governor-General. He cleansed that Augean stable, perhaps a little too sternly, but with the approval of all the independent and righteous men on the spot, especially the American missionaries, with Dr. Judson at their head. Unfortunately Lord Hardinge had left Calcutta for the Upper Provinces, and the ordinary government devolved on the senior member of Council, who was not sorry to recall the too radical Commissioner. The affairs of Moulmein raised a discussion from which he held proudly aloof, in the consciousness of duty well done; but his old ship companion, Dr. Duff, came to the rescue, and established the justness of his policy in the pages of the *Calcutta Review*. The missionaries, wisely abstaining from politics but none the less warmly on his side, accompanied the Commissioner from the rocky shore of Moulmein with expressions of gratitude for his efforts to promote the cause of education and religion among the people, and with the prayer, so touching when read by the light of his subsequent career and lamented end:—"That our Heavenly Father may still direct you in a way in which your labours may be highly useful to mankind, as well as a source of increasing delight to yourself, and that you may finally receive the ultimate reward of those who continue faithful unto death."

Captain Durand's two years' service in Burma were remarkable for more than his administrative experience, although he then sowed the seeds of what is known as the non-regulation system, by which simple and rude peoples are gradually raised to a platform fit for our more elaborate laws and procedure. He learned to know Judson, and they became fast friends. How much is involved in that fact! The old missionary and the young administrator resembled each other in many of the higher qualities of their nature. Fortunately Durand has left us his estimate of the life and labours of the Apostle of Burma, written soon after the saint closed his long and suffering years. No one who would understand both should omit to turn to vol. xiv. of the *Calcutta Review*, where, in 1850, Durand painted at full length a portrait of Adoniram Judson.[1] It is surprising that his biographers have overlooked this valuable contribution to the life of the prince of American missionaries. I am interested in it now chiefly from the light that it throws on the inner life of Durand.

All who knew him, know what an earnest and at the same time catholic Christian he was. He did not in this respect wear his heart on his sleeve; and while devotedly attached to the Church of England, he refused to call any man or any sect master, remembering that One whom he ever sought to follow fully. But though by nature and training averse to mere ecclesiastical talk, there were times when he would open out his heart. I shall ever remember one such occasion, when, as the rest of our party left us in the Himalayas to find a short road over the heights to Nagkunda, we alternately walked and rode along together round the bluff. The glorious October morning, amid scenery which

[1] Reprinted at p. 19, vol. ii., of Durand's *Life*.

the Alps cannot rival, unbent our spirits, and he talked of higher things—of that life to come which is now his for evermore. His picture of Judson is, in many respects, true of himself, if for the missionary we substitute the God-fearing soldier and administrator:—
"He was indeed a mighty champion—mighty in word; mighty in thought; mighty in suffering; mighty in the elasticity of an unconquerable spirit; mighty in the entire absence of selfishness, of avarice, of all the meaner passions of the unregenerate soul; mighty in the yearning spirit of love and of affection; above all, mighty in real humility, in the knowledge and confession of the natural evil and corruption of his own heart, in the weakness which brings forth strength; mighty in fulfilling the apostolic injunction, 'Whatsoever ye do, do it heartily, as to the Lord, and not unto men'; mighty in the entire, unreserved devotion of means, time, strength, and great intellect to his Master, Christ."
And this summing up of an eloquent contrast between the system of the Jesuit Xavier and the *quondam* Presbyterian, afterwards Baptist, Judson may well comfort the many in this country who have been long helping to sow the good seed in our Indian Empire:—

"Far different has been the success of the seven-and-thirty years of Judson's continuous, unflinching labour. His career has not been marked by the alleged sudden conversion of tens of thousands of idolaters. Princes indeed listened, but did not bow their heads to the truths of the Gospel. Brilliant success nowhere attended him. Yet, it may be permitted us to doubt whether Judson has not laid the foundation of a fabric, which, instead of vanishing in the course of the next three centuries, will, should earth last, grow into the stately proportions of an extensive and solid spiritual temple. Driven from Burma, he planted his small, but really Christian, church of Burmese converts on the frontier of the Burman and Peguan Empire; first, at Amherst; subsequently, where Boardman had preceded him, at Moulmein—a position from whence, at any favourable moment, it can with great facility go forth to the work of evangelising the surrounding heathen. His converts and disciples have not been altogether idle, in spite of the stern persecution which awaits them on discovery; and, as most Burmans can read and write, the translation of the Scriptures, their wide dissemination, and the teaching of these converts, few though they be, cannot fail to prepare the soil, and to sow the seed of a future far richer harvest, than the state of this Buddhist stronghold at present promises."

These benevolent and enthusiastic anticipations have been to no little extent realised by our American fellow-labourers. If Buddhism has not yielded an overwhelming number of converts, in the half-century since this was written, tens of thousands of Karens, in whole villages and towns, have been gathered in to the Christian Church. And even Buddhism became so shorn of its intolerance, that in the new capital of Mandalay, not far from the spot where the missionaries suffered such tortures, the king erected a Christian church and sent his sons to a Christian school. Captain Durand's experience of Burma led him to regret the war that forced on Lord

Dalhousie the annexation of more territory, and to declare that, with so vast an Empire as India proper on our hands, it might have been better if the task of civilising Burma had been undertaken by the United States. But in that England has not been its own master, and the present prosperous condition of Burma, now all British, forms a pleasing contrast to the misrule of the independent territory.

After completing in England the furlough which Lord Ellenborough's summons to him had broken, Colonel Durand returned to take part in the Second Sikh War, which he afterwards ably criticised. No one can read Indian history aright who does not study his papers on the Kabul and Sikh campaigns, side by side with Sir Henry Lawrence's Essays on the same subjects. The one corrects the other, the one supplements the other, and from both the Artillery and the Engineer officers, often agreeing—not unfrequently differing—we learn the truth of the policy that guided Lord Hardinge, Lord Gough, and Lord Dalhousie. When appointed Lieutenant-Governor of the Punjab Sir Henry Durand recalled the carnage of its battlefields in which he had taken a part, and eulogised the courage of our enemy of those days, now our loyal subjects, to whom he was about to devote all that was left of his life.

When the Mutiny broke out Colonel Durand was found at Indore as Political Agent of the new Governor-General, Lord Canning. As Lord Napier expressed it, he remained at his post until the cannon balls from Holkar's insurgent troops actually drove him from the Residency with what that Viceroy called a "hopelessly small escort." Going off towards Bombay to bring up Brigadier-General Stewart's column, he took political direction of it, and in spite of the difficulties which he himself afterwards so graphically described, including three days' fighting at Mandlésar and the capture of Dhar, that small body relieved Neemuch, cleared Malwa of mutineers, prevented Tantia Topee from crossing the Nerbudda so as to raise the South, and disarmed Holkar's troops. He well deserved the praise of Lord Canning, who publicly declared that his conduct had been marked by great foresight and the soundest judgment as well in civil as in military matters. In such duties he obtained that grasp of the whole subject of our feudatory nobles and their relation to the English Crown, which afterwards made him the ablest of Foreign Secretaries, the soundest of advisers on questions of native feeling and policy.

The Mutiny left Northern India without a native army. There were 4000 British officers without men to command. Our Indian military system was further discredited by what became known as "the white mutiny," or the discontent caused among the 20,000 English soldiers of the East India Company's local army, by the rash refusal to treat their transfer to the Crown as a new enlistment. As that occurrence had been caused by a want of tact, so its effects were greatly exaggerated by those who desired to see the local army extinguished and India garrisoned only by the ordinary English troops. The first difficulty before Lord Canning, the moment the Sepoy Mutiny had ceased to be vital, was the military one of reorganising the Army. He turned to Colonel Durand as the one man in all India who could best advise him on this subject. That officer was first instructed to ascertain the opinions of all other authorities on the subject, and then to lay them with his own before the Government of India. The Blue-books of 1858-59 show how well he accomplished the task. In his suggestions he carried with him the support of all official India, including not a few Queen's officers. Lord Canning heartily gave in his adhesion to his views. He was sent home to represent them to the authorities here, when the white mutiny, of which we have spoken, and other influences were thrown into the opposite scale, and India ceased to possess a local army. The result has been a serious addition to its military expenditure estimated by some at not less than a million sterling a year, and which is increasing annually. The military difficulties of England and the purely royal army have been greatly increased, by the necessity for recruiting in only one way to supply the Indian drain, and to send out some 3500 officers to such a climate for a force of 72,000 men. Opinion is now fast coming round to the views that Colonel Durand so stoutly urged, in season and out of season, with a persistent patriotism that brought him only enmity. Many of our best military reformers would like to see an Indian local army again. Lord Northbrook and Lord Cromer have always held this opinion.

Durand was one of the first members of the Secretary of State's Council, appointed by the then Lord Stanley on the abolition of the East India Company. There he, Lord Lawrence, and others continued to fight for the views which they had urged when in India. When Sir Charles Wood became Secretary of State, he was not long in finding the personal evil to himself of such independence. When General Outram came home dying, but insisted on returning to his seat in the Calcutta Council, Colonel Durand with his usual generosity at once resigned to make way for Outram, but on the written pledge that he should take Outram's place as Lord Canning's colleague in India. But the pledge was never fulfilled. Sir C. Wood's promise and Lord Canning's request were alike disregarded, and some years passed over before Durand became military member of the Governor-General's Council. On his appointment by Lord Stanley he had given up all thoughts of returning to the East, and was devoting his leisure to the education of his children. But his ripe experience, his sound judgment, and his uncompromising honesty could not thus be buried. The year 1861 saw him again in Calcutta ready to enter on the last decade of his life in and for India.

Colonel Durand, having unselfishly given up his seat in the India Council to Sir James Outram, went out to Calcutta in August 1861, to the inferior position of Secretary to the Government of India in the Foreign Department. That office had always been deemed "the blue ribbon" of the Covenanted Civil Service, to whom it had been confined. Rendered vacant by the lamented death of Mr. Barnes, it had been filled for some time by the Under-Secretary, Mr. C. U. Aitchison, a young Scots Competition-walla of whom Lord Canning declared, in a special Minute in Council, that he would have been permanently appointed to the office but for his junior standing in the service. An Act of Parliament passed in the previous session had rendered it legal for the Governor-General to select any one for certain of the highest offices, hitherto reserved for the Civil Service, subject to the approval of the Secretary of State. Hence the novel spectacle of a military officer filling, for the first time, the most responsible of the Secretaryships, which Warren Hastings had created as the "secret department" nearly a century before. The salary of the office is nominally the same as that of the Premier of England; but in so expensive a country as India, with the frequent necessity of separation from wife and children, and cut off from an English career, it could not then be considered equal to more than two thousand a year in London. Colonel Durand returned to India under the same sense of duty that characterised all his public actions.

In 1861 the tide of Lord Canning's reputation had turned. England had begun to see that he had given it a character for clemency in dealing with mutiny and rebellion, while the crisis, if thus prolonged, had somehow been tided over. India, knowing how much of what Europe pronounced clemency was due to a constitutional slowness in grasping the magnitude of the crisis, yet ascribing not a little of this to the fact that his advisers knew only the Province of Bengal, welcomed the large and generous energy with which the Governor-General addressed himself to the work of rewarding the loyal chiefs and reconstructing the administration. Gradually but firmly had Lord Canning arrived at what was called his aristocratic policy—that of governing the people through their natural leaders. To him this was the lesson of the Mutiny, and especially of the rebellion in Oudh. He carried out that policy alike in ordering a permanent settlement of the land revenue and the creation of a fee-simple tenure of waste lands, which was also the lesson of the famine of 1860 in the North-Western Provinces; in appointing honorary magistrates and justices of the peace; and, above all, in writing on the statute-book of India a new law, which neither Hindu nor Musalman ruler had ever conceded to its nobles—the absolute right of adoption on the failure of natural heirs to feudatory principalities. He even went farther and introduced the law of primogeniture into Oudh, where the barons known as Talookdars might adopt the law in the case of the vast estates that had been regranted to them.

It was fortunate that Colonel Durand's influence was brought to bear on the feudatory part of this policy. This was his highest merit as an Anglo-Indian statesman, for his equally great military policy was negatived, and the necessity for it is only now being recognised. Each is the complement of the other. An army recruited, drilled, armed, and officered as Durand would have had it, is required not so much to keep the peace in India as to guard its gates on the north-west frontier, and to maintain our high *prestige* from Abyssinia and Kabul to Peking and Tokyo. A feudatory policy, such as Lord Canning devised and Durand developed and applied, not only guarantees internal contentment but is fitted to raise that third of the whole area of India and fourth of its population which are administered by native chiefs, to the same level of civilisation as the rest of the country without direct interference on our part. We may pause for a moment over the history and nature of this feudatory policy.

So long ago as 1854, the Maharaja of Patiala, in the Punjab, expressed a wish to visit England, in order to ask from the Queen a *sanad*, or patent, for himself and the other two branches of the same Phoolkean clan, Nabha and Jhind, descendants with him from Baba Phool, their common ancestor. Such patents were even up to that time granted by the puppet pensioner who sat on the titular throne of Delhi, and were valued nominally as honours, but really under the vague idea that some day the Emperor might have power again. When, after their loyal services during the Mutiny, the question of rewarding the Phoolkean chiefs came up, they renewed their request for a patent under the sign-manual of Her Majesty, guaranteeing them the right of adopting descendants of Baba Phool as heirs to the principalities in default of male survivors in the direct line. The request struck not only Mr. Barnes, who on 20th May 1858 sent it up, but Sir John Lawrence as new and excessive, but they recommended an ordinary patent signed by the Queen as highly politic. A year after Lord Canning returned the reply, that any such patent must bear the Viceroy's signature, and this was most wisely approved of by the Crown. Only when Lord Canning began that remarkable series of "progresses" in October 1860, in which at Lucknow, Umballa, and elsewhere, he gave away whole provinces to the loyal, accompanied by even more precious words of haughty eulogy, does he seem to have risen to the full height of the policy involved in the request of Patiala. Selecting every noble, Hindu and Musalman, who had administrative powers over his own State, and adding to the list only one great landholder, the Maharaja of Benares, he gave to a hundred and fifty-three princes and chiefs the *sanad* under which alone they now hold their principalities, subject only to the two conditions of loyalty to the Crown of England, and fidelity to engagements which prevent the misgovernment of their tenantry.

The puppet of Delhi whom we had so long pensioned had disappeared; the butcher of Cawnpore, Nana Dhoondopunt, the last pretender to be representative of the Maratha Peishwa, had vanished in Nepaul. Although this important change in the law of India was decreed in April 1860, the *sanad* was not drawn up till 1862, and Colonel Durand was its author.[1] With

[1] Sir Mortimer Durand thus writes too modestly of his father's share in the great adoption policy, with every detail of which I happened to be familiar, through Durand and Aitchison, at the time :—

"During the remainder of the year 1861 my father remained in Calcutta

hardly an exception, it has given contentment and even loyalty to our Indian nobles of both creeds. Lord Dalhousie having extended the Empire to nearly its natural limits, his successors have had no reason either for annexation or wide conquest. More than once, when the two conditions of the patent were grossly violated by chiefs, might the Foreign Office have applied the penalty. But at Udaipur, the oldest of the Rajpoot States, under Lord Elgin; at Tonk, a Musalman State, under Lord Lawrence, and at Ulwar during the adminis-

working in particular at the very important question of the adoption of successors by Native Chiefs. Owing to a variety of causes, the failure of lineal heirs in the ruling families of Native States is exceedingly common; and if advantage had been taken of every such failure to declare a State escheated to the Crown, the feudatory principalities of India would now be few. Under Lord Dalhousie the British Government had shown a strong inclination towards a policy of this nature; and the chiefs had been greatly alarmed for the extinction of their houses and States. Lord Canning perceived this fact very clearly, and realised the danger which it involved. He determined, therefore, to reassure the chiefs by every means in his power, and especially to grant them the priceless right of continuing their States, on failure of lineal heirs, by adoption or nomination. Accordingly, in 1862, almost all ruling chiefs received sunnuds or warrants, under the signature of the Viceroy, which ran as follows:—

"'*Her Majesty being desirous that the Governments of the several Princes and Chiefs of India who now govern their own territories should be perpetuated, and that the representation and dignity of their houses should be continued, I hereby, in fulfilment of this desire, convey to you the assurance that, on failure of natural heirs, the adoption by yourself and future rulers of your State of a successor according to Hindu law and the customs of your race will be recognised and confirmed.*

"'*Be assured that nothing shall disturb the engagement thus made to you so long as your house is loyal to the Crown and faithful to the conditions of the treaties, grants, or engagements, which record its obligations to the British Government.*'

"The issue of these sunnuds, which my father worked out in communication with the Governor-General, formed a new starting-point in the history of our feudatory policy. Henceforth every Native Chief has the power, whether childless or not, of perpetuating his State and name. It is impossible to imagine a more complete and binding renunciation of any desire on the part of the British Government for the acquisition of fresh territory in India, or to overestimate the effect of such a declaration of policy upon the minds of the chiefs."

tration of both Lord Mayo and Lord Northbrook, the mildest punishment of hopeless misrule or atrocious cruelty has been temporary sequestration in the interests alike of the people and the chief's family. When the history of India since the Mutiny comes to be written, Durand's share in this righteous, this noble, this successful policy will be told.

He was not only trusted as a statesman by the Native Chiefs, he was looked up to by some of them as a father. On every Native State at which he had been Political Agent before the Mutiny he had thus left his mark. His reserved manner, which at first almost repelled those who knew him not, soon gave way, with the Chief whom he respected or sought to influence for good, to warm confidence. We have a striking instance of this in the case of Bhopal, where he had been Resident. When the Begum visited Calcutta in 1870, to receive the honours of the Star of India along with the Duke of Edinburgh, it was touching to see the way in which she rushed at him as an old friend, or was led about by him hand in hand in the childlike Oriental style, at every Viceregal festivity, so that the aides-de-camp pleasantly rallied him on her affection. In one of his letters at this time I find the following:—"The Shah Jehan Begum almost cried after the installation at not being a Knight Grand Commander. I sent her a confidential message that I had never forgotten the appeal made to me when she was a child, by her grandmother, the old Koodsia—that I had been a fast friend of her mother's, and was hers; and that if she ruled her State well, it should not be my fault if she were not a G.C.S.I." It is by such a policy and by such rulers that India is bound to Great Britain by stronger ties than those of conquest.

During the brief administration of the Earl of Elgin, Colonel Durand not only governed the country in all matters relating to his own department, but he was consulted by the new Viceroy on every important measure, especially during the time when His Excellency was away from his Council. Then it was that Lord Elgin spontaneously promised him the Lieutenant-Governorship of the Punjab on the approaching vacancy. But once more his own chivalrous regard for others, based on his scrupulous conscientiousness, prevented the arrangement. Sir Donald, then Mr., M'Leod had filled more than the term of service allowed by the rule of thirty-five years, but he had no desire to go home, and the Punjab Government was anxious to retain him as Judicial Commissioner for one year more. Unwilling to grant this, Lord Elgin consulted the Foreign Secretary, who strongly advised the concession. What was the result to Durand himself? In a few months Lord Elgin was lying in the English-like churchyard which commands the whole sanitarium of Dharmsala, and his successor, Lord Lawrence, appointed Sir Donald M'Leod to the head of the Punjab. Even had Lord Lawrence known the Earl of Elgin's promise, of which there is no evidence, he was not bound by it. And thus, once more, Colonel Durand, who had sacrificed himself for Sir James Outram, virtually handed over the still higher position, for which he was so well fitted, to the fine old man whom he did not succeed till five years had passed away. And then the life of each was suddenly cut off by a violent death.

On the appointment of Lord Napier to the command of the Bombay Army early in 1865, Durand at last took his seat as Military Member of the Governor-General's Council. He became War Minister, with a right to influence by minutes and secret discussions in the Executive Council, and by speeches in the Legislative Council, every part of the policy and administration of the Government. So far as that was possible, he was generally forced to take the part of the opposition in the former. While in the latter he loyally supported the measures of the Government of which he was a part, or was silent when he could not conscientiously give such support, he spoke freely and debated effectively on questions to which the Government was not pledged, or on which it was not unseemly to take a side.

The Government of India may be described as consisting of a Cabinet of Seven, holding office for five years or less. It meets every Wednesday at eleven, and may break up before two, or may sit till evening, according to the extent of the business and the character of the President. During the week important papers are circulated for the opinion either of all the members, or of that one member who has special charge of a department. The Governor-General presides, or, if he is absent in another part of India, the senior member. His Excellency is absolute in the last resort. He may place before the Council only such business as he chooses, and he may override their decision, if he is outvoted, subject to the Secretary of State representing the Crown. Practically the "Governor-General in Council" works well. If he is at once a strong and a good business man, the Council has little discussion to do. If he is influenced by members who are crotchety or able, then the Council obtains undue influence. For, it should never be forgotten, Orientals like to be governed and to be governed by one man. The business of an Empire like India is so vast that the Governor-General, while superintending the whole, confines himself to the detailed supervision of one department. Lord Lawrence looked after foreign affairs, Lord Mayo took public works also, while Lord Northbrook preferred finance. The Governor-General, the Commander-in-Chief, the Law Member, and the Finance Member (till recently) are appointed from England. The Military Member is always an Indian officer, and the other two belong to the Bengal, Bombay, or Madras Civil Service. Each receives ten thousand a year (at par). To them are added two or three civilians from the other Provinces, two Calcutta merchants, and some native personages, all nominated by the Viceroy and in a purely honorary capacity, to form the Legislative Council, of which the Governor of the Province where it happens to meet is also a member. That body is really consultative though *quasi*-representative, and the Executive can always command a majority. To give the Legislature more power in a country like India would be perilous to its peace and good government. All Acts must receive the assent of the Crown through the Secretary of State, as well as of the Governor-General in his executive capacity, who moreover may veto the measures of the Local Councils, and has power to issue temporary Ordinances without his Council, so as to meet a crisis. The Council Chamber, in which both bodies meet when in Calcutta, is a fine room in the Government House, built at the beginning of the century by Lord Wellesley. The walls are adorned with historical portraits of several of the Governors-General from Warren Hastings.

In his own department of military affairs Colonel Durand was a master. The Army trusted him, and he was generally associated with Lord Sandhurst (then Sir W. Mansfield) and Lord Lawrence in pressing those military reforms which the Secretary of State's Council were too long allowed to sacrifice to Presidency jealousies. He stood alone, however, in his opposition to the application of the Irregular system to the whole Native Army. In foreign and feudatory affairs he was most vigilant, here also generally agreeing with the Viceroy. On the great question of Russia in Asia, and her relation to India, which I first fairly raised in the *Friend of India* in 1865, Colonel Durand neither went so far as the party of vigilance who, with himself, scouted Russophobia in its offensive sense, nor did he approve of Lord Lawrence's favourite "masterly inactivity" so far as that related to our own frontier. He urged the spending of money more generously to put the border in a state of defence. In season and out of season he fought for an efficient army, and with all the power of his trenchant pen he opposed, but vainly, the extreme of irregularism. His letters to me on this subject now read like prophecies. Not till Lord Mayo's Umballa Durbar did he see his views fully carried out.

His Minutes show that he had even more to do with the formation and application of Lord Mayo's foreign policy than with the development of Lord Canning's feudatory system. He would not go one step beyond our own natural frontier to meet a possible invader—he had too vivid a remembrance of 1838-42 for that. But he would, by railways and troops, by our relation to the frontier tribes and our own subjects, make that impregnable. And he would place a ring-fence of powerful allies all along our border from Tibet westward to the sea, who should be strong in our support, moral and—if need be—material, alike towards their own nobles who delighted in anarchy, and towards the regions beyond. He rejoiced in the Umballa Durbar, to which I accompanied him, as the beginning of this policy. Shere Ali and he had met twenty-seven years before, when he was with Lord Ellenborough at the Durbar at which the Ameer's father, Dost Mahomed, had been allowed to return to Afghanistan. In one of his letters I find this remark:—"We have done all it was either right or good policy to do; and I trust the Secretary of State and people at home will be satisfied with our proceedings. Lord Mayo has throughout shown admirable good sense; and I think the Home Government, though his political enemies, will be candid enough to say he has done well." That foreign policy was the best part of Lord Mayo's three years' administration. In almost all the rest of his measures, especially in those relating to finance and public works, and in his communistic theories about the land, that Governor-General found his military colleague an independent critic, a wise counsellor, and frequently a stout opponent. All now admit, as not a few of us saw then, how well it would have been for India had Durand's counsels prevailed rather than those of another colleague. No subject was too technical or professional for the Military Member's grasp. Grave bankers tell how his views on currency and finance were far sounder than those which unfortunately prevailed. In debates on land tenures and taxes, or irrigation rates and the intricate questions connected with the application of political economy to the people of India, the early experience, the cultured reading, and the powerful mind of Colonel Durand made him an antagonist whom the boldest of his colleagues feared and the subtlest sometimes tried to circumvent. None of them wrote so forcibly as he. Public opinion in India always supported him, while it admired his fearlessness and trusted his honesty of purpose. Socially retiring, and with but a few friends whom he bound to himself with hooks of steel, often sacrificed to others, long disappointed and baulked of his due, he was amazed at the acclamations with which the fact was received by all classes when he got his right at last.

He did get it, though, as it proved, all too late for the enjoyment of earthly honour, for his duty to his family, for, above all, the highest kind of service to his country. Sir Donald M'Leod's five years' term of office was approaching its close in the Punjab. The Press were discussing the chances of the leading men, and were almost as unanimous in their desire for Sir Henry Durand's promotion—he had been made Knight Commander of the Star of India—as the public, official and non-official. Still Lord Mayo maintained silence. The reason I knew to be His Excellency's revival of a project of Sir John Malcolm's, for uniting the Political Agencies of Rajpootana and Central India into a new Lieutenant-Governorship. Durand alone was consulted on this subject, and he saw it to be his duty to point out the impracticable and useless nature of the scheme in the present day.[1] He did not know that he was meant for the first Lieutenant-Governor, but this would not have influenced his judgment. It seemed as though, for a third time, he was to be denied justice, and India was to be deprived of his services in their proper sphere. But at last, at a farewell banquet given to Sir Donald M'Leod, at Lahore, in May 1870, Lord Mayo made this announcement. The scene is historic, the associations tragic, for in two short years the principal actors—Durand, Mayo, and M'Leod—were suddenly summoned by a violent death from the very midst of their duties:—

[1] Lord Lytton had a similar project, and would have made Lord Roberts Chief Commissioner (see *Forty Years in India*, vol. ii. p. 142).

"GENTLEMEN—Sir Donald M'Leod bequeaths to his successor arduous and most responsible duties. I believe that his mantle will fall upon one who is in every way most worthy and most able to bear it. In Major-General Sir Henry Durand" (the name was received with loud and prolonged cheering) "you will find a Lieutenant-Governor worthy to be the successor of Sir Donald M'Leod; you will have one of the foremost men in the Indian Service; you will find in him all those great qualities which enable men to rule with success; you will find him firm and fearless, honest and brave. He has vast experience, gained in his military capacity, and also in a long period of civil service—experience gained by service in the India Council at home, and in the Supreme Council of the Governor-General of India. He has ability enough to enable him to fill with distinction the highest positions in the public service, and I believe there is not a man in the service of the Queen who would bring to this high office more power or greater experience than Sir Henry Durand. Gentlemen, I ask you, though I know it is almost superfluous to do so —still I ask you to give him your hearty and cordial support. You are justly proud of your Province, and I entirely sympathise with your feelings in that respect. You have every right to be proud of it, for it is one of the most interesting and most flourishing portions of the Empire of India. But I would ask you, in considering the many and varied questions with which every officer in the Indian Service has to deal, to lay aside all feelings of prejudice, and specially to avoid provincialism, to recollect that we are all subjects of one Queen, that we are all fellow-workers together, and that, after all that is said and done, we are nothing more or less than a body of British gentlemen endeavouring to rule for their good a weaker but still a most interesting and intelligent race; and that our mission in this country is to extend to the people of India the blessings of that civilisation which has made us what we are."

This is part of what Sir Donald M'Leod said in reply:—

"I hope to be able to make over this magnificent Province to my high-minded and gallant successor, whom His Excellency has just named to you, prospering in all that is essential to a good administration and a population of good heart, and ever ready on fitting occasion to show their loyalty to it. Most heartily do I second the exhortation which His Excellency has addressed to you, to receive the noble Sir Henry Durand with all cordiality and support. It is perhaps so far a strange coincidence that he and I were fellow-students in boyhood. I can bear testimony to his high-mindedness and the nobility of his great heart, and I am certain that all those who serve him will find in him one prepared to appreciate their services, to reward all merits, to render justice to all men, and to maintain his rule with a vigour which I never could pretend to possess."

After that, midnight brought in the next day, the anniversary of Sir Donald M'Leod's birthday, when Lord Mayo called on the brilliant company to wish him many happy returns of it, and then telegraphed to Sir Henry Durand, at Simla, the fact that the announcement of his appointment had been so enthusiastically received. At the same time, Sir Henry learned from England that his second son, Mortimer, had taken a good place in the list of successful candidates for the Civil Service of Bengal. His answers to the congratulations that poured in upon him show the deep but manly humility of his nature. Dinners from the Governor-General and the Commander-in-Chief, of a somewhat public character, followed. The 1st of June found him at Murree, sworn in as Lieutenant-Governor of the Punjab and its Dependencies.

The new Lieutenant-Governor's first act, after he had fairly grappled the routine duties of his office, was to visit the most important of the feudatories under him, the Maharaja of Kashmir. His letters to me from Srinuggur, the summer capital of that State, are full of wisdom in reference to the relations of the Chief with our Government. His visit had no diplomatic object, and was therefore all the more effective for good. He liked to know the chiefs personally, and that they should know and trust him. His remark to me should be pondered by all our Political Agents in India :—"I go with no purpose of lecturing, or bullying, or interfering, but of treating him as I do all the Native Chiefs, like gentlemen. It is one of the secrets of any little success I have with them, to let them feel and know that they have my sympathy and support, and are treated as I would treat Her Majesty's sons or ministers." He spent the greater part of July 1870 in Kashmir.

As an Engineer, formerly employed on the irrigation works of the North-Western Provinces, Sir Henry Durand took up with interest the consideration of three great water projects. One was a canal from the Swat river, near the fort of Abazai, to run eastward for the irrigation of part of the rich Yusufzai plain; the second, the supply of pure water from the Barra river for the cantonment and city of Peshawar; the third, the water-supply for the station of Kohat. He recorded his opinion on these projects after personally examining the proposed heads of the channels, and obtaining all available local information. These works have all since been completed.

He entered fully into the various military questions connected with the western frontier. He discussed, in a memorandum written on the spot, the provision of some defence for the station of Abbottabad in Hazara. He examined the new barracks at Peshawar forming the first two sides of the proposed fortified enclosure, and the plan which had been ordered at that time for surrounding the whole European cantonment with these large buildings. He inspected, with the civil and military officers, the ground proposed for a new location of a cavalry regiment at Kohat. He had to consider certain matters relating to the positions of the frontier forts, with reference to the work each had to do, and the state of the frontier at that part. An important question concerning these new posts on the Tânk border was to have been taken up, on a visit to the place, which was appointed for the 2nd of January 1871. Before that day came, his eyes had closed in death.

After visiting the Tânk outpost on foot, the Lieutenant-Governor proceeded to see the town and the Nawab's date-gardens. The elephants were waiting at the gate of the outpost. Sir Henry politely motioned the Nawab to ascend to the howdah before him, and smiled at the Chief's reluctance to precede the Lieutenant-Governor. They took their seat together in the howdah, with an attendant on the back. On another elephant five officers followed, seated on a pad, namely, Brigadier-General Keyes, Colonel Graham, Colonel Maclagan, Colonel Kennedy, and Colonel Black. Going to the city first, the Lieutenant-Governor's elephant was turned, after a short pause at the gate, and went on to the date-gardens. It is supposed that he saw the inner gateway was too low to admit the elephant with the howdah. On coming back from the gardens, the Lieutenant-Governor's elephant was taken up again to the gate, and entered the enclosure covering the inner gateway. The outer gateway, the entrance to this little enclosure, was of ample height. The officers waited outside, expecting to see the other elephant turn and come out again. Instead of this, after a short pause, the elephant went rapidly forward through the inner entrance. The officers were horrified to see it pass through, and to hear the sound of the howdah breaking against the flat roof-beam of the gateway. They got down quickly and ran in. Passing part of the broken howdah in the gateway, they found Sir Henry inside, on the ground, lying on his face, with much blood coming from his mouth and nose, and the elephant standing still. A few yards farther on the Nawab was lying back on the broken howdah, with his face turned upwards. Sir Henry was quite insensible. He was carried to the camp. No external injury was perceptible, and he was unable to indicate what he was suffering, or where he had been injured. After having been placed on his own bed in his tent, consciousness began to return. He felt his limbs paralysed; his spine had been injured. He slept during the night, and the next day spoke clearly, and gave specific and distinct expression to his wants. He remarked on the awkwardness of not being able to use his hands, or do anything for himself. He gave directions to his son about informing Lady Durand of the accident. As the day wore on—it was Sunday, 1st January 1871—he became more feeble, but retained full consciousness. In the afternoon, when the doctors perceived that life could not last much longer, his son and two daughters were sent for to come in to him. He told them he was dying; that his life had been a hard and bitter one; and that the only thing which had borne him through it had been the love and fear of God. He begged them as his last advice to look to Christ in all things, to do justice, and to love the right. A few hours later he passed quietly away, and it seemed to some of those about him that "he was glad to go."

The body was borne on a camel carriage to Dera Ismail Khan, and was buried on the 5th of January. It was a soldier's funeral. Fifty-nine minute guns were fired. A simple block of marble covers his resting-place, and on it are graven the words which he had made his rule in life: "He hath shewed thee, O man, what is good, and what doth the Lord require of thee, but to do justly, and to love mercy, and to walk humbly with thy God?"

Thus, in all the ripeness of a long career, just when

the gathered experience of forty years was beginning to be applied to the most important of our Indian Provinces, this Christian soldier and statesman was suddenly taken away. To quote the words of the book published by Lady Durand:—[1]

> "He who here sad heart-sighs soweth,
> Doing right through suffering ill,
> There shall find the joy-ripe harvest,
> All his longings to fulfil."

The Viceroy, who was himself so soon to meet with an even sadder fate, declared in the official eulogy published in the *Gazette*, that "his name will long be revered in the Punjab." The Duke of Argyll, then Secretary of State for India, expressed in equally high terms the sense which Her Majesty's Government entertained of his services. After referring to his "gallantry in the field," and to the "ability and independence of character" by which his life had been distinguished, the official despatch acknowledging the receipt of the news thus closed:—"The life of such a man is an example to the service, and Her Majesty's Government deeply deplore his death."

The Anglo-Indian public, both in India and England, subscribed for an enduring memorial of him. The Secretary of State in Council recognised his great public services by a special grant of £400 a year to his widow.

[1] *Imitations from the German of Spitta and Terstegen.* By Lady Durand. 1873.

VII

LIEUT.-GENERAL COLIN MACKENZIE, C.B., 1825–1881

LAST OF THE E. I. COMPANY'S PURITAN SOLDIERS

AMID the crowd of heroic men, from Clive to Lawrence, to whom the East India Company owes what is greatest in its history, Lieut.-General Colin Mackenzie, C.B., holds a unique position. To the fearlessness of Clive, which Browning has dramatised, and to the dash of Outram, he added the righteousness of Durand and the evangelical fervour of the Lawrences. In Colin Mackenzie Chivalry and Puritanism met. The former was the fruit of his early life, the latter was the deliberate choice of his middle and later years; both combined gave his character a charm all its own, such as has been rare since the days of Coligny.

Sprung from the cadet branch of the Mackenzies of Redcastle, Colin had to make his own way in the world. Landless and portionless, his fathers had sought success in continental and colonial service, adding new lustre to the reputation of the Scot abroad. He, like another large class of our countrymen up to the middle of the present century, found his place in the army of the

East India Company. The beginning of the year 1826 saw him ensign in the 48th Madras Native Infantry, after an education which made him master of his own language and of French, so that he ever wrote a pure and vigorous style, and had the poet Pope by heart. A handsome boy, full of the natural graces of purity and honour, he had passed through the fiery ordeal of Addiscombe as it was in those days, and of brief duty with a royal regiment, unscathed. But he fought two duels. He was adjutant of his regiment when Lord William Bentinck, who could tolerate no longer the iniquities of the Raja of Coorg, sent Sir Patrick Lindsay to remove the monster. As Deputy-Assistant Quartermaster-General, the young lieutenant served with the main column of the force in all the actions which resulted in the taking of Merkara, the capital. After ten years of incessant military experience he sought health at sea. In 1836, and long afterwards, till Raja Brooke struck at the root of the evil, the Malay pirates were a terror to the commerce which swept to and fro through the Straits of Sunda, between China and the West. The young Highlander volunteered for service against them, with Admiral Sir H. Ducie Chads, in the Straits of Malacca and the China Seas, and such were his exploits that he was specially mentioned to Lord Auckland, the Governor-General. On some of those rare occasions when Colin Mackenzie could be beguiled into speaking of himself, I have known him keep us sitting many an hour into the night while he told of adventures by sea and land, which he would not allow to be committed to record beyond the brief summary in the Admiral's despatches.

When, soon after, Lord Auckland in India and Lord Broughton at home entered on the mad policy which shook the Empire to its foundation, Colin Mackenzie, still an unlucky lieutenant, and Major George Broadfoot volunteered, with the result of making the Madras Army as famous in the first Afghan War as Colonel Neill did in the Mutiny which sprang from its campaigns. Each in 1840 became the right hand of George Clerk on the north-west frontier; Mackenzie, first in charge of the Khaibar Pass, as Assistant Political Agent at Peshawar. But, as if that duty were not full enough of danger, he did not rest until he was sent into the thick of the struggle at Kabul itself, as assistant to the Envoy, Sir William Macnaghten. Even there his fiery spirit would allow no danger to present itself which he did not ask to share. The insurrection around Kabul had begun, and Sir Robert Sale had been sent to take the field in the hill country. Edward Conolly, one of three noble brothers, had fallen at Tootundurrah as a volunteer, and the 13th Light Infantry had been repulsed at Joolgah. Dost Mahomed seemed to be everywhere, stirring up the tribes. Mackenzie asked permission to join the Sappers; he led the advanced guard at the forcing of the Khoord Kabul Pass, soon to become a place of terrible memory. He was summoned back only to still sterner work with the doomed force in the Afghan capital, when Dost Mahomed personally surrendered to the British Envoy, and was sent on to Calcutta, with the confession in which Macnaghten condemned the whole war—"We ejected the Dost, who never offended us, in support of our policy of which he was the victim."

From this time of preparation in the young lieutenant's service, when he was still under thirty-five, we now come to the four deeds of daring and suffering in his life, any one of which would have made him the hero of a people and the subject of their ballads in darker ages, all of which duty alone led him to face and to do, because he was not only a soldier but a saint. For a great change had passed within Colin Mackenzie. In 1836 his first wife had died on the fourth anniversary of their wedding day, after a happy union. Gradually, and under Bible teaching, he had come to see that of all lives life in Christ is alone worth living. His courage received a new motive; his sense of duty the highest inspiration. The working of the Spirit had been silently preparing his candid mind for the teaching of Scripture as presented to him by an evangelical missionary. "Chalmers of Beckenham," the brother officer who became soon after the earnest English rector, completed the good work. Colin Mackenzie, the dashing war-loving lieutenant, became thenceforth one of the "saints" of the Indian Army—one, too, of its martyrs, who suffered all his life for the consistency of his Puritanism. The story of the *Storm and Sunshine*[1] of his life has been told, in two charming volumes which every family as well as Anglo-Indian administrator and soldier should

[1] *Storm and Sunshine of a Soldier's Life: Lieutenant-General Colin Mackenzie, C.B.* (Edinburgh: David Douglas.)

read, by his widow, herself a Douglas of the race whom Otterburn first made immortal in our history. Her earliest work, *The Camp, the Mission, and the Zenana,* was justly pronounced equal to Heber's, on its appearance in 1853. When he entered Afghanistan, it was without the dogmatic knowledge of Henry Havelock in somewhat similar circumstances, though he grew into that also. In the lull before the massacre these two stood almost alone among the young officers, in the continence and purity of their lives, while Sir Alexander Burnes was at the head of those who were heaping up wrath against the whole British force, which the imbecility of its military chiefs was impotent to avert. With a perfect knowledge of Persian, moreover, and of the Afghan colloquial, Mackenzie soon became more closely associated with the natives than most of his comrades, being attached to the Kizzilbash force of Shah Shooja, the king. So, by friend and foe alike, he was known as the "Moolla," the Puritan, the priest, the doer of the law. His life was a mystery to the sensual Afghans, and a silent reproach to his own comrades, whom privately he attempted to influence for good. Such was the man, when the horrors of 1841-42 burst on our reduced army of occupation, and financial troubles at Calcutta led the devoted Macnaghten to cut down the subsidy of Rs. 30,000 a year given to the Ghilzai chiefs to keep the roads open.

The first of Mackenzie's four exploits was this:—

Mackenzie and Pottinger had been in vain warning the Envoy of the gathering storm, when, on the 2nd of November, a Kabul mob slaughtered Alexander Burnes and other officers in the city, and plundered the treasury within sight of a passive force of 5000 British soldiers. Having then taken the fort in which all our commissariat supplies were stored, they besieged the camel sheds on the outskirts, where the provisions of the king's force were kept. This so-called fort of Nishan Khan was under Captain Mackenzie's charge. After pressure from Vincent Eyre he wrote what Sir John Kaye justly pronounced "a very interesting and well-written report" of the forty hours' siege. The fort was not capable of defence; it was choked with baggage and encumbered with a host of women and children, and the water was scarce. But he held it, a solitary European, at the head of faithful Mohammedan Sepoys, whom the Afghans, firing through his own loopholes, challenged to give him up for the sake of Islam. In vain for two days did he look for help, "for the glittering bayonets through the trees." All the men were on duty at the same time, but "whenever they could snatch five minutes to refresh themselves with a pipe, one or other of them would twang a sort of rude guitar as an accompaniment to some martial song, which, mingling with the notes of war, sounded very strangely." Ever and anon there rose the wild shrieks of the women over the dead and dying. After fighting and waiting for forty hours without rest, and on the leader's part without refreshment, the only resource was to march the survivors by night to the British cantonments. It was the Ramadan fast; half a mile had been accomplished when

Mackenzie found himself in a narrow lane, met by the cry from a party of Afghans—"Feringhee hust" ("Here is a European"). "Spurring my horse violently I wheeled round, cutting from right to left. My blows, by God's mercy, parried the greater part of them, and I was lucky enough to cut off the hand of my most outrageous assailant. After a desperate struggle, during which I received two slight sabre-cuts, and a blow on the back of the head from a fellow whose sword turned in his hand, which half knocked me off my horse, I escaped out of the crush, passing unhurt through two volleys of musketry from the whole picket. . . . To my horror I perceived my path again blocked up by a dense body of Afghans. Retreat was impossible, so, putting my trust in God, I charged into the midst of them, hoping that the weight of my horse would clear a way for me, and reserving my sword-cut for the last struggle. It was well that I did so, for by the time I had knocked over some twenty fellows I found they were my own Juzailchis. If you ever experienced sudden relief from a hideous nightmare you may imagine my feelings for the moment. During the whole business I had under a dozen killed, whereas about thirty of the enemy had bitten the dust and gone to their place." It was like Colin Mackenzie to spare no pains till "the handful of brave men" who remained faithful to him to the last, though Afghan Mohammedans, received a public reward. Each veteran got a year's pay when Mackenzie's Juzailchis were disbanded at Jhelam. But before that he led the detachment, as General

Elphinstone reported to Government, in almost every fight during the two months' siege of the cantonment, his and their conduct being most conspicuous; and in the disastrous affair of Behmaru, where he was again wounded, he was publicly thanked for his conduct.

We come to the second of the four experiences. The siege ended in the massacre of the Envoy, which Mackenzie's knowledge of the Afghans again strove to prevent. He was to have accompanied Sir William Macnaghten to Peshawar, when the unhappy Minister had been appointed Governor of Bombay by the same irony of fate which marked the whole policy. That had ended in Macnaghten agreeing to pay Akbar Khan, the treacherous son of Dost Mahomed, 30 lakhs of rupees, and an annuity of 4 lakhs, as Wuzeer of Shah Shooja, on the plea that this would give England time to enter into a treaty with Russia, defining the bounds beyond which neither was to pass in Central Asia. On the fatal 23rd December 1841, the Envoy went forth to meet Akbar Khan in conference on this precious treaty, attended by Mackenzie, George Lawrence,[1] and Trevor. Mackenzie had remonstrated, with the warning that it was a plot against him. The deluded Envoy replied hastily, "A plot! let me alone for that, trust me for that!" and so the doomed party proceeded. On the slope of a hillock, which hid them from the cantonment, a carpet was spread where the snow lay least thickly. They dismounted and reclined beside Akbar Khan and

[1] Brother of Henry and John, and afterwards Sir George St. Patrick Lawrence.

his chiefs. Mackenzie could hardly prevail on himself to quit his gallant Cape horse which had before carried him so well, and when on the ground, he rose up as armed men began to gather around the party. Then Akbar Khan gave the signal in the word "Begeer!" ("Seize!") and grasped the Envoy's left hand with an expression of diabolical ferocity, while another secured the right. They dragged him down the hillock as he uttered the words in Persian, "For God's sake!" Akbar Khan struck and then shot him with one of the very pistols which he had once presented to the traitor. Trevor too was cut down, and Lawrence was dragged past his horrified comrade.

Mackenzie had been standing apart talking with the chief of the Afghan police, an old acquaintance, who mastered his right arm, held a pistol to his temple, and amid a shower of bullets hurried him through the snow to a horse. "As I mounted behind my captor, now my energetic defender, the crowd increased around us and the cries of 'Kill the Kafir' became more vehement." After for some time, while at a fast canter, warding off the sword-cuts, with the aid of his followers, the Afghan wheeled his horse round, made the last appeal a Musalman can make by taking off his turban, and implored the devotee Ghazis to respect the life of his friend. The horse fell as it leaped up a high bank, when Mackenzie received a heavy blow on his head from a bludgeon and a fanatic twisted his collar to suffocation. When he recovered consciousness he was being defended by Akbar Khan himself, who then repeatedly taunted him in a tone of triumphant derision, "You'll seize my country, will you?" Insulted and plundered by the men who had slain Macnaghten and Trevor, he and Lawrence were kept prisoners in the city, were then ordered to be blown away from a gun, and were rescued with difficulty by two chiefs. Dressed as Afghans, they were sent back to cantonments to encourage false confidence on the part of the doomed army and its leaders.

The first day of 1842 saw the beginning of the end, when the most disgraceful treaty military commanders have ever signed was ratified, and that retreat began through the winter snow and the far worse Ghilzai bullets, which only one man, Dr. Brydon, survived out of sixteen thousand. In all our history only Cawnpore is blacker than Khoord Kabul and Jugdulluk. Blacker, because the widows and wives and children and a few of the maimed and wounded officers were spared from Khoord Kabul to become the "guests" of the traitor, and, as a matter of fact, survived their captivity with honour, though at the last sent by their "host" to be sold as slaves in Toorkistan. To them had been added Mackenzie, Lawrence, and Pottinger as hostages, on Akbar Khan's demand, after the first had eagerly sought to redeem the errors of Elphinstone and Shelton, as he had done to prevent the infatuation of Macnaghten. The captives, besides these three, and Elphinstone, Shelton, and Johnson, other hostages, were the widows, Lady Macnaghten, Mrs. Sturt and one child; Mrs. Trevor and seven children; Lady Sale, whose husband was holding Jelalabad with Havelock under him; Captain Boyd, wife and child; Lieutenant Waller, wife and child; Lieutenant Eyre, wife and child; Mr. Ryley, wife and child; Mrs. Mainwaring and child; Sergeant Wade and family; and the wounded officers, Colin Troup and Mein, Melville and Dr. Macgrath,—twenty-nine, and fourteen children in all.[1]

All were at first placed under the care of the one Afghan chief who had proved himself at once a patriot and a man, the "good Nawab," as he was called, Zemaun Khan, who was moreover of near kin to Dost Mahomed, then in honourable captivity in Calcutta. To protect them he raised an army of his own, of three thousand men. For nine months they remained in captivity, hurried from place to place, sometimes for their own safety, at others according to the falling fortunes of Akbar Khan, now almost within sight of our troops at Jelalabad, again among the fastnesses of Khoolm, to be sold to the man-stealing Oosbegs. Mackenzie's stories of their prison life, their kindly intercourse, their hopes and fears, their trust in God, their Sunday service, and the use of the one Bible and Prayer-book picked up on the field of slaughter, of the gambols of the children to whose number more than one birth added, their attempts at recreation, their tricks on the 1st of April, their speculations as to relief and the

[1] In 1843 Mr. Lowes Dickinson prepared beautiful lithographic drawings from the portraits of the captives, made by Eyre for their amusement when in prison. The Editor of his *Journal* (John Murray) published them. Colin Mackenzie wrote much of Eyre's *Journal*. Havelock's *Narrative* (2 vols., Colburn) stops at 1839.

course of events in India, where Lord Ellenborough was so far reversing his predecessor's policy as to be willing to sacrifice its noble victims—all this and more he could never be persuaded to put on record, nor to allow his friends to do so. But three years after, when it was still vividly printed on the memory, he was persuaded to tell to a loving writer one episode in his *Recollections of a Journey to Jelalabad.*

This is the third of the deeds to which we referred at the outset.

Major Pottinger, who had succeeded Macnaghten, fearing that the defeat of Akbar Khan before Jelalabad might tempt him to murder the whole party, proposed to him to send one of the captives to treat with General Pollock, who had halted at that city. Mackenzie, who was tending the dying Elphinstone in a fort in Tezeen, the only drugs available being opium and boiled pomegranate, was sent for when the old man breathed his last, and told to prepare for a journey to Jelalabad. No one save Pottinger believed he could survive a mission of such danger. The Afghans reasoned that if any of the captives would return in such circumstances it would be the English Moolla, whose word they could trust, for when, with some confusion, Akbar Khan asked him if he intended to return, Mackenzie answered, "Are you the son of an Ameer and ask me, an English gentleman, such a question?" Akbar Khan's private request was an amnesty for himself and followers, and a grant of land, in which case he would help Pollock to reconquer Afghanistan;

the public letter proposed an exchange of prisoners and the withdrawal of the English from the country. Dressed in a sheep-skin cloak full of vermin, with his white face hidden up to the eyes, and mounted on Lady Sale's horse with a native saddle, Colin Mackenzie set out. He was attended by two of Akbar Khan's troopers, and guided by the notorious Batti, "the thief," and three of his gang, on foot. Batti was the Rob Roy who had eased Sale of several hundreds of his camels, which he resold to the General! The three horsemen and four thieves struggled up the bed of a torrent till they came to a cascade, which barred advance. Laughing at the troopers' abuse, Batti guided Mackenzie up and round by a goat's path till they surmounted hills "to which Ben Lomond is a joke!" He knew Persian and beguiled the way with Pushtu war-songs, till the Scottish Highlander was lost in sympathetic admiration at the man whose nostrils were not even expanded as he clomb the tremendous ascents, his heavy matchlock behind his back with the ends resting on the inside of his elbows. When the snow was reached the danger increased, for the track sloped to the torrent at an angle of forty-five. Even the Afghan troopers protested they had never seen such a road, while the perspiration streamed off them like rain in spite of the wintry wind. So they crossed the Khurkhuchar Pass; but in the easy descent on the other side the icy blast cut through them. To the left they passed the fatal barriers of Jugdulluk, where, untouched by decay, lay the bodies of Mackenzie's brave comrades, of whom he specially mentions Dodgin as having fought so desperately, though he had but one leg, that the enemy were obliged to shoot him from a distance.

As he passed along the narrow ridge in the bright moonlight, with the mangled remains below and the everlasting hills towering in front, he says, "My sense of weakness and absolute inability in any way to control the progress of events which were rapidly hurrying to a crisis, and which were fraught with safety or destruction to myself and my fellow-captives, and with honour or dishonour to my country, had the good effect of leading me to Him whose arm is never shortened to uphold and save all who put their trust in Him." And this follows: "Before we reached the Valley of Zinganeh we had to cross a shallow stream, whose pure waters I shall ever remember with gratitude, for my tongue clove to the roof of my mouth, and there on three subsequent journeys did it quench my thirst." As day dawned and they came to a hostile tribe, Batti carefully smothered the white officer in the Afghan dress and mounted before him, passing him off as a sick chief of Peshawar sent home by Akbar Khan. Every eminence was topped by a robber fort, notably that of the murderer of James Skinner, whose men pursued the party. At the ford of a river, opposite the gate of the chief, Mackenzie, worn out by fatigue, fairly tumbled off among the henchmen who had rushed out with the cry of "Strangers!" "For the first time," he said, "I felt the anguish of mortal fear, notwithstanding the awful extremity in which I had twice stood before when surrounded by the Afghans, in cutting my way into cantonments, and again at Sir William Macnaghten's murder." But Batti, the thief, was equal to the crisis. He harangued his countrymen on the exploits of Akbar Khan over the infidels, while his followers dragged the "sick chief" away up the mountain path.

After a week of hairbreadth escapes and exhausting toil, amid the filth of Afghan surroundings, Colin Mackenzie and his horse, in a state which he used Scotch to describe, as "sair forfoughen," rode into Pollock's camp. So black and haggard had he become that the Sepoy vidette would not believe he was a European. He was received by the General and his old friend, Sir George Macgregor, as an apparition. But the camp was soon alive with the news he brought, and each little fact about the captives spread away over India into every cantonment, and tardily westward to the British homes where hope deferred had sickened many a loving heart. Mackenzie's information helped the avenging army to the rapid success which in due time enabled the captives to free themselves. He did not need to advise Sir George Pollock to scorn all overtures from the murderer of Macnaghten. But he went further, he urged an immediate advance on Kabul as the first and only step necessary to leaving the people for ever to their own independence. And after twenty-four hours he returned into captivity, only to be sent back again on a second though less perilous mission, after seven hours' repose, while Pottinger was preparing another letter to the General. The second journey resulted in an attack of typhus under which he nearly sank, so that his friend, Colin Troup, was despatched on the third and last of these missions by which Akbar Khan sought in vain to save himself from the fate which his deeds deserved. His defeat at Tezeen led the Afghan jailor of the captives, who was conducting them over the wastes of the Hindu Kush to be sold as slaves, to let them free themselves, on Mackenzie, Johnson, Pottinger, and George Lawrence becoming personally bound, "in the presence of God and Jesus Christ," for the amount of their ransom, Rs.20,000 at once and Rs.1000 a month, "In our prison at Bameean, 11th September 1842."

To Kabul, where Pollock's army represented at once the triumph and the atonement of British power, Sale's 13th Regiment led the delivered ones. But work had yet to be done, and Colin Mackenzie must be at the doing of it, though hardly recovered from the Jelalabad perils. Istalif, the virgin fortress of the Afghans, still defied us, and it fell to Henry Havelock to storm it. Mackenzie was by his side at the head of a large body of Kizzilbash horsemen. Then, then at last, he sought home, where were his motherless daughters, away out of all the theatrical rejoicings of Lord Ellenborough, to whom the captives were odious. The still youthful Captain was welcomed as the hero he was, for England did not agree with Lord Ellenborough. Wedded to the eldest daughter of Admiral J. E.

Douglas, the accomplished authoress, who still survives him, he returned to the north-west frontier, raised the 4th Sikh Regiment in 1847, and with it kept the peace of the border during the last Sikh campaign. In him the Marquess of Dalhousie, visiting the new Province of the Punjab, found a man after his own heart.

"Colin," as the Governor-General always called him, was hastily summoned to council at that critical time when the great Proconsul could not make up his mind whether the Indus River or the base of the Sulaimans should be the limit of British supremacy. "Don't give up Peshawar," said Mackenzie; "it is the gate of India." Offered a rich civil appointment in the new Province, the much-enduring soldier preferred the Army still, and in 1850 the Madras Captain was appointed senior Brigadier of the Haidarabad Contingent. But a political and administrative duty of the most important kind fell to his lot. Berar, the fertile cotton valley now pierced by the Bombay and Calcutta Railway, was transferred to the British by the Nizam, and the Brigade was ordered to take it over. Mackenzie's junior, Brigadier Mayne, was eager to provoke a collision, that they might win their spurs. Colin Mackenzie kept him in check, prepared careful statistics of the districts, advanced on his own responsibility the sums which prevented the peasantry from migrating elsewhere and the State losing a year's revenue, and so acted that Lord Dalhousie declared he had taken possession of the Province "without losing a rupee of revenue or spilling a drop of blood."

It was at the close of six years of such service that, as if Kabul had not been enough, he was personally forced to suppress the mutiny of a cavalry regiment in Bolarum, one of several ominous mutterings of the storm which burst in 1857. This is the fourth of his great deeds of daring and devotion to duty.

In September 1855, on the occasion of the Muharram, or ten days' fast observed by the Shia Mohammedans, he directed that the usual orders should be issued, under which processions with music and noise were forbidden during the twenty-four hours of the Christians' day of worship and rest. As it turned out that Sunday was the great day when alone the Muharram processions could take place that year, the Brigadier at once issued a second order permitting them, but only in the lines of their respective corps, and not in the barracks or along the roads. This "usual" police regulation, to prevent a religious procession from interfering with the comfort of the citizens of another creed, as the press described it at the time, was deliberately disobeyed. The 3rd Cavalry Regiment, notorious for opium-eating and for the murder of both a European and a native officer, sent a procession quietly along the road to the Brigadier's garden, where it began making a hideous din. Mackenzie sent first his orderly and then the sergeant of his guard to warn them. They continued, when he himself went to exercise his personal authority, and, in the last resort, to prevent all bloodshed but his own. He could not, as he afterwards said, "skulk under hatches," that being contrary to his nature and his oath. He would not turn out his Hindu infantry guard, for that would have led to a widespread conflict. So he walked out quietly, and, only after remonstrating in vain, he returned with the small standards carried in defiance of the law. The natives, fleeing to their lines with shouts of "Deen! Deen!" ("the faith in danger"), returned with a mob of troopers, who broke in the gate and sprang upon him with sabres. One cut split his skull down to the brain, another severed the outer bone of the left arm, a third cut the deltoid to the bone, and two others took off the middle finger of the right hand. The unarmed Brigadier staggered into and through the house bleeding profusely; the doctor gave up all hope of his recovery, and he himself exclaimed in the pauses of exhaustion, "It is all God's doing, and therefore right." We have Henry Lawrence's verdict on the affair at the time, given in that famous article of his in the *Calcutta Review*, in which he said of a general mutiny—"Come it will, unless anticipated; a Clive may not then be at hand." That wisest and best of Englishmen who ever went to India, declared the Muharram order to be perfectly legitimate, looked on the attack as premeditated by fanatics, and, while doubting the wisdom of Mackenzie's personal interference, said of him, "He possesses much of the Covenanter spirit." His wounds were frightful; few men could have survived them. His dauntless spirit sustained him. Read in the light of 1857, Henry Lawrence's eulogy may be taken even without his doubt. Then we suffered for the weakness which in 1855 sought to extenuate open mutiny, because Colin Mackenzie was a saint as well as a soldier.

The great Mutiny found him in England recovering from his wounds, and the counsellor of the *Daily News* and the authorities, on whom he urged at once the despatch of an army of 30,000 men—a movement too long delayed. He succeeded his friend Sir George Macgregor as Political Agent at Murshidabad, and after that held various military appointments till his promotion to be Major-General in 1871. In all he showed the same "gallantry, ability, and endurance" which Lord Dalhousie extolled in the *Gazette* in 1849. But he would never ask for a reward. It is a satire on the honours which are thickly showered on men now that the age of Indian chivalry is past, that Colin Mackenzie received no more than the first Kabul medal, the Companionship of the Bath, and a special annuity of £300 for his "varied and distinguished services, especially in Afghanistan." Wherever he went, in India, he was the warm friend of Christian missionaries and converts. Wherever he resided, in Edinburgh, London, or the Continent, he sought out Christian friends, he helped philanthropic movements, he made himself beloved by the poor, the dependent, the humble. He was a true soldier of Jesus Christ, who ever held in his heart, and rejoiced in the divine saying, "Him that cometh unto me I will in no wise cast out."

We close the story with a loving admiration of its hero. He was the friend of Havelock, who did in

Jelalabad what Mackenzie was enabled to do amid the disasters of Kabul and captivity. Of him his younger comrade, General Haughton, wrote when he died, referring to a ride for life from Charikar: "He ministered to my spiritual comfort when none else attempted to do so. I have lost the most chivalrous, the most warm-hearted, the most public-spirited, and above all, the most earnest and Christian friend I ever had!"

Colin Mackenzie's final visit, when in 1881 he had found his home in Edinburgh, is thus described by his widow: "At our last visit to our faithful friends, Dr. and Mrs. George Smith, he said to her, 'Well, good-bye, dear; if we do not meet here again, we shall meet at Headquarters.'" On the 20th October he walked upstairs to bed, quite strongly, only the great scars on his wounded head throbbed painfully. Calling for the hymn "Sun of my Soul," and correcting his wife when she said "cannot" instead of "dare not" in the line—

"For without Thee I dare not die,"

he said "Pray for me," and so passed away. A Presbyterian always, and an active friend of every free and evangelical Church, his death called forth this eulogy from Canon Liddon, who had learned to love him: "Simple, fearless, affectionate, chivalrous, he took possession of people's hearts as a matter of course." And it is fitting that this Scottish chief and Christian gentleman should lie side by side with one who, of the Queen's as Mackenzie was of the Indian Army, most resembled him—his friend General Sir Hope Grant. As you enter the Grange cemetery and pass between the tombs of mighty dead like Duff and Chalmers, turn to the far left and see the twin graves of the Indian heroes called to be saints, soldiers in a double sense, as were Havelock and Durand, Henry Lawrence and Herbert Edwardes. May God send our Empire, at home and abroad, a succession of such men!

VIII

SIR HERBERT B. EDWARDES, K.C.B., K.C.S.I., 1819–1868

A Knight of the Faith

UNDER the title of *A Knight's Faith*, John Ruskin published those "passages in the life of Sir Herbert Edwardes"[1] which relate the experiences of the young subaltern when, alone, he civilised Bunnoo, used its wild Levies to defeat Moolraj twice at Kinyeree and Suddoosam, and shut him up in Mooltan until the Commander-in-Chief was ready to take the city. Ruskin describes Edwardes as "a modern military bishop, differing from the military ecclesiastics of former ages in that they, officially bishops, were practically soldiers; but the hero of this my Christmas tale, officially a soldier, was practically a bishop. Practically indeed both, and perfectly both; a first-rate fighter of men in war; a first-rate fisher of men in peace; a captain whom all were proud to follow, a prelate whom all were eager to obey. I really remember nobody quite like him—since St. Martin of Tours." General Gordon,

[1] *Bibliotheca Pastorum*, vol. iv. Collated by John Ruskin. George Allen, 1885.

Havelock, and Stonewall Jackson were all men of his stamp, "only there is a vein of gaiety and natural humour in Edwardes which makes him like St. Martin of Tours, in a sense the others were not."

A year later Lady Edwardes published *Memorials of the Life and Letters*[1] of her husband, dedicating the volumes in the words he had written for his *Life of Sir Henry Lawrence*, which he did not live to complete:—"To all my Countrymen who care for India, and especially to the young whose lot is to be cast in it; to show how possible and good it is to unite the Statesman with the Soldier, the Philanthropist with the Patriot, and the Christian with all, in the Government of a Subject Race." To these books must be added that of Edwardes himself, *A Year on the Punjab Frontier in* 1848-49.[2] No such literary tribute has been made to the reputation and the deeds of any of the Indian heroes of Great Britain up to the present time as these five volumes all unconsciously bring. Herbert Edwardes was equally good with the pen and with the sword. He was the most eloquent of public orators, as well as the most successful of administrative statesmen and political officers. He was a joyous and energetic Christian all his life, as well as the idol of the native tribes whom he tamed, and of the officers whom he attached to himself for ever. He was the favourite disciple of Sir Henry Lawrence, and, above all, the sole master of John Nicholson, who when dying spoke only

[1] London: Kegan Paul, Trench and Co., 1886.
[2] London: Richard Bentley, 1851.

of him and his own mother. Yet Herbert Edwardes was never more than a Commissioner of a Punjab Division, though he was virtually its Provisional Lieutenant-Governor. He left India at forty-six, and he died before he was fifty years of age, too soon for the highest honours to reach him and for the good of the peoples he loved. He was of the chosen ones of whom it is said,—

> "In secret love the Master to each one whispers low,
> 'I am at hand, work faster; behold the sunset glow!'
> And each one smileth sweet who hears the Master's feet."

In the eighteen crowded years between the first Sikh War and his retirement from the Punjab to die, Herbert Edwardes did these memorable deeds, any one of which would have sufficed for a soldier-statesman's reputation:

He tamed Bunnoo and took Mooltan.

He secured the treaties of 1855 and 1857 with Dost Mahomed, which kept Afghanistan and the north-west border quiet.

He held Peshawar, raised the Levies, and sent Nicholson with the movable column to take Delhi.

He gave sympathetic toleration to Christian missions from Peshawar along the whole frontier, and he roused England to do its imperial duty to India.

Born on the 12th November 1819 at Frodesley, near Shrewsbury, son of the rector of the parish, and grandson of Sir John C. Edwardes, Bart., Herbert Benjamin Edwardes studied modern literature hard at King's

College, London, and was the ornament of its debating society side by side with Charles Kingsley and Fitz-james Stephen. Denied Oxford by his guardians, he went to an old friend of his family, Sir Richard Jenkins of Nagpoor fame, and asked him for a direct appointment to India. At twenty-one he joined the crack regiment of the East India Company, the 1st Bengal Fusiliers, and soon found himself in the Punjab. The first Kabul War was just over, and the young Lieutenant, whose unselfishness and wit had made him the darling of the regiment, and who had passed the interpreter's examination in three languages, became the famous critic of the military and political system which had led to its disasters. For weeks the *Delhi Gazette* delighted the Anglo-Indians and outraged the authors of the war by his "Brahminee Bull's Letters in India to his Cousin John Bull in England." Henry Lawrence, after long search, discovered the anonymous writer, who had been in the thick of the battles of Moodki and Sobraon as Sir Hugh Gough's aide-de-camp, and carried him off to Lahore as one of his assistants in the hopeless attempt to help the Sikhs to govern the country. The fruit of his experience of those stirring times was seen in two articles in the *Calcutta Review* on the "Sikh Invasion of British India"[1] and the "Lahore Blue-Book."[2] Livelier writing and wiser criticism are not to be found in those early volumes of the then great Quarterly. As Henry Lawrence's private secretary, even sleeping in the same room with him for five months,

[1] Volume vi. No. 11, 1846. [2] Volume viii. No. 15, 1847.

Edwardes learned how to govern the martial races of the Punjab, and ever after delighted to describe his master as "the father of my public life." Lawrence at this time wrote to his wife in England: "Taking him all in all, bodily activity, mental cultivation, and warmth of heart, I have not met his equal in India." When Kashmir was sold to Gulab Singh for a crore of rupees, Edwardes was sent to do his first independent work—to suppress the rebellion which naturally followed, the only act of Sir Henry Lawrence's we can never approve. What Edwardes would and could have done there has, after a long interval of misrule and decimation of the people, been accomplished by a younger generation of "politicals" like Neville Chamberlain and Walter Lawrence. Edwardes wrote:—

"Oh, what a field is that valley at this moment for that noble animal, *a just ruler!* In five years I would undertake to raise its revenue to a million, and its people from Irish poverty to what Providence designed them to enjoy—scriptural milk and honey.

"I am on my road to Lahore, in charge of the Sheikh and his army—leading, in fact, my own bear into town.

"If I were an ancient Roman I should be entitled to 'a triumph,' and should enter the city in a gold chariot (the original of our 'glass fly'?) with Sheikh Imâm-ud-din and his lieutenants darbied and muffled, and a shopful of Kashmir shawls held up on yard-measures waving gloriously cheap in the air. A band of Kashmir virgins—or mayhap old women, for lack of them—would announce my advent with songs of 'Io triumphe! Io triumphe!' and the senators (now called Lal Singh, Tej Singh, Deena

Nath, Bhuggut Ram, and other unpatrician names) would be Manlii and Fabii, coming out in snowy togas—or what moderns vulgarly call clean shirts—to welcome my return! As it is, I shall be challenged by a black sentry, who, ten to one, won't let me into Rome—I mean Lahore—without the countersign. This comes of not being one's own ancestor!

"These barbarous phases of society, into which an educated man descends as into a pit of lions, have, after all, a wild, almost terrible interest. There is something noble in putting the hand of civilisation on the mane of a nation like the Punjab (if I may borrow Spenser's allegory), and *looking down* brute passions. What a victory! to bind a bullying people with a garland—to impose security of life, good order, and law as fines, upon a whole nation, for their offences against the tranquillity of the human race!"

To do this on a grander scale and on juster principles, to teach the happier lesson "how man may be won; what affection there is to be had for the asking; what truth for the trusting; what perennial honour for a moment's justice; what life-long service for a word of love," as Ruskin puts it, Edwardes was deputed to pacify the Afghan valley of Bunnoo which had defied even Runjeet Singh. Backed by only five hundred men and two troops of Horse Artillery, in three months he levelled the walls of four hundred forts, built one strong castle in their stead, and ran a military road through the heart of the country. The close of the year 1847 saw the Wuzeerees paying tribute. The bloodless conquest was just in time to supply a force with which to avenge the treacherous murder of Vans Agnew and

Lieutenant W. A. Anderson, sent to Mooltan to do the same work there which had been done at Bunnoo.

On the evening of the 22nd April 1848 Edwardes was in camp on the Indus, doing justice among Baloochi peasants, who were either robbers, robbed, or witnesses of robbery, when a messenger rushed in with the dying Agnew's letter announcing the rebellion of Moolraj. Concealing the disaster for a time he sent the man back with the reply—"God will bring an honest man out of worse straits, so trust in Him and keep up your pluck. Rely on it, it shall not be my fault if we are a day later than the 27th." He had but one Sikh infantry regiment, two guns and twenty camel-mounted guns (Zamburuks), and three hundred horse. In his treasury were a few thousand rupees. Commissariat he had none, but the country was fat. The hot weather was on in all its power. For nine months the young Lieutenant carried on the war, and after two victories shut up Moolraj in the city till General Whish chose to take him. He spent two lakhs of rupees each month. He held up his hand and the soldiers came to his side. He fed and paid them out of the rebel district. Reviewing the whole position eight years after, Sir Henry Lawrence wrote:[1] "Since the days of Clive no man has done as Edwardes, nor do I know of many who could and would have acted as he did on the Mooltan outbreak." His first battle of Kinyeree has been called the Waterloo of the Punjab, having been fought on the 18th June. In that of

[1] *Calcutta Review*, No. 43, April 1854.

Suddoosam, a fortnight after, Lieutenant Lake and Cortlandt helped him to drive Moolraj precipitately from the field, when that traitor to his own Government turned his guns on his own soldiers to stop them following his example. This was what happened before the battle.

"Sadik Mohammed Khan was a servant of the Maharaja, appointed to do duty with the Nazim of Mooltan, and, when the rebellion broke out, was drawing pay from both. . . . Moolraj expected him to side with him, but, though unable to escape, on account of his house and family, he refused to set his seal to the oath of rebellion on the Koran, and the very day that I arrived before Mooltân, Sadik and his father took their hawks on their wrists, and, under pretence of hunting, issued forth from the city and joined me. It is an incident illustrative of those strange uncertain times that, two days afterwards, he was my faithful henchman at Suddoosam, and, being well mounted, was often the only man by my side. Had he been a traitor, he might have killed me at any moment. But I heard his story, believed it, trusted him, and was rewarded by invaluable service throughout the rest of the rebellion. Yet it was as hard to trust in those days as it was necessary.

"The very moment before this battle of Suddoosam I was dipping my head into a pail of water, preparatory to putting on a thick turban, so as to keep my brains cool as long as possible in the sun, when Sadik Mohammed's own uncle insisted on speaking to me. Lifting my dripping head out of the pail, I listened to the old man's solemn warnings to be on my guard; 'for,' said he, 'all these men, like my nephew, who have come over from the enemy are here by Moolraj's orders and consent. You are drawn into a trap. Half your soldiers are friends, and half are foes, and, like rice and split peas, they are all mixed up in one dish. If there is not some treachery in this day's fight, my name is not Surbulund Khan!' The idea was not pleasant, and I soused my head under water again, desperately; but soon came up, wrung out the water, clapped a turban over my wet hair, and thanked the old gentleman for his information, which was too late to be useful, mounted my horse, and—never found out any of the traitors from that day to this!"

Accidentally Edwardes shot off his own right hand, but otherwise he seemed to lead a charmed life. Once a bullet passed through his sleeve from wrist to elbow without touching him. Again a gun held up against him in a conflict, when he thought nothing could save him, flashed in the pan. A third time, when writing in his tent, he was approached by an assassin whom the sentry was just in time to seize. A fourth time, an emissary of Moolraj poisoned his soup, and he and his guests narrowly escaped fatal consequences.

He returned to England, ill, to find himself a national hero. When feasted at the Mansion House in 1849, along with the Duke of Wellington, he was replying to the toast of "The health of the Indian Army," when he electrified the guests by turning to Major Nicholson with the exclamation—"Here is the real author of half the exploits which the world has been so ready to attribute to me." England then heard for the first time the name of his friend and attached follower, who was to prove the hero of Delhi. To this time, eight years before the Mutiny of 1857, we owe the curious "Memorandum" which reveals a foresight and even a genius not inferior to Sir Henry Lawrence's graver prevision.

"A good story might be written by way of prophecy, or I would rather say *warning*, of the sudden and unexpected overthrow of the British Indian Empire by the British Indian army. Scene—Lahore. Time—Fifty years hence, or A.D. 1900. Materials as follows:—

"The native army, according to a system introduced by a Lord Napier, who was Commander-in-Chief about 1850, has been for the last forty-five years massed upon great points, such as Kabul (annexed about 1880), Peshawar, Lahore, Umballa, Delhi, Dinapoor, and Calcutta, in Bengal; in Madras . . ., and in Bombay. . . . The extension of the Empire by the annexation of Khorassan has rendered a vigorous economy necessary, and prevented the increase of the European army. Pressure of parties in England has transferred the Government of India from the East India Company to the Crown, which has introduced the same colonial system as prevails over its other dependencies, and has lately lost Canada.

"'Lord Frederick Verisophts' are now Commissioners of provinces, and young barristers come out as magistrates. To meet their convenience, law is administered in English, and English education has superseded vernacular through all the Government schools. The people, in consequence, are oppressed and discontented. The courts, in the hands of a few Bengali Baboos, are not resorted to, except by the rich. The country is consequently ripe for evil designs. The army, for the sake of economy, has continued to be increased from the same classes of Hindustanis, and the only balance is between the Hindus and the Musalmans.

"About the year 1855, an extensive scheme, organised by Rani Junda, Bhaie Maharaj, Raja Deena Nath, and others, to restore the Rani to the throne of Lahore by means of our own soldiers, was discovered by Bhaie Bikrumah Sing (jealous of Bhaie Maharaj) to the British Government, and the ringleaders hanged or imprisoned. But the secret of unlawful organisation could not be so easily unlearnt; and the ambitious spirits of the country, who could nowadays find no native court to which to resort for service, commenced and gradually matured a secret confederation of the whole native army, which was much favoured by the system of military centralisation now in force. The large European society in the great cantonments has withdrawn the officers more than ever from their men, and few are now left who can discourse with them in their own language.

"Still, indications of the conspiracy creep out through officers of irregular corps, which at first hold aloof, though tempted. Midnight meetings of the Native Divisional Committees, under pretence of native festivals, should be described. Their correspondence in Persian, which has become 'cypher.' The outbreak on the first of a month at muster; massacre of all European officers at parade; ineffectual stand of few European regiments; retreat to the sea and embark; division of the Empire; upstart princes, etc.

"This sketch of a prophetical Indian novel was written on or about 21st December 1849, in my boat, dropping down the Sutlej River, with John Nicholson, on our way to England after the second Sikh War. The inspiration of it was drawn from the experience we had lately had in the Punjab of the Sikh army; the fear of similar results in our own native army, on which Sir Henry Lawrence was so often talking to us all; and the views of discipline entertained by the then Commander-in-Chief, Sir Charles Napier."

Lieutenant Edwardes returned to India Brevet-Major and C.B., with a special gold medal struck for him alone by the Court of Directors, and with the thanks of Parliament. A peer having remarked that these were unprecedented honours for so young a man, the Duke of Wellington exclaimed: "My Lords, Lieutenant Edwardes's services have been unprecedented, and his rewards must be unprecedented too." The 20th March 1851 was his last day in England, and he wrote to John Nicholson: "I cannot tell you how good it is for our best purposes to be helped by a noble wife who loves you better than all men and women, but God better than you."

The Governor-General had marked him, and chose him as Commissioner of the Peshawar Division to take the place of Colonel Mackeson, struck down by an assassin in court in October 1853. "Holding it, you hold the outpost of Indian empire," wrote Lord Dalhousie. ". . . You have a fine career before you. God speed you in it; and for your own sake and for the sake of this empire." Now Edwardes began the second of his unique acts of statesmanship.

The Punjab had now become a British Province, but only for three years. British prestige had not recovered from the disasters of the Kabul War. Mackeson had governed the tribes on the frontier by the spy system, spending money on natives of doubtful allegiance and character, who moved about among the hill races making them uneasy and suspicious. Edwardes felt that such a policy was in itself unfair as well as injurious. He began in 1853 the system which, as carried out by his successors during the subsequent forty years, has ended in the peace of the border and its delimitation, so far at least as human nature in such conditions allows. Sir Robert Sandeman applied the same policy to Baloochistan with still better results. Calling together the chiefs and tribal representatives, he declared his determination to treat them with a generous friendship so long as they lived as good neighbours, but warned them that the new power which he embodied would at once crush the disturbers of the peace. What he had begun in Bunnoo, so as to check the Mooltan rebellion and bring about the submission, ultimately, of all the Punjab, he extended over the whole border.

The same open, honest, and straightforward policy which, under the personal fascination of his character, won over the independent tribes, he saw must be applied to Kabul. Without an avowed and active friendly attitude on the part of Dost Mahomed, the border would never be at peace—a truth only now completely worked out by the Durand Convention with Dost Mahomed's grandson. He first wrote to Lord Dalhousie, describing the advantages of a treaty signed on both sides under which "bygones should be bygones" between England and Kabul. The Governor-General's reply was characteristic in its frank promptitude: "I give you *carte-blanche*, and if you can only bring about such a result as you propose, it will be a feather even in your cap." The Chief Commissioner, on the other hand, discouraged the proposal, saying, "I have two good reasons against it—you will never be able to get the Afghans to make a treaty; and, if they make it, they will not keep it." John Lawrence adhered to the same inactive policy towards the Afghan ruler, whoever he might be, all throughout his public life; which policy Mr. Wyllie, the Foreign Under-Secretary, afterwards defended, in the *Edinburgh Review*[1] against my correspondence in *The Times*, as "masterly inactivity." So Edwardes was instructed to correspond demi-officially with the Governor-General, but the formal correspondence went through Lahore, Lawrence writing his adverse views in pencil on the margin of his Commissioner's letters.

The negotiations resulted in the famous Treaty of March 1855, stipulating, to use Sir Charles Aitchison's authoritative words, that there should be peace between the British Government and the Ameer, that each should respect the territories of the other, and that the friends and enemies of the British Government should be the friends and enemies of Kabul.[2] This Treaty was confirmed by that of 26th January 1857, equally brought about by Edwardes. The Shah of Persia's aggression on Herat, and insults to the British Mission at Teheran, led to our war with that country in 1856, and made it

[1] For January 1867.

[2] *A Collection of Treaties, Engagements, and Sanads*, vol. ix. 3rd edition. Calcutta, 1892.

desirable to subsidise Dost Mahomed that he might advance against the Persians. It became necessary to depute British officers to see that the subsidy was so appropriated, and to maintain a native envoy at Kabul and Peshawar respectively of the British and Kabul Government. The two Lumsdens accordingly resided with a staff and escort at Kandahar during the fateful year 1857. *The Mission to Kandahar*, by Major H. B. Lumsden, of which a hundred copies were confidentially printed at Calcutta in 1860, forms a record of peculiar value which might now be given to the public.

By these Treaties Herbert Edwardes proved to be (1) personally the turning-point of our change of policy towards Afghanistan, which, up to Mackeson's death, was still Suddozai and hostile, and therefore was reversed so as to become Barakzai and friendly. On the occasion of each Treaty, with unselfishness almost superhuman, at least in public affairs, he successively resigned the legitimate opportunity offered to him by the Governor-General, of being the representative of the British Government in the formal act of signing the Treaties, urging Government to depute John Lawrence alone to make the first Treaty, and to associate him with himself in making the second. But (2) these Treaties had a much more far-reaching influence, when, three months after the latter was concluded, the Sepoy Mutiny threatened the temporary extinction of our Empire over Northern India.

At the end of March 1857 Edwardes, having accompanied his sick wife to Calcutta on her way to England, had more than one interview with the Governor-General, Lord Canning. The first muttering of the storm was heard there, when the 19th B.N.I. was disbanded at Barrackpoor; and this gave urgency to his advice that the lesson should not be unheeded, as, however, it proved to be. Still Lord Canning learned to know the man to whom he was not long after to telegraph, "Hold on to Peshawar."[1] On his way back he had many conversations with Henry Carre Tucker at Benares, Sir W. Muir, C. Raikes, Valpy French, and Dr. T. Farquhar at Agra, and, above all, his beloved chief, Sir Henry Lawrence, at Lucknow. He inspected the Lawrence Asylum at Sunâwur, "a perfect parish clustering round

[1] He enjoyed a conversation with Dr. Duff, who told him—

"There were numbers of Hindus of good family who were Christians in belief, and who meet regularly for prayer, but will not openly profess. The educated Bengalis who are not Christians appear to be very disaffected to Government, and to talk freely of what they will do with India when they have got rid of us."

In a letter to his wife he records this experience:—

"*April* 1857.—At night I got into the railroad again, and turned my face once more to that troubled post, Peshawar. . . . A well-dressed native got into the carriage with a writing-desk, took out a Bible, and began to read by the light of the lamp over his head. I entered into talk with him, and asked if he was a Christian. 'Not exactly; that is, I have not declared myself.' Did he approve and believe Christianity? 'Yes; I have given up all *modern* Hinduism, but I adhere to pure deism, and agree with your English Unitarians.'—'It was impossible,' I said, 'to read the Bible and not acknowledge that it came from God.'—'Yes,' he said, 'the Bible is the only religious system I know of that tells men to love their enemies and do good to those that despitefully use you. It certainly spiritualises all the relations of life.' I asked him why so many young Baboos became infidels; and he said he could only suppose that it was because 'The fool hath said in his heart, There is no God.' I looked into his Bible, and found it copiously annotated in pencil. It had been given him by a clergyman of the Free Church named Milne."

That was the saintly Free Church of Scotland Minister, first of Perth and then of Calcutta.

a most English-looking church." At Umballa the muttering at Barrackpoor had been followed by the lightning flashes—"the disaffected portion of the Sepoys were giving trouble, burning houses." At Lahore he found John Lawrence able to work only "by constant application of chloroform" to his head. On the 5th May he rejoined his friend, John Nicholson, in the Commissioner's house at Peshawar.

Six days after that came the Delhi telegram of the mutiny at Meerut, and the march of the Sepoys to the Musalman capital. Edwardes wrote that night to his wife: "We must expect the mutiny to spread to every station if not put down with the bayonet at some one cantonment. If it comes here we shall, please God, make short work of the mutineers, for we have three European regiments in the valley and all the artillery is European." The first act of Edwardes was to wire to John Lawrence, then at Rawal Pindi, to order a movable column ready to march on any station in the Punjab where disaffection might show itself. His second was to write, with Nicholson's approval, urging this and the further step of raising a levy of a thousand Mooltani horse at once. As to Peshawar, he reported, "it will be just as in 1848, the last to go; and not go at all if the intermediate country be occupied by a good field force." He wrote from the fulness of his experience of the Bunnoo and Mooltan days, when from the whole length of the Derajat border levies of the men he had attached to himself—wild swordsmen, matchlock-men, and cavalry—enabled him, in the awful heat, to shut up Moolraj and hold one of the most fertile divisions of the Punjab. To his wife he wrote:—

"*June* 1857.—I am overwhelmed with offers of men for service from every wild tribe on the surrounding hills. Doubtless it was fortunate that we invited these offers; for it has drawn into our pay all those who, if idle, might have been led into opposition. It must be a dull heart, indeed, that does not acknowledge that nothing but God's mercy has saved us. One turning-point in the crisis was the persecuting spirit shown by the elated Mohammedans at Delhi. The Hindu Rajas took alarm, bethought them of former Mogul times, and rallied round John Company. So the setting-up of the king excited the Musalmans against us and the Hindus for us. The most seditious letters have been intercepted, preaching the extermination of the infidels. The devil has certainly done his best to get rid of us; and, depend upon it, it shows that Christianity is working at the very foundations of Hinduism and Mohammedanism.

"Sir John Lawrence has steered his Province through the storm with courage, and I hope the Punjab has set a good example to the rest of India. . . . It has been a struggle for empire. It was, I always thought, one of the standing wonders of the world that we held India by an Indian army. The fabric of a hundred years, piled up unreflectingly, province on province, kingdom on kingdom, on the bayonets of a single race, has subsided in a month, like a snow-palace in the sun, and nothing short of this dissolution would, I believe, have ever brought about the reorganisation of the army of India on a more solid footing. So it's all for the best, but, alas! the price that has been paid. What mourning and grief there will be in England!"

The British Empire was fortunate not only in

Edwardes, but in the officers who worked with him on the Peshawar frontier in those days. When, forty years afterwards, I visited the station which is now, with Pindi and Attok, the impregnable base of the frontier advanced to Landi Kotal, Quetta, and Chaman within seventy miles of Kandahar, the historical spot which I first sought out was the bungalow,[1] where under the trees, morning after morning, these men held their council of war, which resulted not only in holding the gate of India, but in sending Nicholson and his movable column to sweep the Province of the disaffected, and at last to capture Delhi. The story has become history, told for the first time with critical accuracy in the pages of Mr. T. R. E. Holmes[2] and Lord Roberts.[3] The latter pronounces Edwardes "one of the most remarkable men that the Indian Army has ever produced." Edwardes himself wrote home:—

"You cannot think what a change the fall of Delhi has worked among the natives. Everybody comes up to the house to congratulate me, as if the victory was his own. A world of old systems, old traditions, and old credulities has passed away, and now a new era lies before the Anglo-Indians. In the gap between the two lie thousands of English men, English women, and English children, and a hundred thousand once faithful native soldiers. No doubt an overruling God has some vast good in store that all this bloodshed is to usher in. The natives are confounded. They don't know what to attribute it to. They say it is

[1] In 1897 the Deputy Commissioner's.

[2] *History of the Indian Mutiny*, 2nd ed. 1885.

[3] *Forty-one Years in India*, 20th ed. 1897.

our unanimity, our extraordinary resolution, our individual devotion to the public service, our good destiny, and so on; and I then wind up by saying, 'Yes, it is all these, no doubt. But who gave these virtues to us rather than to you? Why, God. And those who counted the English as few at the beginning of the war forgot to ask on which side God was to be counted.' Their own habitual piety (which is very great and sincere—after its own fashion) in referring all the results of life to the immediate operation of Providence, carries this deduction of mine home to them at once."

This brings us to the greatest of his imperial services, which underlay all the rest. We have already[1] recorded how he was the first to raise the question of the attitude of the British Government to its national and universal Faith, so long misrepresented, and with such consequences, by the East India Company. His Memorandum, written on 23rd January 1858, two months before John Lawrence's, has the special merit of having anticipated the Queen's own declaration of a Christian and tolerant policy nine months after in the Royal Proclamation of November 1858. For he wrote it "not for Government, but for parties at home interested in the question"; and he sent it, in the first instance, as a letter to the Earl of Shaftesbury. It resulted in giving an impulse and an intelligence to the movement in Great Britain for making Christianity known to the peoples of India with a zeal which promises the most valuable political and social, as well as spiritual, results. Sir Herbert Edwardes was the last man to expect con-

[1] Page 85.

currence in all his suggestions. Of Sir Donald M'Leod's letter to Sir John Lawrence on his Memorandum Edwardes wrote: "It does not go quite so far as mine in some respects, but goes a great way, and has some valuable new propositions. The angelic tone of it contrasts very favourably with the vehement and often ironic tone of mine." Edwardes was no fanatic. The spirit of Christ permeated all he thought and felt and did. His life was his religion, which he received through no ecclesiastical school, but straight from God and His revelation in the Bible.

When he became Commissioner of Peshawar in 1853 the first official question he had to decide was whether he would follow his predecessor, the murdered Mackeson, in declaring that the first missionary who crossed the Indus at Attok to enter the Peshawar valley should be turned back by his orders. Colonel Martin of the 9th Bengal Native Infantry, whose offer of £1000 to the Church Missionary Society had called forth this distinct refusal, asked Edwardes for his sanction. On 19th December 1853 the Commissioner called a meeting of the European residents, whom he thus addressed:—

"As Commissioner of this frontier, it is natural that of all in this room I should be the one to view the question in its public light, and I wish to state what I understand to be the mutual relations of the Christian Government and Christian missions of this country—our duties as public and private men in religious matters. That man must have a very narrow mind who thinks that this immense

India has been given to our little England for no other purpose than for our own aggrandisement—for the sake of cadetships for our poor relations. Such might be the case if God did not guide the world's affairs; for England, like any other land, if left to its own selfishness and its own strength, would seize all it could. But the conquests and wars of the world all happen as the world's Creator wills them; and empires come into existence for purposes of His, however blindly intent we may be upon our own.

"And what may we suppose His purposes to be? Are they of the earth, earthy? Have they no higher object than the spread of vernacular education, the reduction of taxes, the erection of bridges, the digging of canals, the increase of commerce, the introduction of electric telegraphs, and the laying down of grand lines of railroad? Do they look no further than these temporal triumphs of civilisation, and see nothing better in the distance than the physical improvement of a decaying world? We cannot think so meanly of Him with whom 'one day is as a thousand years, and a thousand years as one day.' All His plans and purposes must look through time into eternity; and we may rest assured that the East has been given to our country for a mission, neither to the minds nor bodies, but to the souls of men.

"And can we doubt what that mission is? Why should England be selected for this charge from the other countries of Europe? The Portuguese preceded us, and the French followed us here. The Pope of Rome gave India to the one, and the God of War was invoked to give it to the other. Yet our Protestant power triumphed over both; and it is a remarkable coincidence, that the East India Company was founded just two years after the great reformation of the English Church. I believe, therefore, firmly, and I trust not uncharitably, that the reason why

India has been given to England is because England has made the greatest efforts to preserve the Christian religion in its purest apostolic form, has most stoutly protested against idolatry in any shape, and sought no other mediator than the One revealed in the Bible.

"Our mission, then, in India is to do for other nations what we have done for our own. To the Hindus we have to preach one God, and to the Mohammedans to preach one Mediator. And how is this to be done? By State armies and State persecutions? By demolishing Hindu temples as Mahmud of Ghazni did? Or by defiling mosques with Mohammedan blood, as Runjeet Singh did? It is obvious that we could not, if we would, follow such barbarous examples. The thirty thousand Englishmen in India would never have been seen ruling over two hundred millions of Hindus and Mohammedans, if they had tried to force Christianity upon them with the sword. The British Government has wisely maintained a strict neutrality in religious matters; and Hindus and Mohammedans, secure of our impartiality, have filled our armies and built up our Empire.

"It is not the duty of the Government, as a Government, to proselytise India. Let us rejoice that it is not; let us rejoice that pure and impure motives, religious zeal and worldly ambition, are not so lamentably mixed up. The duty of evangelising India lies at the door of private Christians; the appeal is to private consciences, private effort, private zeal, and private example. Every Englishman and Englishwoman in India is answerable to do what he can towards fulfilling it. And this day we are met to do so—to provide the best means we can for spreading the gospel to the countries around us. They happen to be Mohammedan countries of peculiar bigotry.

"Sad instances of fanaticism have occurred under our

eyes; and it might be feared, perhaps, in human judgment, that greater opposition would meet us here than elsewhere. But I do not anticipate it. The gospel of peace will bear its own fruit and justify its name. Experience, too, teaches us not to fear. The great city of Benares was a far more bigoted capital of Hinduism than Peshawar is of Mohammedanism; yet it is now filled with our schools and colleges and mission, and its pundits are sitting at the feet of our professors, earnestly and peacefully, though doubtless sadly, searching after truth.

"What may we not hope to do with the Afghans? *They* have much more in common with us—a one and a living God; Mosaic tradition; nay, a belief in Christ.

"For these reasons, I say plainly that I have no fear that the establishment of a Christian mission at Peshawar will tend to disturb the peace. It is, of course, incumbent upon us to be prudent, to lay stress upon the selection of discreet men for missionaries, to begin quietly with schools, and wait the proper time for preaching. But having done that, I should fear nothing.

In this crowded city we may hear the Brahmin in his temple sound his shunkh and gong; the Muezzin on his lofty minaret fill the air with the azan; and the civil Government, which protects them both, will take upon itself the duty of protecting the Christian missionary who goes forth to preach the gospel. Above all, we may be quite sure that we are much safer if we do our duty than if we neglect it, and that He who has brought us here with His own right arm will shield and bless us if, in simple reliance upon Him, we try to do His will.[1]

[1] The Rev. Robert Clark, who was present, writes:—

"It was the day of the Peshawar races, and it was suggested that the missionary meeting should be deferred. 'Put off the work of God for a steeplechase?' exclaimed Colonel Martin, fresh from his closet of prayer. 'Never!' The meeting was held on the appointed day. There

When, five and a half years afterwards, he went home on leave, his last act was to make over to the Mission his own house. In England he was honoured and welcomed. He refused to stand for the representation of Glasgow in Parliament, but went everywhere making eloquent orations in the spirit of his Peshawar speech of 1853. In his own county of Shropshire, at the inauguration of the statue of Clive in Shrewsbury market-place, after sketching the career of the man to whose genius and greatness we owe the Empire of India, he rebuked the faction who hounded him to death. In Exeter Hall and again in Manchester his brilliant outline [1] of the history of India and the duty of Britain has not been surpassed. March 1862 saw him again in harness as Commissioner of Umballa, where it fell to him to trace out eleven of the Wahabi conspirators, who, from that city and Patna, were sentenced to penal servitude in the Andaman Islands.

His wife's health and his own drove him finally home in 1865, where he gave his energies to more than one of the missionary and philanthropic societies, home and foreign. A good-service pension of £100 a year was the reward given him for "distinguished and meritori-

were comparatively few present, but God's Spirit had been invited by prayer, and He was present, and He made His presence unmistakably felt, and men's hearts, and women's hearts, too, then burned within them, as they spake one to another, and heard the words of Sir Herbert Edwardes, which seemed to be almost inspired, when he took the chair at the meeting. His speech at the time 'thrilled through all India.' After the meeting the following words were read: 'Not unto us, O Lord, not unto us, but unto Thy name give the praise, for Thy mercy and for Thy truth's sake. Wherefore should the heathen say, Where is now their God? As for our God, He is in heaven.'"

[1] "Our Indian Empire, its Beginning and End." Delivered to the Young Men's Christian Association in Exeter Hall, 1860.

ous service" by Her Majesty's Government. While, in 1868, lying ill at Kinloch, near Dunkeld, he was asked if he would be Lieutenant-Governor of the Punjab, when a vacancy seemed at hand. Before that year closed he died, on 23rd December, in London, with this confession: "I put full confidence in Jesus, and I couldn't do more if I lived a thousand years." His body lies in Highgate cemetery. Beside the monument of Warren Hastings in Westminster Abbey the Secretary of State for India in Council erected the national memorial of Herbert Edwardes. The Edwardes Gateway of Peshawar, on the high-road to Kabul; the Edwardes Memorial School in the former city; the Edwardes well and resting-place at Bunnoo, now officially called Edwardesabad, perpetuate his name among the races he loved.

Khummah, the Mohammedan water-carrier, who had served him in war and peace all through his Indian life, was "baptized for the dead," saying when the news reached Peshawar, "My master was such a good man. I have seen him under all circumstances, and I have never seen him make a mistake. He can't have made a mistake in his religion. Will you teach me his religion? I should like to believe what he believed."

IX

JOHN CLARK MARSHMAN, C.S.I., 1794–1877

HISTORIAN AND JOURNALIST

"MR. JOHN MARSHMAN, of Serampore, whose own pen is consistently guided by a love of civil order and religious truth." So Sir Herbert Edwardes characterised him, when writing of a copy of the Pashtu Bible, which was found treasured by an Afghan chief on the Punjab frontier.[1] John Marshman is the only non-official of the twelve Indian statesmen of the century, and as such he was one of the first to receive the Order of the Star of India. He was in some respects the most remarkable of them all. For more than fifty years he lived in India; for nearly three-quarters of the century he sacrificed himself for the good of its peoples. He was the colleague and successor of the Serampore brotherhood—Carey, Ward, and Dr. Joshua Marshman, his father. He founded and long edited the first Bengali and English weekly journals in India. He worked incessantly for the education of the people in

[1] Ali Khan of Gundapoor. See *A Year on the Punjab Frontier in 1848-49.*

their mother-tongue and in English. He did more than any other single pioneer for Indian railways, telegraphic communication with England, and forestry. His personal benefactions for the spread of Christian civilisation in the East were larger and more unostentatious than those of any other philanthropist, save only his father and William Carey. While guiding the Administration and the public of India alike by his experienced pen, from the days of Lord Hastings to those of the present Earl of Northbrook, he wrote *The History of India* (1867), which is still the best and must remain the most authoritative for the British period.

John Clark Marshman was born on the 18th August 1794, at Broadmead, in Bristol, where his father kept a school, which sent forth such men as Rich, the Bombay civilian and son-in-law of Sir James Mackintosh, who became British Resident at Baghdad. He was six years of age when, on the 13th October 1799, he knelt on the strand at Serampore, as his parents thanked God for having landed them in safety on the soil of India. To his father's classical and Oriental training, the boy added the influence of his mother, Hannah. The life of this first of woman missionaries in modern times has yet to be written. She spent almost every day of her long Indian life of forty-eight years in educating the girls and the women of Bengal to be good and cultured Christians. She supplied to the Serampore Brotherhood the domestic comfort and harmony, without which its busy members could not have accomplished half of what they were enabled to effect for the elevation of Southern Asia.[1] That noble organisation started from the first on the only plan known last century, that of self-support like the community of the Moravian Brethren. For seven years William Carey had spent his indigo-planter's income on the Mission. When he was transferred to Danish protection the Brotherhood consisted of nineteen persons in all, of whom ten were children. All these had to be housed, fed, and clothed, so as to become efficient soldiers in the conflict with idolatry; the children must be educated, and, if God called them, be trained to be the missionaries of the future. The immediate expense was found to be above £600 a year, and that owing to Mrs. Marshman's "greatest frugality."

First, after solemn prayer and renewed dedication to God, laying it down as a fundamental rule "that no one shall engage in any private trade, but whatever is earned shall go into the common stock," the missionaries divided the work according to the special fitness of each. As Carey had the translation of the Holy Scriptures, and soon was made Professor in Lord Wellesley's college; as Ward, with two of Carey's sons, had the press, the schools naturally fell to Joshua Marshman, and to his wife far more than to him, as the event proved. The pecuniary result of this splendid organisation, as it extended during the next forty years, was unique in the history not only of all Christian missions,

[1] See my sketch in the *Missionary Review of the World* for December 1896.

but of all philanthropy. The one woman and the three men, with their children and assistants, were the means of earning at least £90,000 sterling for the work of God right across Southern Asia from the Persian Gulf to the Pacific Ocean. Of this enormous contribution, besides the self-support of the workers, Carey gave half, and Hannah Marshman alone gave at least one-fourth.

In such circumstances the young Marshman received the training which, with a visit to Europe, when he resided for a time in Rome and made the grand tour of those days, developed his scholarship and literary powers. In 1819 he was formally admitted a member of the Brotherhood. From that time he became the active director of its most extensive affairs, and the generous supporter of its numerous missions. In the painful controversy forced on Carey and his associates by the Baptist Missionary Society, he conducted the correspondence with wonderful charity; and it fell to him to buy back, out of his own earnings, the Mission property, which they had created and surrendered with almost quixotic generosity. Before his death he made over the famous College and the properties, thus twice his own, to a new generation of the Society, and all with a quiet, albeit righteously proud, reticence, which concealed the nobility of his action. Left sole representative of the Brotherhood, and undertaking its enormous responsibilities, John Clark Marshman created the income necessary to meet them by his literary labours,—his paper mill, the first in India; his educational and law text-books, and his official salary as Government translator. In all this he became an expert Oriental scholar, mastering Chinese like his father, as well as Sanskrit and Persian. The Bengali language and literature he followed Carey in almost creating, his knowledge and style surpassing that of the Bengalis themselves with two exceptions.

A few years before his death, I induced John Marshman to tell the story of his founding the first Bengali newspaper, though not without a protest against intruding his own name. On the 31st May 1818 the first number appeared, and fifty years after he thus wrote:—

"In the early stages of the Company's Government, the question of enlightening the natives of India was regarded not only with indifference—the same feeling was manifested with regard to education in England—but with dread, and with that strong feeling of aversion to which it gives birth. . . . The communication of knowledge to our subjects in India might endanger the stability of the Empire. It was affirmed that our Empire was an Empire of opinion, though I must confess that I have never been able to discover the point of this. To the Mohammedans we appear as unbelievers, to the Hindus as *mlechas* who slaughter kine, and both classes consider that we have no business in India, and would be delighted to get rid of us, and to establish a government after their own hearts.

"No efforts were made by the various Governments in India, or by the Court of Directors, to impart instruction to the natives, or to elevate the native character, throughout the currency of the Charter of 1793, when, at the earnest instigation of the India House, the House of Commons negatived Mr. Wilberforce's benevolent resolution to allow schoolmasters to be sent out to India. The Charter was renewed in 1813, and when the Bill came to be read for the last time, a rule was carried to appropriate a lakh of rupees a year from the revenues of India 'to the revival and promotion of literature, and the encouragement of the learned natives of India, and for the introduction and promotion of a knowledge of the sciences among the inhabitants of the British territories.' The question was considered one of such small import, that it was not deemed necessary by the reporters to give the name of the gentleman who brought forward the clause; but I have every reason to believe that it was Mr. Robert Percy Smith, commonly called Bobus Smith, the school-fellow of George Canning at Eton, and likewise the father of Lord Lyveden. He was for six, seven, or eight years Advocate-General in the Supreme Court in Calcutta, where he amassed a large fortune, and as usual obtained a seat in Parliament. It was on this occasion, as far as I can recollect, that Sir John Anstruther, who was Chief Justice, and on his return to England found his way into Parliament, inquired whether it was really intended to educate the natives of India, and whether it was altogether safe to do so. The grant was interpreted in Calcutta to be intended for the encouragement of Hindu and Mohammedan literature, and for ten years whatever portion of it was expended—which was not large—was devoted to those objects under the patronage of Dr. Horace Hayman Wilson, the great champion of those creeds.

"During this period of total neglect of education on the part of the public authorities, the Serampore missionaries took up the question in real earnest, and made the most strenuous efforts to create an interest in it in the European community. In 1814 Dr. Marshman drew up a brief pamphlet under the timid and modest title of 'Hints for the Establishment of Native Schools.' This was the first time the subject had been brought distinctly before the members of Government and the European gentry in Calcutta, and it was received with no little cordiality. Under the enlightened administration of Lord Hastings the tide was turning; but in England the idea of setting up schools in India appeared so great and remarkable an innovation in our Indian policy, that the whole of the little brochure was transferred to the pages of the most popular encyclopædia of the day as one of the wonders of the age. The 'Hints' were followed up by active exertions. A circle of schools was established, and a series of elementary school-books compiled in history, geography, and arithmetic. Dr. Marshman took charge of this department of labour, and I was employed in translating into Bengali the books used in the schools. More than half a dozen of those treatises were brought into use before the year 1818, and a spirit of eager inquiry was created in native society. It appeared that the time was ripe for a native newspaper, and I offered the missionaries to undertake the publication of it. . . . The jealousy which the Government had always manifested of the periodical press appeared, however, to present a serious obstacle.

"The English journals in Calcutta were under the strictest surveillance, and many a column appeared resplendent with the stars which were substituted, at the last moment, for the editorial remarks, and through which the censor had drawn his fatal pen. In this state of things it was difficult to suppose that a native paper would be tolerated for a moment. It was resolved therefore to feel the official pulse by starting a monthly magazine in the first instance, and the *Dig-Dursun* appeared in April 1818. It was composed of historical and other notices, likely from their novelty to excite the attention of the natives, and to sharpen their curiosity. In the last page, in a smaller type, some few items of political intelligence were inserted. Two numbers were published and copies sent to the principal members of Government, and the fact of the publication was widely disseminated by advertisements in all the English papers. As no objection appeared to be taken to the publication of the magazine, though it contained news, it was resolved at once to launch the weekly paper, and to call it by the name given to the earliest English news-letter, the 'Mirror of News,' or the *Sumachar Durpun*. But Dr. Carey, who had been labouring fifteen years in India during the period when the opposition to missionary efforts and to the enlightenment of the natives was in full vigour, was unfavourable to the publication of the journal, because he feared it would give umbrage in official circles and weaken the good understanding which had been gradually growing up between the missionaries and the Government. He strenuously advised that the idea of it should be dropped, but he was overruled by his two colleagues, Dr. Marshman and Mr. Ward. When the proof-sheets were brought up for final examination at the weekly meeting of the missionaries the evening before the day of publication, he renewed his objections to the undertaking on the grounds he had stated. Dr. Marshman then offered to proceed to Calcutta the next morning and submit the first number of the new gazette, together with a rough English translation of the articles, to Mr. Edmonstone, then Vice-President, and to the Chief Secretary, and he promised that it should be discontinued if they raised any objection to it. To his great delight he found both of them favourable to the undertaking. At the same time he transmitted a copy of the paper to Lord Hastings, then in the North-Western Provinces, and was happy to receive a reply in his own hand highly commending the project of endeavouring to excite and to gratify a spirit of inquiry in the native mind by means of a newspaper. And thus was the journal established. A copy of it was sent with a subscription book to all the great Baboos in Calcutta, and the first name entered on the list was that of Dwarkanath Tagore. On the return of Lord Hastings to the Presidency, he endeavoured to encourage the undertaking by allowing the journal to circulate through the country at one-fourth the usual charge of postage, which at that time was extravagantly high.

"A fortnight after the appearance of the *Durpun*, a native started another paper in Calcutta with the title of *Timirunasuk*, 'the destroyer of darkness,' but it did not continue long to shine. At a later period arose the *Sumachar Chundrika*, or 'the moon of intelligence.' It was projected and edited by a Brahmin, Bhobani Churn Banerjee, a man of extraordinary powers of intellect and humour, and of the greatest energy, and master of a Bengali style of surpassing ease and elegance. He was a Brahmin of the Brahmins, and his journal became the organ of the orthodox Hindus, of which the late Raja Radhakant Deb became the great champion, after the death of his father. For more than ten years the *Durpun* and the *Chundrika* fought the battle of progress on the one side and of Hindu conservatism on the other. At length came the great event of the abolition of Suttees, which agitated native society to its profoundest depths. The *Durpun* supported the abolition, the *Chundrika* denounced it in no measured language. In order, at this critical period, to increase the popularity and the influence of the *Durpun* I gave it in Bengali and English, in parallel columns, and the circulation immediately rose beyond the level of its rival.

"Both journals have left a numerous and flourishing progeny, which is continually on the increase. I feel confident that this notice of the lineage of the family will not be devoid of interest in this the third generation of Editors."

Mr. Marshman did even more for Bengali literature by his text-books and weekly translations. When in 1871 I was asked by the Duke of Argyll, then Secretary of State for India, to report [1] on the Educational Works and Appliances in the London International Exhibition of that year, over which the Prince of Wales presided, I submitted the collection of Bengali books to the venerable expert, whose comparative review has now a historical value, going back to the year 1820.

"The catalogue of works, published in the vernacular language of Bengal, affords a gratifying proof of the rapid development of intellectual life and animation among the natives. They are not distributed gratis, but sold at prices varying from four pence to four shillings. With the exception of a small number published by the Calcutta School-book Society, they are printed at native presses and sold by native firms of booksellers. At the beginning of the century a metrical abridgment of the two great epics, the Ramayan and the Mahabharat, and one or two minor poems, were to be found in manuscript in some families, but there did not exist a single prose work in the Bengali language. The Serampore missionaries, the pioneers of Christian civilisation in Hindustan, and whose establishment was formed in the last year of the last century, were the founders of the Bengali press. Dr. Carey, from his connection with the college of Fort William, induced the head pundit—Mritunjuy, an Orissa Brahmin, and the first pundit in Bengal—to compile several works in Bengali, which became models of vernacular prose. Dr. Carey's colleagues at Serampore also employed other natives to

[1] Indian Department: *Report on Educational Works and Appliances*, Class X. London: J. M. Johnson and Sons, 1871.

compose prose works on different subjects, which they issued from their press. In course of time a native, who had been trained at the press, set up a printing establishment of his own at Calcutta, and continued for six years to publish works on speculation. Others followed his example, and in 1820 I made a collection and an analysis of all the works which had down to that time been issued from the native press, and under purely native patronage, and they amounted to twenty-seven. Of these works, one was a treatise on law, one on astronomy, one on music, one on materia medica, two dictionaries, a satire on physicians, or rather empirics; two treatises on women—not over-chaste; one on the duties of men; one on the instruction of youth; and three describing the three kinds of men and women in the world. The rest were popular legends of the gods and goddesses of the Hindu Pantheon. A comparison of the two lists will show how greatly the native taste has improved, and how much wider is the range of subjects which are now found to be interesting to the native mind. The character of the works is, moreover, of a higher standard. The style is less primitive and more classical; there is a much larger introduction of compound words of Sanskrit origin; and the learned language of the East—which is, perhaps, the most refined and perfect instrument for the expression of human thought—is thus brought to bear on the improvement of the language of the people.

"It is particularly noteworthy that the cultivation of the vernacular language, of which these various treatises afford evidence, is coeval with the introduction of English education, and corresponds with its progress. At a previous period all the knowledge existing in the country was monopolised by an educated caste of priests, and sealed in the sacred language which the people were forbidden to approach. The learned fraternity of Brahmins kept this knowledge entirely in their own hands, and never made the slightest effort to communicate it to the people through their own language. They disdained even to use the vulgar tongue, except in the indispensable intercourse of life ; an impassable gulf divided the two sections of society —the learned Brahmins from the ignorant multitude. When English was adopted, under the auspices of Lord William Bentinck, as the language of education, it was surmised that the creation of a new educated class, drawing its knowledge from the sources of a foreign language, would produce the same result—that we should have an English caste of Brahmins and pundits, who would equally despise and neglect the vernacular tongue, and that the million would equally be left without the means of access to the stores of knowledge possessed by the upper ten thousand. This apprehension has not been realised. It is those who have received a complete education, literary and scientific, through the medium of English, to such an extent as to be able to maintain a fair competition with European students, who are thus communicating the knowledge they have acquired to the country through the national language, improving it by the aid of its parent the Sanskrit, and enriching it from the treasury of European knowledge. They are manifestly diffusing a taste for intellectual pursuits among the subordinate classes, and gradually creating a vernacular literature; and thus the Government is doubly rewarded for the encouragement it has given to the cultivation of English."

Mr. Marshman's life-long services to, and sacrifices for, the education of all classes of the peoples of India culminated in the Despatch of the Court of Directors of 19th July 1854. He had left India in 1852, and reached London just in time to take a prominent part in the discussions which preceded the last, or 1853, Charter of the East India Company. Along with Dr. Duff, whose educational system in 1830 developed and reinforced that of Carey and Dr. Marshman, he gave elaborate evidence before the Parliamentary Committees. Sir Charles Wood, afterwards Lord Halifax, was then President of the Board of Control, and Mr. Baring, now the Earl of Northbrook, was his secretary. They were so powerfully influenced by the evidence of these two veteran reformers, that they drafted that Despatch frequently in the very language of Marshman and Duff. That Despatch, followed by Lord Stanley's of 1859 on vernacular education, and improved by Lord Ripon's Commission since 1884, has given the millions of our fellow-subjects a more perfect system of public instruction than the United Kingdom itself enjoys with its ecclesiastical and party divisions. By his articles in India, and pamphlets addressed to Cobden and Bright in England, no publicist had so great an influence for the highest good on the improved administration of India, and especially of Bengal, which became a Lieutenant-Governorship now consisting of seventy-five millions of Hindus, Mohammedans, and Christians. The seeds he sowed, political as well as educational, continue to bear a harvest of peace and ever-increasing prosperity.

His action was especially direct and personal in the three great State departments of applied science—

forestry, cable telegraph, and railways. When the second Burma War had given us the teak forests of Pegu, Lord Dalhousie sought the co-operation of Mr. Marshman, then travelling in Germany, to secure a skilled and practical savant, who would carry out the work of conservation and extension which they both had at heart. The selection of Professor (now Sir) Dietrich Brandis, of Bonn University, was most fortunate. That distinguished expert, after organising the forest system of Burma, as Director-General of all the Forests of India wrought such results that these now yield a net annual revenue of nearly a million sterling, while the climate, the public works, and the villages are all alike benefited. Mr. Marshman's long advocacy of telegraphic communication between England and India, the need of which was dangerously illustrated in the delays of the Mutiny year, resulted in the Red Sea cable, since superseded by the Indo-European system.

But it is to him, along with the late Sir Macdonald Stephenson, that the still greater triumph of Indian railways must be traced. For years he advocated the movement which resulted in the submission to the authorities in Calcutta and London, in 1844, of specific offers to construct one or more of the strategic and commercial trunk-lines which, with their feeders, now cover 22,000 miles, and are planned to extend to 64,000 miles. Even his enthusiasm, alike in Bengal and as the principal financial director of the East India Railway Company in London, undiminished by years of official obstruction, did not dare to anticipate the magnificent results which are slowly revolutionising the conservative East, while the stocks form a most attractive investment for rupee as well as sterling capital, yielding an average five per cent. It was he who obtained from the orthodox Brahmin Sanhedrin, the Dharma Sabha of Calcutta, the authoritative decision that the Hindu devotee might ride in a railway carriage without losing the merit of his pilgrimage. That fatal blow at caste and tradition, applied by such a reduction of fares that the native travels at a farthing a mile or less, is telling, in a way they cannot define but readily admit, on the varied millions who daily crowd the carriages and stations. In the *Quarterly Review*, in 1868,[1] Marshman recorded the history of India's railways in their first or Dalhousian stage, extending over fifteen years, with the one omission of his own share in the enterprise.

All these statesmanlike services to humanity and the Empire were made possible and very fruitful by his literary powers as journalist and historian. At once to enable him to carry out his philanthropic charities, and to move public opinion in England and India, he started *The Friend of India*, "published every Thursday morning." On the 1st January 1835 the first number appeared. The prospectus appealed to the volumes of the quarterly and monthly *Friend of India*, through which the Brotherhood had for some years fought the good fight of humanity, with such effect that

[1] Article ii. of No. 249, vol. cxxv. (John Murray).

much of these successive periodicals was reprinted in London. Mack and Leechman, his associates in the college on which he alone spent £30,000, signed the manifesto, which contained these significant passages: "The welfare of India, the country of our adoption though not of our birth, is the grand aim of our labours. And the means by which that aim can alone be realised are the diffusion of correct information and just views respecting her interests, and the encouragement of right feeling towards her. . . . The prosperity of a country is made up of many elements; but they will all be secured when the blessings of good government are enjoyed, knowledge is diffused, and true religion prevails. . . . Governments, especially where their members have civilised and cultivated compatriots, are more ruled than they rule. . . . The true function of public writers (and it is, at the same time, their reward) is, in company with their readers and supporters, to help on this march of general improvement, not so much with the dogmatism of teachers as with the kindliness of fellow-students." It is significant that the first article, after two and a half columns in this elevated strain, is devoted to the "Digest of the Civil Regulations," by F. Millett, for "the reformation of the laws in any country is one of the most unequivocal indications of the progress of political improvement." Macaulay was soon to land at Calcutta as the first Law Member of Council, with a draft of the Penal Code in his pocket. By his own law-books, especially the most profitable, *Guide to the Civil Law of the Presidency of*

Fort William (1845-46), Marshman superseded all other digests until he left India.

The famous Weekly of Serampore soon became the most powerful journal in the East, and on Indian affairs was without a rival in the English language. Under Mr. Marshman's nephew, Mr. Meredith Townsend, from 1852 to 1859, its reputation and circulation increased as the Mutiny introduced the new order of things. From 1859 to 1875, when I chiefly conducted it, Mr. Marshman was one of the three valued London Correspondents, Mr. Townsend, then and still of the *Spectator*, and General Maurice being the others; with Sir George Birdwood also for a time. The three Editors further enjoyed the influence of *The Times* as, in succession, its Calcutta Correspondent. For forty years they were the independent and trusted interpreters of the Government of India to the people and to India, and of the Anglo-Indian and Native public to the Government.[1] The position was as unique as it was most honourable and influential for good in the history of journalism. Without the forty volumes the history of India for the period cannot be accurately written.[2] When Sir John Kaye established the *Calcutta Review* in 1844, Mr. Marshman became one of the most frequent contributors to its pages, and he was certainly the ablest historical and political writer it had. From the first to the fifteenth volume he wrote ten articles. His archæological papers on the "Right and Left Banks

[1] See X. (Sir Henry Sumner Maine) and the Appendix.

[2] I know of only three complete sets—in the India Office Library, in Serampore College, and in my own library.

of the Hooghly River," and on "Bengal from the Earliest Times," stand alone in the value of the facts which they embalm. Equally authoritative and of singular authority are his two volumes on *The Life and Times of Carey, Marshman, and Ward.*[1] The life of his heroic brother-in-law, *Memoirs of Major-General Sir Henry Havelock, K.C.B.,*[2] followed a year after. Meanwhile, in the retirement of Kensington Palace Gardens, broken only by his duties as Chairman of the East India Railway Company's Committee of Audit, he elaborated his *History of India* in three volumes (1863), which I urged him to complete in a popular form for the Indian Universities. The two Indian volumes, dedicated to the native youth of Bengal, ran through many editions. From Wellesley at least to Dalhousie the historian had seen and known every Governor-General, and of the continuous course of events which he recorded he was a living part. In an abridgment, published four years before his death, he brought down the history from the earliest period to the close of the East India Company's Government.

No one has ever had, before or since, so profound a knowledge, or so just a judgment on Indian affairs, political, financial, and administrative, as John Clark Marshman. Nor has any one ever used his powers with more self-denial for so long a period for the good of India, notwithstanding detraction on the one hand, and neglect on the other. In both respects Sir

[1] Longmans: London, 1859. A popular abridgment appeared afterwards.

[2] Longmans: London, 1860.

Henry Durand was like him. Of the eighty-three years of his life he spent seventy-seven in or for India, from his early boyhood. There has been no such continuous career, all on a high level. He had one just ambition, to utilise his experience for the good of the people of India, by entering Parliament, and so to become Under-Secretary of State for India. He would not wink at electoral corruption, as was the fashion at one time, and so he lost the representation of Ipswich, his wife's town, by three votes. For Sir Charles Wood he wrote an exhaustive paper, during the Mutiny of 1857, on the transfer of the Government of India to the Crown; and was surprised to read it as the speech of the President of the Board of Control in the House of Commons. Privately grateful, Sir Charles asked what he could do for the writer, and was answered that he wanted nothing. But when it fell to the Conservative Government to appoint to the new Council of India, he was offered only the office of Secretary in the Political and Secret Department. Replying that he could go to the India Office only as one of its masters, that is, in Council, he left the offered appointment to Sir John Kaye. So literature, the East India Railway, and philanthropy occupied his later years, while he had begun a work on Charles Grant, and a history of each Governor-General, which would have been precious contributions to Anglo-Indian history.

So, on the 8th July 1877 he passed away, more honoured by the few who knew the nobleness of his nature, and the proud humility of his sacrifices, than if he had at the last[1] submitted to harness. He died, after a blameless and self-sacrificing life, the great Non-official Statesman and Friend of India.

[1] The *New York Times* (July 1877), then edited by the late Mr. Louis Jennings, M.P., published an adequate obituary notice of Mr. Marshman, of which I have failed to find a copy.

X

SIR HENRY SUMNER MAINE, K.C.S.I., 1822–1888

Jurist and Legislator

India has been most fortunate in at least five of the English Jurists, who have made it the envy, and in some respects the model, of law reformers not only in Great Britain, but in Germany. Lord Macaulay, Sir Barnes Peacock, Sir Henry Maine, Sir James Fitzjames Stephen, and Mr. Whitley Stokes, who held the office of Law Member of the Council of the Governor-General of India for varying periods during the half-century ending 1883, have given British India, and Southern Asia which it influences, codes of substantive law and procedure, criminal and civil, which, next to Christianity, form the most searching and permanent of all the dynamical forces of Western civilisation in the East. Of the five, Macaulay and Maine stand out, each as the most notable juridical statesman of his generation, not only in the United Kingdom but in the United States of America, and in Europe.

India was indeed fortunate to have enjoyed the services of two such thinkers and writers, at the two most formative periods of its history. Macaulay for three years, under the great Charter of 1833, was the most powerful colleague of Lord William Bentinck, and the author of the Indian Penal Code, though it was left to Sir Barnes Peacock to pass that through Lord Dalhousie's Legislative Council long after. Maine, during the seven years after the Mutiny and Indian Councils' legislation of 1858-61 by Acts of Parliament, worked out and almost completed the codes and civil law of India with the hearty approval of his successive colleagues—the eighth Earl of Elgin, Sir John Lawrence, and the sixth Earl of Mayo. Of the two, it cannot be questioned that Maine was the greater in the value and permanence of his services to India and to the Empire. He fruitfully originated and profoundly influenced, for all time, the progress of three hundred millions of people. His works, which, with the style of a master, apply the historical method to the philosophy of institutions, promise to be more enduring than even the History, the Essays, and the Lays of his brilliant predecessor. As a boy, I received an eloquent charge from Thomas Babington Macaulay when, just before his rejection by the city of Edinburgh, he took part in the annual commemoration of its High School. As a young man it was my privilege to spend a day every week during the greater part of seven years with Maine, in Calcutta and Simla, discussing public affairs when I was India Correspondent of *The Times*, and conducting the weekly journal of Serampore. In all my experience, in East and West, for half a century, Sir Henry Maine was, with Sir William Hamilton, the most lucid thinker, the most powerful intellect, the most persuasive reasoner, and the man of practically the widest influence I had met. As the centuries go on, it will be proved that no one administrator has done so much for the people of India as he.

Son of a Scots physician of Kelso and an English mother, and godson of the Archbishop of Canterbury, Henry Sumner Maine was born near Leighton on the 15th August 1822. The effect of an overdose of opium in childhood was to make him delicate and reserved all his life, but his temper was winning and his character attractive from the first. He gained his education and had his character formed in the school of Coleridge and Charles Lamb, in Christ's Hospital, which, after them, Thackeray has made memorable in English literature. There the boy learned two things: his mastery of English, on which, above all, he prided himself; and his knowledge of the ancient classical languages. Hence, when at Pembroke College, Cambridge, he became Senior Classical Medallist, and Craven University Scholar, and then Tutor at Trinity Hall, he, at the early age of twenty-five, sought a career as Rector of the High School of Edinburgh in succession to Dr. Carson. Being, fortunately, as he told me with a smile, defeated by Dr. Schmitz, he was at once, at that early age, appointed Regius Professor of Civil Law. When he had been for some years Reader on Roman Law and Jurisprudence to the Inns of Court, he was one day surprised by the urgent solicitation of Sir Charles Wood to go out to India as Law Member of the Governor-General's Council, on £12,000 a year. His duties as Reader had brought him into contact with Anglo-Indians, at a time when to be a barrister was thought by civilians the best means of becoming a High Court Judge. But the Secretary of State had two better reasons for selecting the pale and sickly jurist, who had no objection to offer to the princely salary save delicate health. Henry Maine was one of the brilliant band who, under Mr. Cook and the old *Morning Chronicle* staff, started the *Saturday Review*, giving it an Attic flavour and an English manliness which long made it a power in periodical literature; and he had published the first-fruits of his life-long study and thought in that still remarkable treatise on *Ancient Law*, wherein he showed its connection with the early history of society and its relation to modern ideas.

After much hesitation he declined, but on the death of Mr. Ritchie, who had thereupon been appointed, he then resolved to banish himself for a few years to India, as Sir James Mackintosh had done before him. Never was a legislator more needed. The Mutiny had forced on the Empire the reorganisation of both laws and courts. Sir Charles Wood had just, in 1861-62, got Parliament to pass the Indian Councils Act, and Maine was wanted to carry it into effect. He reached Calcutta in the interregnum filled by Lord Elgin between the death of Lord Canning and the appointment of John Lawrence. It is not too much to say that, for a time, owing to Lord Elgin's illness and death, he and

Sir Henry Durand governed India. For seven years, broken by only one short visit home, at Calcutta and at Simla, of which his delicate health made him always a passionate defender, the new Law Member continued to pour forth a stream of most enlightened legislation, while he was the responsible adviser of the Executive on a multitude of questions having a legal bearing. All this time, too, he was studying the people, their Hindu and Mohammedan institutions, the so-called prehistoric customs of the millions of Aborigines in the hills, and the progress of his own countrymen under new conditions of climate and commerce, of labour and social surroundings. While he legislated he observed, and as he observed he corrected, modified, and adapted his legislation, till he came to possess every qualification that a practical jurist ought to manifest in such circumstances—save a mastery of any vernacular of the people. To the last he had to accept his knowledge of the natives through interpreters, and hence his reluctance to deal with the most delicate of all the questions concerning them—those relating to the customs, tenancy, and taxation of the land. The great measures passed in his time affecting the tenures of Northern India were promoted and prepared by civilians with not a tenth of his brains, but with all the experience he necessarily lacked.

When he went out, there was in existence a curious body of commissioners for drafting laws for India, whose work he was expected to induce the Legislative Council of Calcutta to accept. That body consisted of a paid secretary, and of unpaid members like Mr. Robert Lowe (Lord Sherbrooke) and several of the judges. What could these do in ignorance of India? They practically left the work to the secretary, whose drafts they hastily glanced over, when taking the office on their way to the train on Saturday afternoons. All through his seven years' career, Sir Henry Maine was hampered by these projects of law, but his impetuous successor, Sir Fitzjames Stephen, got them abolished by the threat that he would resign if these were continued in force. It was this body that prevented Maine from giving India a fair and workable law of contract. But he took all the codes in hand, revising the Penal Code, and improving the two Procedure Codes.

His chief merit, however, lay in the additions which he made to the code of substantive civil law. Drawing on the stores of the law of France and America, especially of New York, he gave India reforms for which the ablest lawyers in this country vainly sigh. He could not, indeed, touch the religious usages of the natives, in so far as these form their laws and affect all their civil rights as well as social prejudices. But when such prescriptive customs operated intolerantly on other religions, or on converts to other faiths, he completed that writing of toleration on the Statute-book of India, which it was the glory of Lord William Bentinck to have begun and of Lord Dalhousie to have developed. For he was ever on the watch against the otherwise inevitable effect of our legislation in giving rigidity to the barbarous usages of the intolerant creeds of India, and in fossilising evil customs that might perish of themselves. Nor is it only as a legislator that Sir Henry Maine left his mark on Indian history and progress. As Macaulay had done at an earlier period, he threw himself into the good work of the higher or English education of the natives. He held the office of Vice-Chancellor of the Calcutta University for a period of four years, and he signalised his administration by public addresses and private influence which stimulated the thousands of students of all creeds and classes to more accurate and fruitful labours.

But it is as a legislator and codifier that he has left a name greater than that of all European and American jurists, for, all other things apart, none could wield as he had the privilege of doing, the almost autocratic power of a Government like that of British India. From that point of view Henry Sumner Maine stands beside Constantine, Theodosius, and Justinian. During his tenure of office 209 Acts were passed.

When he took the place suddenly left vacant by the death of Mr. Ritchie, a distinct period in the work of codification, begun by Macaulay, had been brought to a close by Sir Barnes Peacock. The Penal Code and the Criminal and Civil Procedure Codes were law. A great work had been accomplished, the magnitude and difficulty of which only posterity will appreciate. It was necessary that the operation of these Codes should be carefully watched, as they affected the life and customs of a people who were not only under alien rulers, but who shut themselves up within the recesses of a social and religious system unlike anything in the Roman or the Western world. The Codes had also to be adapted to that official machinery which had been created by regulations of the vaguest legal character, and had in many Provinces been directed by still vaguer orders from the Executive. If the work of the early Law Commission of Macaulay and Sir Barnes Peacock was to prove at once a potent and a silent civilising agency, it must be thus adapted and completed by one who, while equally accomplished as a lawyer, had proved himself a master of all juridical systems, especially in their relation to the earlier stages of society.

The time of Maine's arrival in India was the close of a period in its political constitution also. The legislature created by Lord Dalhousie had been abolished, to the regret of all who saw in it a safe and prudent means for teaching the people and residents of India the art of self-government. By the Indian Councils Act Parliament had given full legal effect to the assumption of the government of India by the Crown in 1858, and had fairly broken with the traditions of the East India Company. All India was brought under the sway of legislation. Non-Regulation Provinces, won by the sword and tamed by the will of individual Englishmen, had been so far developed as to make it advisable to put them under the yoke of law. As on the abolition of the Dalhousie Council, the Act was here also undoubtedly too sweeping, and before Maine laid down his office he had to press on the Home authorities the necessity of restoring to the Executive the power of legislating for frontier districts by absolute ordinances. Finally, the legal tribunals, through which the East India Company had worked from the days of Warren Hastings and Wellesley to Lord Canning, had just been reorganised and adapted to the new order of things. The Supreme and Sudder Courts were amalgamated at the Presidency Towns, a High Court was given to the North-Western Provinces, and soon a Chief Court was planted in the heart of the Province which boasted that its prosperity was due to a system that kept law at a distance and governed only by men. It was at such a critical time, when the working of the Codes had to be watched, the codification had to be carried on, and the recent improvements in English law had to be applied to India; when the Government of India had been placed in a new relation to the Crown and to the various Provinces; and when the Courts had received a new organisation, that Maine became Law Member of (the first) Lord Elgin's Council.

He found Sir H. Harington in charge of the legislative department, and was assisted by the technical knowledge and experience of that civilian. The first great duty which devolved upon Maine was the amendment of the Civil Procedure Code. A long and bitter controversy as to the relation of indigo-planters to the peasantry on the estates which they leased, had been terminated by the extinction of a valuable industry in some of the richest districts of Bengal, and by a promise that the Government of India would supply such laws and such courts as would prevent the recurrence of the evil. Maine had no bias, or if he had it was not in favour of the planter. But as a jurist and a practical lawyer he knew—he had written very forcibly about—the importance of a just law of contract justly administered. All Sir H. Harington's prejudices were against the planter, but he, too, felt that such evils as those which had rent a Province would be prevented only by legislation, at once to protect the ignorant in making a contract and to give speedy relief to those who suffered by its fraudulent breach. The fresh English jurist and the old Indian civilian agreed on provisions which would have secured both ends, under which only registered contracts intelligently made and fraudulently broken would be liable to be dealt with by the *civil*, not the criminal, courts as fraudulent debtors are treated, and that at the cost of the employer who sued the contractor. But the old Indians of the Law Commission prevailed with the Secretary of State to forbid the amendment of the Civil Procedure Code, into which the compromise, accepted by all parties in India, was to be introduced, and this reform still remains to be conceded. What Maine could not do, however, in reforming the law of contract, he attempted to effect by improving the procedure and largely increasing the number of Small Cause Courts.

Though baffled, but never answered, by the Law Commission, he did his duty in dealing with the chapters of the Code of substantive Civil Law, which they sent out. The Indian Succession Act, which contains the first instalment, owes much to his knowledge of the position of Englishmen in India, to whom it applies the most enlightened provisions of the law of France and that of the United States as to the property of married women, while it sweeps away the unjust feudal distinctions regulating the descent of land and the shares of the children of intestates. Hindus and Buddhists received some of the benefits of this Act.

It would be difficult to over-estimate the importance to its growing trade and capital of those Acts, by which Maine has given India the best fruits of recent English legislation on commercial questions. The two Trustee Acts, framed for England by Lord St. Leonards and Lord Justice Turner, the Mercantile Law Amendment Act, and the Indian Companies' Act, remove the reproach that in this respect Indian legislation had lagged far behind the English Parliament. There may be still a difference of opinion as to the Partnership Amendment Act, which goes in advance of England in so far as it protects the commanditarian loans so familiar in France and America, for we are not aware that the Act has in any case been applied. But looking at the whole of Maine's commercial legislation, it has been gratefully accepted by mercantile men, and it did much for public credit and the rights of joint-stock shareholders in the mad days of Bombay insolvency and limited liability companies. We may take along with this class of measures the Grand Jury, the Divorce, and the Vagrancy Acts. The first, though received with disapprobation in Calcutta, as likely to cause the very failure of justice it was intended to prevent and as interfering with an old privilege and a venerable institution, was approved in Madras and Bombay, and it has worked successfully. Ordinary juries are now supplied from a more intelligent class. But the real merit of this Act was, that it provided means for the trial of European offenders in other places than the Presidency towns, without interfering with that privilege which cannot be taken from European British subjects, until the courts of the interior have been raised to a level with those presided over by trained barrister judges. The Divorce Act has given to Christians in India the same relief which is within their reach in England, while it has done more for morality than the English law, by allowing the judge to hear cases with closed doors. The Vagrancy Act had the unanimous approval of all classes.

Perhaps Maine's greatest merit as a legislator, in the eyes of all who value civil liberty and free thought, lies in the measures he has produced, and the constant efforts he has made, to relieve the rigidity given by our legislation to the barbarous usages of the intolerant creeds of India. None has shown more eloquently or clearly than himself how the reign of law which we have introduced, and the Indian Councils Act of Parliament carried to an extreme, has, on the one hand, a tendency to perpetuate customs and rights which are intolerable and infamous, while it stimulates progress on the other. So long ago as 1832 the same Governor-General who would not allow Hindus to burn their widows, decreed that a man's religion should not, according to the very essence of Hinduism, be permitted to operate so as to deprive him of his civil rights. A clearer provision became necessary by 1850, when the *lex loci* Act was passed by Lord Dalhousie's Government, declaring that change of religion should not in any case "impair or affect any right of inheritance." Maine might well say of this, that it is "still the charter of religious liberty in India." But the principle laid down in 1832, and repeated more clearly in 1850, remained still inoperative in two very important classes of cases. The Hindu who changed his religion was still in the eye of the law bound to the child who had been betrothed to him in infancy, whom he might never have seen and who steadfastly refused to live with him. The civil right of lawful marriage was denied to him, and this Maine and Sir John Lawrence restored. The Act by which this amount of justice was done, when passing through Council, elicited from Maine the very ablest of the many able speeches which he delivered in India. It has proved most effectual in promoting the union of betrothed persons, who were kept apart only by the cruel bigotry of the Hindu parents. In the second class of cases, enlightened Hindus who objected to the filthy ceremonies which attend the celebration of betrothals and marriages, sought recognition of the legality of unions attended with less revolting rites, for that legality had been called in question by the Advocate-General of Bengal. Maine introduced a Bill giving to all the same option which Christians only enjoy, of marrying before a civil registrar and afterwards according to such rites as they prefer.

Maine was a scholar, and as such he enjoyed the rare honour of holding the office of Vice-Chancellor of the University of Calcutta for twice the usual time. His annual addresses are still remembered. His English style, whether as a writer or a speaker, has always been as perfect as his thought, of which it was the expression, is clear. In him, in all his capacities, a reverence for authority has been happily blended with a continual reference to first principles and a logical deduction from these principles. Even more characteristic of Maine than his *Ancient Law*, is his critique of Mr. Buckle's first volume in the *Edinburgh Review* of April 1858. While admitting the fearless love of truth which Mr. Buckle's admirers discover in his work on the history of civilisation, Mr. Maine defends morality and religion against his clumsy assaults, and exposes his hasty generalisations and inaccurate statements with a skill superior to that of all other critics on the work whose productions we have seen. In his executive capacity, for one on whose professional opinion great practical issues depended, Maine may sometimes have been subtle where plain common sense would have been better, or too much of a lawyer when he was called on to act the statesman, or too pliable in the hands of one who at once was and was not a colleague, like the Governor-General. But as a legislator who, to use his own words written long before he expected to hold such a position, "solves old problems under new shapes," there are few that have done so much for Indian progress, none that have done it so well.

Of all Sir Henry Maine's services to the people of India and the civilisation of British Asia, the greatest is to be found in the principles which he laid down and applied when passing through the Legislature Act XXI. of 1866 on the Remarriage of Native Converts. That measure has a meaning and an influence far beyond the local circumstances or even the rapidly increasing community affected. Maine laid down the law of toleration, in all its breadth and consequences, in a way unknown from the Emperor Constantine's days to the Viceroy Lord Lawrence's. His exposition of the true principles of the government of varied races, creeds, and cults, by an imperial or any other Power, is beyond price. It was made just at the time of the transition from the intolerance of the Company to the direct rule of the Queen-Empress, who had strongly insisted on these words, and had written them with her own hand in the Proclamation of 1st November 1858: "Firmly relying ourselves on the truth of Christianity, and acknowledging with gratitude the solace of religion, we disclaim alike the right and the desire to impose our convictions on any of our subjects."

In Northern India at least the origin of the Native Christian community lies within this century. Ever since the great Charter discussions in 1833, benevolent laymen as well as missionaries had been led to demand for the convert the same civil rights which all others enjoy before the law. Not till 1850 was his property protected, and not till soon after Bishop Cotton landed in Calcutta was a deliberate proposal made legally to release him whose partner refused cohabitation from the penalty of an indictment for bigamy in the event of remarriage. So great have been the hardships and immorality attending a life of celibacy, that there are few missionaries, except such as are more High Church than Roman Catholics themselves, who have not been in the habit of remarrying their converts in defiance of all penalties. The result had been that of all regulations which are contrary to the voice of nature and the ineradicable facts of society. The law to prevent bigamy never interfered; the authorities, both spiritual and civil, winked at what was equitably right, however legally wrong. Nay, so pressing was the necessity and evident the justice of relief, that the Law Member of Council hesitated not to say in his place, and to say truly, that there are missionaries who would brave the penalties of even the new Marriage Act for the sake of the purity of the infant Church. Nor was the necessity of legislation only a question for the present. Maine taught the objectors that this difficulty was not unknown in the early history of the Church, and that relief was always granted to the convert by men whose very nearness in time to Christ and the Apostle Paul entitled them to understand the words of Scripture at least as well as modern theologians. These objectors had not breadth of view and strength of faith enough to look forward to the time when the preparatory forces now at work in our schools, our Government, our English example, and our Missions will have destroyed caste and the Hinduism which has so long rested on that foundation.

Even if we allow the cases under the Act to be few and obscure, which was not the fact, what will they be when education has been so extended that succeeding generations will display a boldness their fathers lacked? If Christianity is to make any progress in the next two centuries commensurate with the preparatory work already done, we must expect the cases to which the Remarriage Act will apply to be exceedingly numerous for a time. Were the education of girls to keep pace with that of boys the difficulty would not exist, although of this there is more hope in the future than there has been in the past. The present necessities and the future growth of the Native Church demanded the removal of the last civil disability under which native Christians suffered, and the morality of a fast-increasing and actively loyal class of Her Majesty's subjects was being sapped.

Whether the spirit of Christ's teaching and the "let her depart" of St. Paul is, when interpreted by the *abi, discede* of Roman law, sufficient scriptural sanction, as we believe it to be, or not, need not trouble any clergyman's conscience. So far as he is concerned the Act is optional. It merely prevents the weak brother, who will not remarry a convert under excessive safeguards, from putting a yoke on missionaries more experienced and of broader views. The question is one capable of reduction to the simplest principles. Among all nations, savage and civilised, every married man has a right to his wife's society, and every law, however barbarous or refined, enforces the right. The right rests with the husband, the crime of separation—even on the ground that she has become Christian—is the wife's. But as public opinion in Europe would not justify a husband in compelling a wife who loathed him to live with him, so in India it is still less for the good of morality, nor is it in accordance with native law, that the wife should be forced to rejoin him, as was in one instance decreed by a Judge of the Madras Supreme Court. The only just remedy, fair to both parties, is that provided by the Act. And it has this advantage, that the recusant party is in the eyes of both Hindu and Mohammedan law dead to the converted partner. Native law has freed the former from the marriage tie, and our courts would be forced to recognise this fact. Is the latter to labour for life under a disability, which to an Asiatic is so serious that no inhabitant of the Tropics believes in the possibility of continence?

Maine's keen interest in the principles and provisions of this great Act is seen in the following letter which he addressed to me:—

"CALCUTTA, 18*th January* 1866.

"I hope you will be able to support the amended Bill in its integrity. I do not expect much active opposition to it in the Council, if any. But I do look for some coldness, and the Bill might be endangered if its supporters quarrelled about details. Cust has, however, written to say he should not oppose it if he were here in time—some proof of the state of opinion in England.

"I long since thought it probable that the Roman Catholics would have to be exempted. The line we have taken effectually puts an end to Banerjea's absurd insinuation about Romish influences. The fact is, the Roman Catholics bitterly opposed the Bill from the first.

"I would have left them out from the first draft, but they had not then furnished proof of their really having a procedure, and so I was afraid of being told that the proper way of dealing with the whole subject was simply to repeal the penal sections of Anderson's Acts. They have now shown that they have a procedure regular enough for there to be frequent appeals on doubtful points to the Pope and the Propaganda. Whether indeed this procedure is not sometimes relaxed in favour of conversion, is a point on which one cannot be sure. But, taking India as it is, it is not for us to scrutinise too closely any form of Christian propagandism, and besides, all we do is to leave them alone, *i.e.* to place them in the position they were in two years ago. They are satisfied with it, and that should be enough for us.

"I myself would have preferred the same course, if I had to deal with a number of organised religious bodies. If the Protestant Churches had been all organised Churches, as are the Roman Catholics, I would have left them to their own procedure, as we have done the Roman Catholics. But, as things actually stand, the result would have been anarchy. Few Protestant Churches are in a position to obtain new rules of discipline, and the Anglican Church is totally debarred from obtaining them. All these Churches habitually resort to the State when difficulties of this sort occur, and I think we have done well to provide all communities but the Roman Catholics with a common secular procedure, but to declare that no clergyman shall be compelled to celebrate a remarriage of which he disapproves.

"The Roman Catholic procedure doubtless dates from the time when their Church was the sole missionary Church, *i.e.* the period of the conversion of the Northern Nations. Had the Protestant Churches addressed themselves to missionary labour while their discipline was being organised, I have no doubt they would have had a similar procedure; and, indeed, I see that the aversion of any religious community, or portion of such a community, to the measure is proportionate to the lateness of its contact with missionary operations.

"[Sir W.] Muir's examination of the Arabic authorities places the correctness of the view we take of Mahometan converts beyond question. I suspected it was so before, from the positiveness of statement in such books as Baillie's *Mahometan Law.* The only difficulty which struck me was founded on the notorious fact that a Mahometan may marry a Christian wife, or semi-wife, without converting her. The explanation is to be found in the exclusive view taken by Mahometans of marriage as *a contract.* If a Mahometan marries a Christian, that is the contract; but if he marries a Mahometan and she turns Christian, that is a fundamental violation of the terms on which the marriage was originally contracted.

"I can scarcely conceive anybody arguing that, though the Mahometan law, which the Courts are bound to apply, may dissolve the marriage, a Christian must regard it as subsisting. Not to speak of other difficulties, that arising from Mahometan polygamy seems fatal to such reasoning.

"The establishment of the point as regards Mahometans seems to me pretty nearly to reduce the case of the opponents to an absurdity. It being *ex concesso* impossible to respect the previous Mahometan marriage, is the previous Hindoo marriage to be respected to the extent of absolutely forbidding remarriage? It may be a question whether we do not pay it too much respect.—Very truly yours,

H. S. MAINE."

When pressed to strike out the sections which provide a procedure to be followed before divorce, Maine replied in the closing passage of a speech which rises to the highest region alike of juridical eloquence and ethical principle:—[1]

"I cannot give up that procedure. I cannot give it up, in the first place, in justice to the wife. I do not think the situation of a Hindu widow so happy, or that of a Christian wife so unhappy, that I can consent to leave her to her family unless in deference to her fully ascertained free-will. The missionaries and the converts are well informed as to the causes which generally keep the wife apart from her husband. It is no fanciful opinion about his outcaste condition; it is misapprehension about his new mode of life—some miserable fable about meat, drink, or raiment, by which she has been deluded—which deters her. I cannot agree to leave her to her widowhood until at least an opportunity has been given of explaining these delusions away. Again, I cannot abandon the procedure in justice to the husband, for, if in law she is still his wife (which is the case supposed), I do not choose to assume that his sole object in suing her is to obtain facilities for marrying

[1] *Sir Henry Maine.* A Brief Memoir of his Life. By the Right Hon. Sir M. E. Grant Duff, G.C.S.I. With some of his Indian Speeches and Minutes. Selected by Whitley Stokes, D.C.L. (John Murray, 1892.)

somebody else. Lastly, I am not ashamed to say that I will not surrender the procedure, because, while it is equitable in itself, it is in harmony with the theory of divorce in which so many Christian Churches have concurred, and by which the native converts and their advisers are, presumably, guided. That theory I understand to be, that while divorce on the ground of persistent heathenism is lawful, it is not lawful in cases where the civil law maintains the validity of the marriage unless some serious attempt is made to recover the wife's society. It is the more reasonable to make some concessions to the doctrines held by the converts, because I am convinced that, in regard to this particular matter, they obtain less than fair treatment simply because they are Christians. It is not only that we forget that they are a native race, with many of the characteristics of all native races, but we actually show them less consideration than other native races. I am completely convinced that if conversions had been going on in some parts of India from Hinduism to Mohammedanism, and if the convert to Mohammedanism had entertained the same feeling as the Christian convert about his first wife (which one knows he would not), and if the disturbances which would be the probable consequence had compelled us to legislate—I feel sure that a Bill applying this carefully guarded procedure would have been praised by all as eminently prudent, moderate, and equitable. But because the converts are Christians every point is taken against them. For this reason I have been compelled to prove, I fear at tedious length, that they are entitled by their own religious laws to demand relief. Contingencies on which not a thought would have been bestowed if another native race had been in question have to be carefully weighed and taken into account; the very molehills of Hindu prejudice are exaggerated into mountains, and difficulties which in everyday Indian life crumble away at a touch are assumed to be of stupendous importance. I know, of course, that we do this because the converts are of our own faith, and because we are tender of our character for impartiality. But I do not know that we are entitled to be unjust even for the sake of seeming to be impartial. Surely the duty of the British Government to the Christian converts is too plain for mistake.

"*We will not force any man to be a Christian; we will not even tempt any man to be a Christian; but if he chooses to become a Christian, it would be shameful if we did not protect him and his in those rights of conscience which we have been the first to introduce into the country, and if we did not apply to him and his those principles of equal dealing between man and man of which we are in India the sole depositaries.*"

The great Christian principle of equality Maine applied in the other region of the position of woman, in his speech on the law of succession. Even Hindus and Mohammedans, though exempted from its operation, were roused by its tendency towards such protection as deeds of settlement secure to a wife's property. In conclusion he said:—

"If I had no data to go upon other than these discussions supplied, I should be led to the conclusion which I have arrived at independently, that if there exists any test of the degree in which a society approximates to that condition which we call civilisation, it is the degree in which it approaches the admission of an equality of right between the sexes. In this country I am sure that by simply applying this criterion you could construct a scale of barbarism and civilisation which would commend itself to every man's perceptions. . . . I once had a conversation with a very able native member of Council on some project of law, and I observed to him that if his view were correct there would be no difference between wifehood and slavery. 'Well,' said he, 'but that is the very doctrine from which we take our start.'"

In March 1867 Sir Henry Maine closed his four years' administration as Vice-Chancellor of the University of Calcutta, at the annual convocation for the purpose of conferring degrees, by an address, the most fruitful passage of which, on the Greek origin of all modern progress, he elaborated in 1875 in the Rede Lecture delivered before the University of Cambridge. Bishop Cotton had just been drowned in the Ganges. Recalling the departure for India of Alexander Duff just before he delivered the first of his four addresses, the Vice-Chancellor said: "Dr. Cotton and Dr. Duff belonged, so to speak, to the opposite poles of the British religious system. Dr. Duff was the voluntary emissary of a great endowed religious body, Dr. Cotton was the chosen representative of a great hierarchy. Yet now, when I wish to speak of the one, I am unable to find any other words than those which I used four years since of the other. Each believing his own creed to be true, believed it to possess the great characteristic of truth—that characteristic which nothing else except Truth possesses—that it can be reconciled with everything else which is also true. Each united the energy which springs from religious conviction with the most absolute fearlessness in encouraging the spread of knowledge."

The Vice-Chancellor naturally bade farewell to the thousands of Bengali graduates with the compliment that their intellectual performances "are rapidly approaching the highest European standards." Years of experience as a Fellow and Examiner of the University of Calcutta enable me to endorse this opinion. But it is only as *intellectual* performances that the papers of India graduates are equal to the average of the passmen of the British Universities. The Hindu or Musalman student works at a frightful disadvantage. All his studies are conducted in a foreign language, and he begins the grammatical use of that language at a comparatively late period in life. This, however, is the least of his difficulties. For the few hours five days a week that he is in contact with an English scholar, his remarkable imitative power, his unexampled patience, his intense desire for knowledge, and his subtle intellect enable the Hindu lad to learn at a rate which would have satisfied even John Stuart Mill. But for more than three-fourths of his life every day he is exposed to all-powerful influences in his own home which tend to make him unlearn the spirit, at least, of what he has acquired. The best part of an Englishman's education is gained out of the class-room. But when the Hindu leaves that he is exposed to influences of caste, idolatry, Orientalism, and dense darkness which threaten to quench the rushlight in his soul. As an illustration of this take the Hindu graduate who has four hours given him at a University examination to answer ten stiff questions in political economy. As a rule, the rapid pace at which he must write will force him unconsciously to violate idiom, to misapply the Article—his great difficulty—and misspell even technical terms. But he will show a vast amount of knowledge of his subject, while his more carefully prepared English paper will display familiarity with all the rules and principles of its grammar. It is surely unjust to sneer at the Hindu Bachelor of Arts because he neither speaks nor writes a foreign tongue with the grace and accuracy of one who learned it from his mother's lips, and because he manifests some intellectual independence or swagger. A little reflection and experience will convince those who are indifferent to a kind of progress with which they have no sympathy, that there is little or no intellectual inferiority on the part of Hindu graduates to the mass of Cambridge, Oxford, or Scottish University men.

Yet their inferiority as men and scholars is great. All that we include in the idea of moral training, of the creation of right motives, is wanting. The Hindu intellect, even when steeped in English literature and Western thought, has no bloom. The Hindu character, when polished by English scholars, loses its natural grace and too often becomes repulsive. Your graduate of Calcutta, Bombay, or Madras may beat the Oxford or Cambridge man, on the same conditions, in a mathematical or metaphysical examination. Yet the defeated Englishman will rise to be a master of men, for he is a master of self, and will carve out a great career, for he has great motives, while his victor will subside into a Government clerk, an oppressive zemindar, or a mere sensualist. We shall be told that this is only because the native is comparatively denied the career in his own country which the Englishman enjoys both in England and India. It is not true, so long as the mere sacrifice of caste is all that is required to enable Indian graduates to enter the Civil Service. But even if it were, the only reason for not more rapidly conceding to the natives of India that official career which a few ask, is their moral unfitness. No one doubts the intellectual ability of many to take the place of the highest Englishmen in the land. But their whole past history, the present condition of one-fourth of all India which natives alone govern, the experience of districts under covenanted and statutory native civilians, and the whole judicial records of the country show that the rule of the native would be corruption and oppression intensified, because directed by intellectual power. The salt has no savour, and till it acquires *that*, it will be fit for nothing but to be kept out of every place into which it would introduce evil.

This, of course, Sir Henry Maine could not plainly tell the Bengalis from his place as Vice-Chancellor. But hints of the facts underlie his four addresses. And in 1887 he wrote all his mind in the seventy pages which he contributed to Mr. T. H. Ward's volumes on *The Reign of Queen Victoria: A Survey of Fifty Years' Progress.*[1] Nothing quite so wise and

[1] London: Smith, Elder, and Co., 1887.

complete on the meaning as well as the facts of our administration and education of India has ever appeared, and we marvel that it is not reproduced, along with his Rede lecture on "The Effects of Observation of India on Modern European Thought." Quoting the saying of an eminent Anglo-Indian, that the British rulers of India are like men bound to make their watches keep time in two longitudes at once, he adds, if they are too slow there will be no improvement; if they are too fast there will be no security. "The British dominion in India is much too wonderful a creation for despair to be justifiable, but a man must have a very superficial conception of what Indian government is if he thinks that it has been made easier by the necessity for reconciling these two conditions."

I have preserved not a few of Sir Henry Maine's letters on Indian questions, addressed to me at Serampore, from Calcutta and Simla. Some have a peculiar value as reflecting his experience and opinions as an old journalist, when with the hearty consent of Sir John Lawrence and Sir William Mansfield, his colleagues, he made the proposal—most attractive in some aspects—that the weekly *Friend of India* should be transferred to the Government, and I should continue as the Editor of the *Moniteur*. That was impossible, and it turned out afterwards that the plan was opposed—most properly I still think—by Sir Henry Durand and the Secretary of State. The correspondence is of interest now only as illustrating his conviction of the power of the Press, especially in a country where its liberty always tends to license.[1] The Journal of Serampore for forty years loyally strove to support the British Government of India—sometimes against the Secretary of State, as in the notorious case of Sir C. Wood and the Mysore annuities, and kept its independence; differing from weak Governor-Generals like Lord Auckland and Lord Canning in the early mistakes of the latter, and from John Lawrence in his "masterly inactivity," but always honourably.

May 1871 saw Maine a member for life of the Council of India, on the nomination of the Duke of Argyll, and K.C.S.I. There he carried out his legislative system almost to completion. To his early work on *Ancient Law* he added his six lectures as Corpus Professor of Jurisprudence in the University of Oxford on *Village Communities in the East and West*,[2] and thirteen lectures on the *Early History of Institutions*. In 1883 appeared his *Dissertations on Early Law and Custom*. In 1885 he rewrote from *Quarterly*

[1] See Appendix.

[2] *7th December* 1870.—"Down to Oxford to hear the last of Maine's lectures in the hall at Corpus, which were afterwards published in his volume on *Indian Village Communities*. Maine then lived in Cornwall Gardens, whence the name given, I think, by Sir Henry Thring to the whole neighbourhood, which is now full of people who know each other—'Maine's Village Community.' It is odd how the Government of India was, in 1870, carried on from Kensington. The Duke of Argyll lived at Campden Hill. My permanent colleague Merivale was within a few doors of me in Cornwall Gardens. Close to him was Sir Robert Montgomery, and farther along in the same line Stephen, then in India, had a house, while Halliday was, like me, in Queen's Gate Gardens."—From *Notes from a Diary*, 1857-72. By the Right Hon. Sir Mountstuart E. Grant Duff, G.C.S.I. (John Murray, 1897.)

Review articles, and published them under the title of *Popular Government*, the nearest approach he made to the discussion of politics under his own name. He was far above party, since in the early days of the *Saturday Review* he had castigated Mr. Disraeli. Other magazine articles followed, and twelve lectures on International Law published after his death. All are precious; but the most fruitful of his works, affecting the millions of India now and for all time, is *The Anglo-Indian Codes*, which in 1887 Mr. Whitley Stokes, D.C.L., edited, and the Clarendon Press printed at Oxford.

Unanimously elected Master of Trinity Hall, Cambridge, in 1877, he saw his works translated into many languages, and formally recognised by European jurists in 1883, for he was made Foreign Associate of the Institute of France. I last parted with him early in 1888, in Regent Street, when he was in the fulness of his intellectual powers. The winter drove him to Cannes, where he suddenly died on the 3rd February 1888. Except the missionary, who applies the divine dynamics of Christianity to its people and their progress, India has never had a statesman who has more widely or permanently influenced it for good through the irresistible pressure of Law.

XI

HON. SIR HENRY RAMSAY, K.C.S.I., C.B., 1816–1893

The "King" of Kumaon

No Scottish family has done so much to extend and to consolidate the Empire of British India as the Ramsays of Dalhousie. The founder was ennobled by his sovereign, James VI., whom he rescued during the death-grapple in the secluded chamber of Gowrie Castle. The ninth earl, whose brother also succeeded to the baronetcy and estates of Panmure, was made a peer of the United Kingdom for his services at Waterloo, and followed Lord Combermere as Commander-in-Chief of the Indian Army. His son was the greatest of all—the first and the last Marquess of Dalhousie. When hardly out of his boyhood, he was Sir Robert Peel's President of the Board of Trade, and virtual author of the English railway system. Sent out to India, the youngest, and, as it proved, the last of the Company's Governor-Generals, in the self-denying administration of eight years to which he sacrificed his life, Lord Dalhousie added to British territory an empire as large as Clive's, gave to its millions all the latest reforms of the age, scientific, social and educational, and would have left it stronger than ever had not the home authorities turned a deaf ear to his military requests. Not a few of his kinsmen commanded in the British and the Company's armies. General John Ramsay had a Division in Bengal; Colonel James Ramsay was long well known as Commissary-General there; Colonel U. Maule Ramsay was Brigadier at Gwalior.

But the last of all the Ramsays, and second only to the great Marquess in ability, was the Hon. Sir Henry, popularly known as the King of Kumaon, who spent forty-four years as an administrator in the North-Western Provinces of India. When his elder brother succeeded to the united honours and estates of Dalhousie and Panmure, as the twelfth earl, Henry was living in all simplicity in the heart of his Himalayan province, one of those patriarchal rulers who, as soldier-statesmen, won and then civilised the martial races of our extended frontier. Born in 1816, he went out almost direct from the Edinburgh Academy as a Company's cadet to Bengal in 1834. In the six months' campaign of 1848-49, when, for the second time, the Sikhs contested with us the supremacy of the Punjab, Henry Ramsay won his spurs in a style of which his kinsman, the Governor-General, four years his senior, was proud. But the Marquess of Dalhousie was no nepotist; and it fell to Mr. Colvin, the Lieutenant-Governor of the North-Western Provinces, to reward the young soldier long after. In the year before the Mutiny, Major Henry Ramsay was sent to the non-regulation districts of Kumaon and Garhwal as Commissioner. There he lived and there he reigned, amid the blessings of the people, and to the admiration of all men, till he came home to die. He had married the daughter of Sir Henry Lushington, Bart., who survived him, and he left more than one son in the Indian military and political services.

The country with which his name is for ever identified is just the size of Switzerland, but still more beautiful, with a million of hardy mountaineers. From the once rebel plains of Rohilkhand the Kumaon division rises up to the main range of the mighty Himalayas, and is arrested only by the border of Chinese Tibet. Lakes are rarely met with in the stupendous mountain system of North India, but this Province contains one of the most beautiful in the world, Naini Tal. Around it, as a sanitarium of rare beauty, the Europeans of the North-Western Provinces cluster in the hot season, and not far off, at Ranikhet and Chowbuttia, our British troops with their families find health and acclimatisation in the first years of their tropical service. From Almora, the capital, whence Henry Ramsay governed the million of his children for nigh forty years, thirty snowy peaks can be seen, all much loftier than Mont Blanc, while the giant Trisul (trident) and the two mightier Nandas tower up to almost twenty-six thousand feet. It is a land of great rivers, frequented by thousands of the

Hindus from the parched plains below to worship at their sacred fountains.

Here, three-quarters of a century ago, Bishop Heber found the only rest and refreshment he knew during the two tours over the wide extent of his diocese, which then included not only all India, Ceylon, the Straits Settlements, and China, but Mauritius and Australasia. In his bright letters to his Oxford and Chester friends, Heber described himself as "enjoying frosty mornings, cool breezes, and the view of the noblest mountains under heaven." As the guest of Traill, the first Commissioner, and the friend of Sir Robert Colquhoun, commandant of the local troops, Heber explored the vicinity of Almora and Havelbagh with the same zest which had carried him over Russia and the country of the Don Cossacks. And there, on Sunday, 29th November 1824, he thus filled up his Journal:—"This day I enjoyed the gratification of being the first Protestant minister who had preached and administered the Sacrament in so remote yet so celebrated a region. I had a very respectable congregation of all the Christian inhabitants." Afterwards, Sir Robert Colquhoun expatiated on the then little known military virtues of the Goorkhas, of whom he spoke, and who have since proved themselves to be, as the smartest and most European-like soldiery of India. Then, adds Heber, "we had family prayers." The work thus begun fell to the catholic-spirited Scot, Henry Ramsay, to continue, and to apply to the natives of Kumaon.

From two sources in Garhwal the Ganges takes its

rise, and where the two affluents unite amidst everlasting snows, the shivering sun-stricken children of Mother Ganga find the holiest spot of pilgrim asceticism in all the Brahmanical world.

Just before the crowning victory of Waterloo this land, which had been long ravaged by the Goorkhas, came under the British peace. First Traill, and then J. H. Batten, two administrators worthy of the noblest traditions of the Indian Civil Service, reduced to order the chaos caused by their Nepaulese predecessors, using the iron hand of a personal autocracy, tempered by equity and kindliness, to all who loyally obeyed the ruler. Henry Ramsay developed the policy of patriarchal administration, which Durand had been the first to embody in Tenasserim, under the name of "non-regulation," and which had been splendidly carried out by the Lawrences and their officers, like Ramsay himself, after the Second Punjab War. He was soon recognised as the father of the people. In a region where roads and navigation, and even riding, was impossible, Ramji Sahib, as he came to be called, first fearfully and then affectionately, would suddenly swoop down on an offending village, or for the comfort of a suffering hamlet, like a bird from his eyrie. He could out-walk even his favourite *paharees*, or Highlanders. Promptly to right some wrong, he would emerge from the ravines or the forests of his kingdom before it was known that he had left Almora.

It was well that such a man had been for even so short a time as twelve months in charge of Kumaon when the Mutiny of 1857 blasted the plains of Northern India and, in the neighbouring division of Rohilkhand filled with Mohammedans, became almost civil rebellion. An Act was in due time passed to disarm the population. Mr. Colvin and his Government were shut up in the fort of Agra, where he soon afterwards died. Between him and Ramsay in their mountain fastnesses it could not be said that government existed at all. They could not be in touch. Ramsay heard of the disarming Act, but would not believe that could apply to him. Were not his million of subjects peaceful and even actively loyal? The Commissioner of the neighbouring rebel division of Rohilkhand remonstrated with him, but in vain. Ramsay referred to Lord Canning and his Council the question whether he was to reward his Highlanders, Hindus, and Goorkhas for their loyalty at such a time by taking away the arms which they had used in our service. By that time the first Viceroy of India was learning to see facts for himself, and the Government of India decided in the indignant Commissioner's favour. The *paharees* kept their muskets, and continued to use them against our enemies.

Henry Ramsay was his own engineer and forester and public works secretary for many a year. Perhaps the finest enterprise that he undertook and carried out single-handed was the revenue settlement of the waterless districts known as *bhabar*. The hill-tracts contained only some five hundred square miles of arable land, while the magnificent water resources of the country were running to waste, or became pestilential swamps as they collected at the plains. The streams found their way under the dry forests, and emerged below only to create malaria. Building drains and reservoirs on the higher uplands, he regulated the supply, and he carried it down to form small irrigating canals. He gradually wrought such a change on the face of the country that verdure and health everywhere prevailed. The people flocked to the new holdings, and they gladly paid an increasing rent to the State landlord and improver. The Public Works Department cast its eye on the enterprise, and sought to bring it under its own regulation control; but Ramsay long maintained his independent management, and was allowed to do so until the waste forest area ceased to exist, and the malarious swamps became smiling gardens. Lord Mayo, when Governor-General, visited the country, being himself an experienced agriculturist. He so admired the forest reclamation that he resolved, had his life and term of office been continued, to make it the model of similar works all along the lower Himalayas. His Excellency's only complaint of the autocratic Commissioner was that he would not dine with him on Sunday evening, but preferred to keep to his custom of attending divine service. The Viceroy admired him all the more, and it was well known among both his native and European subordinates that Ramji Sahib would do no business between six and seven every morning, for that hour all through his life he gave to God.

The "non-regulation" system, under which the territories recently acquired by conquest or occupied by simple hillmen were governed outside of the elaborate codes and procedure and appellate courts of India proper, was necessarily temporary in its action. As a system it had its own codes, but these were simple, and were administered by civilians and soldiers of marked individuality of character and righteousness of aim, who feared no responsibility save to their own conscience and to God. The system was also educative, preparing the new subjects and their officials alike for the time when they must be absorbed into the Imperial machine of law and procedure. Henry Ramsay fully recognised this, with his marvellous tact and sweet reasonableness. At first he kept law, in the technical sense, far from him. "In my opinion," he once remarked, when on the spot he was deciding a boundary dispute, "law is too often injustice. It can be twisted in any way, and can be made to defeat its own purpose. The best administration is that which deals out justice on intelligible principles, which never change." But he, too, made mistakes, which he was the first to admit; and as every judge and magistrate cannot be a Henry Ramsay, or a John Lawrence, he paved the way for the High Court jurisdiction all over his territory. What Traill began he completed, till he left the Kumaon division of the North-Western Provinces a model administration.

At an early stage of his government Sir Henry Ramsay followed Henry and John Lawrence in doing Christian things in a Christian way. He would not deny to the leal-hearted Highlanders whom he loved, the best that could be given them—the truth, the hope, the life of Christianity. His own example was to many the most powerful argument. He insisted on complete toleration and fair play. For the rest he wished the evangelical missionaries God-speed; and as a private gentleman he helped them in his leisure hours and Sunday rest. Was he not ruler, in immediate contact with the Hindu people, of the holiest of all lands in their eyes, of the Meru Mountains of their mythology, the Ganga fountains of their daily worship? The temples of Kedarnath and Badrinath drew millions to their shrines. Hourly, night and day, the sin-burdened people were toiling up the rugged hills to wash, if perchance they might be clean. In his own capital of Almora, like our ancient city of Chester, the Commissioner had rejoiced in the work of a man like the late Mr. Budden, of the London Missionary Society, whom he himself supported, with the Mission, from the first. But he longed to see the true worship of the one living God in Christ nearer the degrading nature-worship of mountain and stream, of stock and stone, that the earnest, longing seeker after peace might have a chance to learn of Him who hath once for all taken away sin. So he offered the Bishop of the Episcopal Methodist Church of America, which Dr. Duff had urged to undertake the evangelisation of that part of North India, £300 to found, and £70 a year to carry on, a mission at Pauri, the administrative headquarters of the shrine-country of Garhwal. The two principal public buildings in the Province—the Ramsay Hospital in Naini Tal and the Ramsay College in Almora—most fitly bear his name. When opening a Government High School at Almora in 1894 the Lieutenant-Governor, Sir Charles Crosthwaite, exhorted the supporters of the new scheme never to forget the debt of gratitude which they owed to the missionaries and the Ramsay College, but for which they would now have had neither the ability nor the desire to establish such a school. He further reminded them that through the training received at the Ramsay College they now held their well-paid positions under Government. They had been willing enough, he said, to take the advantages offered them by the missionaries in days when Government was not in a position to supply the same benefits, and their sudden desire for non-sectarian education had come very tardily. The High School is the offspring of the Ramsay College, and the Government would never forget what was due to that institution, but would always continue to encourage and aid it. Henry Ramsay's best monument is the loyalty and reverent regard of a grateful million of people.

He ceased to be Commissioner in 1884, but so attached was he to the people and their interests, that he felt as if he could not leave. He remained for eight years afterwards, in a non-official capacity, doing them all the good in his power.

Before he left India, in 1892, Sir Henry Ramsay received what he publicly, and in all simple sincerity, declared to be the greatest honour of his life—he was elected by the missionaries of all India Chairman of their Decennial Conference, held at Calcutta in 1882-1883. He resisted the summons with characteristic humility, and when compelled to obey, he struck the keynote of that successful gathering in these words: "The true president of this Conference is the Lord Jesus Christ, and the promise of His presence is the surest guarantee we have of success. Let us, therefore, look to Him for that guidance, wisdom, and grace we all need." The veteran Christian outlined the progress made by the varied peoples of India under his own eyes, through Christian teaching and Western truth. "Even the moral character of the people has undergone a considerable change." "There is now more life in the Christian Church than there ever was before. Forget all differences of opinion; look to Him who is the light of the world. God has sent us to India for the all-important work of saving souls—that is the essence of mission work. By God's Spirit alone that work can be done well."

Always a wise and reasonable Christian, modest, self-distrusting, and becoming all things to all men that he might win them, Henry Ramsay was tremendously in earnest during the last third of his long life. The American Episcopal Methodist, Bishop Thoburn, tells us how, in 1861, he visited his dying friend the late Sir William Richards, who had preferred to spend his last years in India. The departing soldier had ceased to hear distinctly, and Sir Henry bent over him. Throwing his arms around his neck, and drawing him down upon his breast, the dying man poured into his ear a story of holy triumph, which made those who witnessed the scene feel as if the gates of heaven were opened and its glory were filling the room. Softly, but distinctly, he told his friend of his joy, of his hope, of his vision of God. As they left the house, Sir Henry Ramsay exclaimed to the bishop: "I would not exchange what I have learned in that room for all the coronets that were ever worn. I have heard of such scenes, but I never thought that I should witness the like."

From that day the Commissioner of Kumaon lived and worked for the Master, not indeed with new, but with more intense zeal; he seemed to live a second life, extending over other thirty-six years, till to him, also, the summons came at the ripe age of seventy-seven years. So another was added to the golden book of the Anglo-Indian Knights of the Faith.

XII

SIR CHARLES UMPHERSTON AITCHISON, K.C.S.I., C.I.E., 1832–1896

Student and Foreign Minister

Sir Charles U. Aitchison was one of the first, and he was the most distinguished, of the Competition-Wallas of what is now called the Indian Civil Service. His active administrative career covered the term of office of eight Viceroys and Governor-Generals, from the beginning of Lord Canning's to the close of Lord Dufferin's—a period of more than thirty years. His official relation to each, as Foreign Secretary, Chief Commissioner, Lieutenant-Governor, and Member of Council, at different times, and the personal influence of his high character, experienced counsels, and ripe judgment, brought it about that for nearly a whole generation he was more continuously and intimately associated with almost every great event in the recent history of our Indian Empire than any other man. From the reorganisation of Feudatory as well as purely British India after the Mutiny of 1857 to the conquest and pacification of Upper Burma, when he resigned Council in November 1888, he might have said with truth, *Quorum magna pars fui*, but a dignified modesty was too marked a feature of his character. He never sought a favour, never asked for an appointment; notwithstanding his rapid promotion and unconscious influence, he rarely made an enemy. He was to the new Imperial system of Indian administration what the Hon. Mountstuart Elphinstone was to the old *régime* of the East India Company. Would that he had been longer spared to the Empire to assist the ruling class in the Secretary of State's Council, and in India, by his wise judgment, his cautious conservatism in all things Eastern, and his sympathetic care for the peoples of India.

Charles U. Aitchison was born in 1832, in Edinburgh. Through his mother, the seventh Lieutenant-Governor of the Punjab sprang from the old Scottish Covenanter family of the Umpherstons, memorable for their sufferings in the "killing" period of the seventeenth century, and of the Cameronian Church almost to the last.[1] Fearing God and loving righteousness, trained at Lasswade with De Quincey's children, and lads like

[1] In 1869 Aitchison printed at Belfast (Marcus Ward and Co.), for family use, a remarkable collection of original MSS. and papers in the possession of Francis Umpherston, Esq., Elmswood, Loanhead, under the title of *Passages in the Lives of Helen Alexander, and James Currie of Pentland; and other Papers.* The little quarto has as its frontispiece a photograph of the Martyrs' Monument in Greyfriars Churchyard, Edinburgh, which his mother's predecessors erected in 1706, and others renewed in 1771. The collection is further valuable because of the letters from the Right Honourable Sir Robert Hamilton to Helen Alexander and James Currie. The famous Baronet of Bothwell Brig was an ancestor of the great metaphysician, Sir William Hamilton, Bart., in whose classes Sir Charles Aitchison took honours in the years 1849-50.

Colonel Baird Smith, the engineer who took Delhi, first in a Scottish parish school, and then in the Royal High School of Edinburgh, Aitchison became one of the foremost students of its University, where he took his M.A. degree.

The good work of learning to think, begun by the Rector, Dr. L. Schmitz, was carried on by Sir William Hamilton in the class of Logic and Metaphysics, then by far the greatest living force in the University, which suffered from effete teachers. One of a set of brilliant fellow-students, Aitchison and they long after in India used to recall the days of Sir William Hamilton—the fire of his hazel eye, brilliant almost to blackness, and the magnificent Olympic head dominating the broken and palsied frame, the living embodiment of the motto on the panel above his chair:—

> "On earth there is nothing great but Man,
> In Man there is nothing great but Mind."

The book which moulded Aitchison's life was *Die Bestimmung des Menschen*, or *The Destination of Man*, by Fichte. The intense earnestness of the practical morality into which the great German idealist's system resolved itself, not essentially different from that of Berkeley, captivated him. Fichte's doctrine of faith as the ground of all conviction, moral and scientific, seemed to him the complement of Hamilton's great law of the Conditioned; and the two together placed him, in regard to the principles of religion, on intellectual ground which no metaphysical speculations were ever after able to shake.

What these two thinkers began, Tholuck completed at the University of Halle, where Aitchison spent the summer session of 1854, following a winter session at Berlin. Tholuck was then, as he had been for twenty years, in the forefront of the few evangelical theologians of Germany. He exerted a wonderful influence over the students whom he attracted from all parts of Reformed Christendom. Daily he walked with one or two of them in the arbour of his garden, or in what he called the "pratum theologicum" on the banks of the Saale. Then, throwing off the professor, he became a student again, entering into the studies, the projects, the difficulties and perplexities of the young men as if they were his own. This produced a more profound impression on Aitchison than even his lectures. In Edinburgh, alike at the University and at the New College of the Free Church of Scotland, Charles Aitchison's pure young manhood and lofty character placed him in the front rank of his fellows, and attracted their admiration. It was while holding the highest scholarship at the New College, where at that time there was a lack of sympathetic divines, that he was urged by Miss Napier of Coates Hall to compete for one of the Indian appointments thrown open by the Charter of 1853 under Macaulay's persistent influence. He was twenty-two years of age; it was the middle of April 1855, and the examinations were held a few weeks after, so that there was no time for special reading, even if there had been anything to indicate what it was advisable to read. Only twenty appointments were offered, and there were 113 candidates, of whom fifty-one were from Oxford and Cambridge. The Scottish Universities and Colleges sent twelve. In the mathematical paper Aitchison did so badly that he gave up all hope of passing. But his Greek and Philosophy brought him out fifth on the list. Alone he represented Scotland, to which he returned to find himself lionised. The venerable Principal Lee sent him forth from Edinburgh with much information and friendly counsel. After a year spent in London in the study of Law and Hindustani, he landed in Calcutta on the 25th September 1856, where I welcomed my old school and college companion.

After passing his Persian and Hindi examinations in three months, he entered on his official experience at Hissar, a dreary district of sand, coarse grass, scrub and brushwood, relieved with intervals of green at the tail of the Western Jumna Canal. It was the 19th March, and in a month he found his name in the *Gazette*, transferred to Lahore, where John Lawrence, who was one of the few Haileybury men that believed in the competitive system, wanted four of the new-comers. Riding a camel to distant Karnal from the 4th May, he reached Lahore just in time to learn that he had unconsciously escaped the massacre of nineteen Christian officers and their families at Hissar on the 29th May. He never saw the place again till he visited it in 1882 in the course of his tour as Lieutenant-

Governor of the Punjab. At Amritsar, the pivot on which the loyalty of the Sikh Khalsa turned in 1857, Aitchison found himself in the thick of the Mutiny events. For four months he and his comrades never slept save half-dressed and within reach of arms. He held the Bhairowal ferry on the Beas river against the Jalandhar mutineers, and he was Frederick Cooper's most trustworthy assistant. One deed of personal daring and beautiful comradeship at this time must be recorded. An old High School fellow of his and the writer's had been shot through the head at John Nicholson's action of Najafgarh beneath the walls of Delhi, and was officially reported dead.[1] Believing that this was premature, Aitchison found his way through a dangerously disturbed country to the camp on the famous Ridge, sought out his dying friend, nursed him through days of unconsciousness, arranged for his conveyance to the hills, and then returned to his own duties. That officer still lives to bless the name of his friend, who, years after, secured for him the share in the Delhi prize-money, of which he had long been deprived unrighteously.

After taking part in the stirring exploits of the time, he became personal assistant to the Judicial Commissioner, and drafted the code of the criminal law of the Punjab. He worked side by side with the great John Lawrence, whose disciple he thenceforth became, especially in all questions of Central Asia politics, and the

[1] Dr. Ireland, author of the *History of the Siege of Delhi, by an Officer who served there* (Edinburgh, A. and C. Black, 1861), and valuable professional works.

social prosperity and contentment of our native subjects. On the promotion of Mr. Robert Simson, Aitchison was selected by Lord Canning's Government to be Under Foreign Secretary. The time was epoch-making. All North India had to be reorganised, from Allahabad to Peshawar. The Native Sovereigns and great landholders had to be dealt with according as they had loyally helped the Paramount Power, or had, like Holkar, passively obstructed its action while secretly encouraging revolt. The new Under Secretary was foremost of all the officials who accompanied and advised the first Viceroy and Governor-General in the great tour which he made in 1859-60. In a series of the most splendid Durbars ever held in the name of the Queen-Empress, Lord Canning lavished whole districts and provinces on the most loyal chiefs, and in sonorous speeches drafted by the Secretary, or read out by him in Persian, rebuked the disloyal. Joined soon after by Sir Henry Durand, R.E., as his immediate chief, Aitchison developed the policy of adoption to a Raj on the failure of natural heirs, which has ever since bound to us the feudatory potentates of India, and taught them to rule the sixty millions of human beings, who are their subjects and the Queen's, wisely and well. When Sir John Lawrence became Viceroy, in 1864, Aitchison was more trusted than ever. He had issued his now famous *Collection of Treaties, Engagements, and Sanads relating to India and neighbouring Countries*, each prefaced by a lucid historical narrative of the highest impartiality. His treatise on *The Native States of India* (1875), with the leading cases illustrating the principles which underlie their relations with the British Government, is the most important contribution to that new department of international law. So valued had his office minutes been found, that he may be said to have written most of the despatches relating to the great questions of foreign and feudatory policy from Lord Canning to Lord Northbrook. After an interval of practical district and judicial work in the Punjab, where also he acted as local secretary, he returned to the Foreign Office in Calcutta and Simla as full Secretary, shaping events all along our north Asiatic frontiers, and especially in Afghanistan, on the lines laid down by Lord Lawrence and accepted by Lord Mayo and Lord Northbrook.

Aitchison's volumes suggest to the careful student a new division of the history of British India into periods corresponding with the policy which dictated our treatment of the Native States, and the consequent growth of our Eastern Empire. These seem to be six:—

1. The period of commercial engagements, from 1611 to 1757.

2. The period of political subordination, from 1758 to 1798.

3. The period of real but unacknowledged political supremacy, and of subsidiary alliances, from 1799 to 1805.

4. The period of political isolation and non-interference, from 1806 to 1817.

5. The period of acknowledged political supremacy, from 1818 to 1858.

6. The period of the fusion of complete supremacy and non-interference, from 1859 to the present time.

The first period began with the establishment of the first English factory in 1611 at Surat in the Soobah of Ahmedabad, after Sir Henry Middleton's naval victory over the Portuguese fleet, and ended with the triumph of Plassey. In 1613 a firman from Delhi confirmed a treaty for the establishment of factories at Surat, Cambay, Ahmedabad, and Gogo; and the year after King James's Ambassador, Sir Thomas Roe, obtained the right for English merchants to trade throughout the Great Moghul's dominions, said Great Moghul thus replying to King James, who had addressed him as "the high and mighty Monarch the Great Moghul, King of the Oriental Indies, of Chandahar, of Chismer and Corazon, etc., greeting":—"Unto a King rightly descended from his ancestors, bred in military affairs, and clothed with honour and justice; a Commander worthy of all command, strong and constant in religion, which the great Prophet Christ did teach, King James, whose love hath bred such impression in my thoughts as shall never be forgotten, but as the smell of amber, or as a garden of fragrant flowers whose beauty and odour is still increasing, so, be assured, my love shall grow and increase with yours."

The gallant defence of Surat against Sivaji by the English in 1664 gave them political influence with Aurangzeb, and in 1685 the Government was removed to Bombay. Meanwhile, soon after their establishment at Surat, the English had formed a station on the Coromandel coast at Armagaon, between Nellore and Pulicat. In 1639, on the invitation of the Hindu Governor of the district, the English went south to Madras, which in 1653 as Fort St. George was made a separate Presidency. In Bengal the English in 1624 obtained a firman to trade with the one port of Piplee in Midnapore; in 1642 a factory was established at Balasore; and in 1652, for the sum of Rs.3000 a year, the right of free and unlimited trade was conceded. Clive's victories at Arcot and Plassey, and the consequent humiliation of the Nawabs of the Carnatic and Bengal, put the traders in a totally new position, and our power entered on its second stage. We were now conquerors and exercised political influence, but still in subordination to the shadow who occupied the Delhi throne, and even to his representative at Murshidabad. Even in 1767, before his departure for Europe, Clive thought it necessary to obtain from Shah Aalum a *blank firman* for the Soobahship of the Deccan, and he thus wrote of the necessity for maintaining the name of the authority of the Nawab of Murshidabad, in order to crush the rivalry of the other European factories:—

"Be it therefore always remembered that there is a Soobah; that we have allotted him a stipend which must be regularly paid in support of his dignity, and that, though the revenues belong to the Company, the territorial jurisdiction must still rest in the chiefs of the country acting under him and this Presidency in conjunction. To appoint the Company's servants to the offices of Collectors, or indeed to do any act by an exertion of the English power which can equally be done by the Nabob at our instance, would be throwing off the mask—would be declaring the Company Soobah of the Provinces. Foreign nations would immediately take umbrage, and complaints preferred to the British Court might be attended with very embarrassing consequences."

This lasted till 1798, the close of the first administration of Lord Cornwallis, for though the regulations made by that Governor-General placed the whole administration in the hands of English officials, it was he who first introduced the suicidal system of non-interference with native states. It was, therefore, left for Lord Wellesley to begin the third era of real, though unacknowledged, political supremacy, lasting throughout his administration till 1805. Neither the King's Government, which was occupied with the French war, nor the Court of Directors, nor Lord Cornwallis, could appreciate the policy of "the glorious little man," who saw that by interference alone, followed by subsidiary alliances, could the Marathas be prevented from swallowing up all India, and the Pindaris from preying upon the legitimate states. Lord Cornwallis, who was hurried out to make a ruinous peace with powerful freebooters and then die, fell back on the old policy of political isolation, and that continued till 1817. Its fruit was the Pindari War.

The fourth period, which continued with some intervals of a retrograde policy till the Mutiny, was introduced by the Treaty of 1817 with Sindia. That left us free to make engagements with the Rajpootana

States, and so to save them from both Marathas and Pindaris. The renewal of Lord Wellesley's policy was due to the Marquess of Hastings. After him it certainly slumbered through the weak years of Lord Amherst, the peace-loving time of Lord W. Bentinck—though even he was forced to fight and take Coorg—and the humiliating incompetence of Lord Auckland. But Lord Ellenborough and Lord Hardinge were different men, and it was given to Lord Dalhousie to put the keystone in the arch by establishing the supremacy of the Crown of Great Britain from the Himalayas to the two seas. The work was done when even the shadow of Moghul royalty was removed, and the campaigns of 1858 established our power on a firm basis. The sixth period of British Indian history, which Lord Canning introduced, is still evolving itself.

When Lord Lytton began, unhappily, to reverse the policy of his immediate predecessors since the foolish George, Earl of Auckland, Aitchison was in Edinburgh enjoying the first long furlough he had had. Like Lord Lawrence, the Duke of Argyll, Lord Hobhouse, and the statesmen of all parties, except a small and extreme Conservative knot, he watched with dismay the succession of disastrous events which culminated in the Second Afghan War. The Viceroy, knowing the value of his experience and counsel, kept him nevertheless fully informed of the change of policy, and invited his frank criticism in private or demi-official letters. On his return to duty Aitchison was pressed by Lord Lytton to accept the promotion he had refused at the hands of his friend Lord Northbrook, and in 1878 he became Chief Commissioner of British Burma.

The climate daily injured one accustomed to the dry heat of Northern India, but for more than two years he made his mark upon the Province. The two great moral questions underlying its administration, of the purity of its officials in relation to the women of the country, and the preservation of the Burmans from the temptations of the opium excise, he dealt with on both their personal and economic sides, as Lord Dalhousie and Sir William Muir had ineffectually attempted before him.

After acting as a member of the Governor-General's Council, the hot season of 1882 saw him called to be ruler of the greatest, in a military and political sense, of the twelve Provinces of India, as Sir Charles Aitchison, K.C.S.I., Lieutenant-Governor of the Punjab and its dependencies.

From April 1882 for the next five years he proved himself, as the head of his old and loved Province, a king of men, ruling the twenty-six millions of Sikhs and Mohammedans, from Delhi to Quetta, and from Umballa to Kashmir and Gilgit, with a sympathetic knowledge and thoughtfulness which endeared him to them all. He induced the Central Government and Legislature to found, by charter, the Punjab University, that he might carry out the wise experiment, first suggested by Sir Donald M'Leod, of attaching to our rule the learned and often disloyal leaders of the Hindus and Mohammedans, by teaching Western truth through the classical Oriental languages.

Alternating between Lahore and Simla, the two capitals, and spending the delightful cold season in tours along the frontier or through the districts and feudatory States, the already experienced Lieutenant-Governor made his influence felt for the highest ends in every portion of his great dominion.

The Punjab was administered as it had not been since John Lawrence laid down the office, and Henry Durand fell at the post of duty, because it was ruled by a man of the same high Christian character and force, who had the same regard for the rights of the people in all questions of land, taxation, education, and municipal self-government. As President of the Public Service Commission, he reorganised and reformed the Civil Service of India in its various branches, adding this to the burden of his duties as Lieutenant-Governor. He was the last virtual commander of the notable Punjab Frontier Force, the officers and men of which learned to love and admire him for his vigour and fairness, and for the fine condition in which he passed over the pluckiest little army in the world to Lord Roberts. The new Governor and Lady Aitchison, in their personal capacity, set themselves to the encouragement of all missionary and philanthropic enterprises, in the spirit of the Proclamation of the Queen-Empress, and after Her Majesty's example in the relief of the suffering women of the zananas of the villages. Men like the late Dr. Forman, the noblest missionary the United States of America have sent to North India; Dr. Valpy French, the first Bishop of

Lahore, whose *Life* is full of the good deeds and influence of Aitchison; Dr. Youngson of the Scots Mission at Sialkot; Rowland Bateman of the Church Missionary Society, and women like the late Miss Tucker (A.L.O.E.) of Batala, found in the Lord Sahib or Chief of the Province not only kindly sympathy and help, but a new impulse.

When Sir Charles Aitchison returned home at the close of his Lieutenant-Governorship he would fain have rested, at last, among his own people. But his friend Lord Dufferin prevailed on him to return to his side as a colleague in Council, and so to complete his work for Burma after the conquest of the territory of Ava. He loyally consented, but, in doing so, developed the beginning of the disease which was to make him a sufferer for the rest of his life, and prematurely to cut short his days. It was when the most prominent member of the Government of India—next to the Viceroy himself—that at Simla, on the 12th of June 1888, he made his remarkable speech at a meeting held to interest the European residents in the work of the Church Missionary Society. Lady Dufferin, Lady Roberts, and Lady Lyall were present. After Bishop French had summed up his own address in this saying of a great French bishop when visiting Rome, "When one has seen the catacombs, one understands the great explosion of Christianity under Constantine—the city had been conquered underground," and had added, "That is exactly in a figure what is taking place in India now," the Hon. Sir Charles Aitchison began in these remarkable words:—

"I assume that I am speaking to Christian people—to men and women who really believe that, as our blessed Lord came in the body of His humiliation to redeem the world, so He will surely come again in triumph to reign over His purchased possession; and that all work done here—yours and mine, as well as that of His missionary servants; ay, and the work too of His enemies who scoff and blaspheme the sacred Name—is but the preparation of His kingdom. Those to whom this precious hope is as the marrow of their spiritual life are never disheartened by the slow progress of Missions, or disturbed by the sneers of those who say, 'Where is the promise of His coming?' They remember the weary ages through which the world had to wait for the fulfilment of the promise made to the fathers; but it came all in due time. And so now they are content to tarry the Lord's leisure, to work and wait, rejoicing in every visible sign of progress, but not cast down even when there is no sign, knowing that the Lord is not slack concerning His promise, as some men count slackness."

Then, after remarking that it was the best and most distinguished administrators of the Punjab who had been foremost in the encouragement of Missions, he thus closed:—

"The British dominions have reached their natural boundaries of sea and mountain. But the kingdom of our Lord and of His Christ knows no limit in space or in time. Wherever there is a human soul to be found, however debased and degraded—nay, just because it is debased and degraded—there must His kingdom be set up. His rule is destined to be universal, because it is the only rule of righteousness and peace. Allegiance to Him can alone bring peace to the consciences of men. The sin, one single stain of which cannot be washed away by all the blood of victims ever slain on Jewish or on heathen altars, He has atoned for and forgives; the salvation that no penances, or pilgrimages, or self-tortures can procure, He freely bestows as an unmerited gift; the holiness that no human effort can attain unto, He graciously implants; the wills that are perverse and defiant, He gently bends and turns by His love. This is the faith, not for India only, but for the whole race of sinful and suffering humanity. This is the faith that creates not only pure and gentle souls, but heroic, such as we see in noble men and still nobler women, who, for love of Him, forsake the delights of home, and labour, year in year out, through the depression of the rains and the heat of tropical summer, to extend the knowledge of His Name; little appreciated, often misjudged, yet content to live and labour, and to die, if but the frontier of His kingdom be enlarged."

A bold, a magnificent testimony from an official whose life it expressed. He possessed the qualities which go to the making of a successful and righteous statesman, and all these were directed by daily communion with God. Living and dying, he was the Lord's, but with a reverence, a reticence, a modesty, a humility, which concealed his inner life from all but his immediate associates, save when duty to his own conscience and to his Master led him to declare his convictions. His intellectual force, trained by his mother, his church, and his teachers, gave him a rapid grasp of the facts of every case. His wise and cautious but not slow judgment seemed almost an instinct, and not the result merely of experience. His kindly charity made him more impartial, as virtually a judge in personal questions and great affairs of State affecting the peace of the Empire and the prosperity of Provinces, than if he had been rigidly stern, or always indignant—as he was when merely a spectator of the Second Afghan War. As Foreign Secretary for years, he had much writing of "Notes" and despatches, much compiling of historical annals and documents in many Oriental languages. He wrote slowly, but with a lucidity of style and a weight of authority which never failed to convince his associates and even his opponents. He spoke in public with no less deliberateness, but every speech became the last word on the subject.

How he grappled to himself the friends whom he loved from youth, and whom he made in his long and varied career, by the intensity of his affection and the generosity of his attitude towards them, not a few survive to testify. Nor are these sorrowing friends all of his own people and faith. His long illness and death carried mourning into more than one Sikh Maharaja's castle and Musalman Nawab's palace. Many were the natives of India, plain men as well as hereditary nobles, who consulted him when troubled in conscience, whom his life attracted to higher ideals, and whom he led to become daily students of the teaching of Jesus Christ.

Sir Charles Aitchison finally retired and took up his residence in London at the beginning of 1889. The University of Edinburgh had long before enriched its list of honorary graduates by adding his name as LL.D. Oxford welcomed him with a degree which opened to him all the privileges of the University, when he removed to its suburbs, suffering from the disease to which, after five years of intermittent agony, he succumbed. Nevertheless, he gave all his strength to work for the poor and for Christian missions, in public speeches and committees and in private benevolence. He was constant in his attendance as a director of the Church Missionary Society. For the Baptist and other Societies he more than once spoke in public with the catholicity which the missionary cause ever gives. What he did as President of the Church of England Zenana Missionary Society, the minutes tell us when his last illness compelled him to lay down the office: "It is impossible to express adequately what the Society owes, under God, to his Christian statesmanship, his sound judgment, and his ripe experience in dealing with many delicate problems, and to his advocacy through the Press and on the platform of the cause of India's women."

The lingering death of the strong man was, like his life, a Christ-like lesson. His written farewell to his elder brother was in these words: "I realise now more than ever that the Bible promises are all true, and bring perfect peace whether I live or die." "You must all pray for me," he said, while unconsciousness approached, "as I am too weak to do so for myself." Then this to his wife: "I thought I saw His beautiful face. It was a face of great beauty, and He seemed to say to me, 'If you have ever wandered, you are now at My feet, and you will stay there.' Read me the Psalm about the beauty of holiness" (Psalm xcvi.). Gently at daybreak his spirit was breathed away. It was the 18th February 1896. An Iona cross of Carrara marble rises high above the spot, in the Oxford cemetery at Wolvercote, where his body was laid by his son, his son-in-law, and old Indian friends. Of him, as of his Covenanter mother's death eighteen years before, we may best use his own words: "I would wait for the time when we shall go to her. A triumphant vision of the blessed life beyond scatters all earth-born clouds and doubts. While the eye is blinded with tears I am filled with comfort, and I am exceeding joyful in all our tribulation."

Lord Northbrook visited his old colleague and friend not long before the end. He died as he had lived, a Covenanter of the modern type, pure and upright, loving and gentle, doing good to all men and especially to the people of India, for whom he had spent his days. Adding the evangelical graces to all that has made that other Scot, Mountstuart Elphinstone, a unique personality in the history of British India, Charles Aitchison will long be remembered as in the front rank of the Christian statesmen who have won and then saved our Eastern Empire.

Sir Charles Aitchison's last writing was a remarkable monograph on Lord Lawrence.[1] Especially did he support the two vital policies of fair land revenue assessments based on political as well as economic considerations, and the Russo-Afghan peace. He keenly resented an attempt made, after his retirement, to screw up the periodical settlement of districts like Sialkot, where almost every family of peasant proprietors has given a son to our Sepoy army. His letters to me on the subject are full of political wisdom and administrative experience. John Lawrence's policy, as followed by Lord Mayo, whom he was near on his assassination in the Andaman Islands, he summarised in these three main principles—(1) by frank explanations with Russia to come to a common understanding as to Central Asia, and so to put an end to the intrigues and fancies begotten of ignorance on both sides; (2) to define the boundaries of the States intervening between Russia and India, and to strengthen their internal government so as to enable them to maintain their independence; (3) by the development of trade and commerce to bind those States to each other and to the British Government, by a common interest in the preservation of peace.

Of the TWELVE, as of many others during the three centuries of the conquest and government of India from Queen Elizabeth to the Queen-Empress Victoria, it must be said, that these are they *Who through faith subdued kingdoms, wrought righteousness.*

[1] In Sir W. W. Hunter's *Rulers of India:* Oxford, Clarendon Press, 1892.

APPENDIX

SHOULD THE GOVERNMENT OF INDIA HAVE AN OFFICIAL NEWSPAPER?

SIR HENRY S. MAINE TO DR. GEORGE SMITH

"CALCUTTA, 16*th March* 1868.

"MY DEAR MR. SMITH—You will no doubt recollect the conversation which I had with you at Simla in the autumn of 1866 on the subject of possible future relations between the Government and the *Friend of India*. As you did not renew our conversation, I inferred that you did not think anything could be done in the direction indicated; and I should not now recur to the subject if new facts and circumstances were not presenting themselves.

"I regard it now as all but certain that the Government of India will before long establish direct relations with the Indian Press. It is no longer a question of feeling; it is now one of power. We are beginning more and more to be conscious of the reflex action of Indian opinion, which is mainly formed by the newspapers, which penetrates to England in a variety of ways, which thus leavens or creates English opinion about India, and so becomes a real power with which we have to count. Even more serious is the direct influence of the European Press in India on the now enormous Native Press. Where the native newspapers do not perceive that native interest points the other way (which they constantly fail to do), they merely echo European cries, which, in the vast majority of cases, are liker calumnies on, or misrepresentations of, the policy of the Government.

"It is unnecessary to describe to you the condition of the European Press in Bengal and Upper India, one newspaper, two at most, being excepted. We always knew that it was careless, shallow, and scandalous. We now know all but for certain that it is corrupt. It is not very uncharitable to speak of it as constantly subsidised by one or other of the numerous persons who are conspiring against the Indian Exchequer.

"It would be very unjust not to make an express exception of the *Friend of India.* It is much abler than its contemporaries, and has a very much higher sense of its duty. But, to speak frankly, I do not think it cares to sacrifice or jeopardise its circulation by supporting the Government in a measure which, for the moment, is decidedly unpopular; and it is only justice to its proprietary that it should be reluctant to do so. Yet that the Government does require support, even in that contingency, is plain; and that it is entitled to have it, is an inference from the fact that opinion in India constantly veers right round to the Government side after a month or two of clamour, though not soon enough to undo or prevent the collateral mischief which is caused by the temporary discredit of the Government.

"You know that I have always doubted the expediency of founding a wholly new organ of Government. Yet if a less extreme measure is not practicable, I believe that a new organ will be founded.

"I must ask you, therefore, to reconsider the subject of our Simla conversation, and to mention it to any whom it may concern, of course in strict confidence. You will, doubtless, be careful to recollect the assurances and explanations which I gave you at the time, and which made it clear to you, I think, that nothing was intended which implied disrespect on the part of the person making the proposal, or which would lead to dishonourable conduct on the part of the person to whom the proposal was made.

"The English Government does not subsidise newspapers, because it is ordinarily the representative of a party which pays for their support by subscribing to them and taking them in. The Government of India, though constantly maintaining against attack the interests of millions upon millions, has no such newspaper-buying party at its back; on the other hand, the party opposed to it is getting to consist less and less of mere grumblers, or of persons who honestly entertain non-governmental theories. It is coming more and more to consist of persons who seek to obtain pecuniary advantages at the cost of other classes, or of the public Treasury. Under such circumstances, it seems to me equally right and natural that the Government of India should seek to create a real and essential, and not a merely apparent and nominal, analogy between itself and the English Government.

"Perhaps you will acknowledge the safe receipt of this, even if you defer your reply till you return.—Very sincerely yours, H. S. MAINE."

The proposal was necessarily submitted to the joint proprietor of the *Friend of India*, Meredith Townsend, Esq., of the *Spectator*, by Dr. Smith when on a visit to Great Britain. The result was the following reply:—

DR. GEORGE SMITH TO SIR HENRY S. MAINE

"SERAMPORE, *4th December* 1868.

"MY DEAR MR. MAINE—You have asked my opinion on the subject of the propriety of the Government establishing a *Moniteur*, or of entering into such relations with an existing newspaper as would result in the same thing. The danger and uselessness to Government of *secretly* subsidising a newspaper are so evident as not to be worth discussion. Such a transaction would be dishonourable alike to Government and to the Journal; the fact could not be concealed in the long run; the support of a paper pretending to be independent but known to be paid would not be worth having; bitter opposition to Government would be created in the case of every other journal. Moreover, the experiment has been tried all over Europe and has failed everywhere. I will confine my remarks, therefore, to the question of an acknowledged official paper.

"This question has cropped up several times, always to meet with the same fate after discussion. Mr. Marshman tells me that he was consulted on the subject in Lord Auckland's time. It was that Governor-General's opinion, as well as that of Messrs. Mangles and Halliday, that the project was inadmissible. Lord Auckland remarked that it would be more prudent to give any journal disposed to deal fairly with the Government the information which was necessary to keep it in the right path. With a knowledge of the history of the Journal which I have edited now for ten years, and of Journalism and the position of Government in India generally, I would adopt that opinion. In addition to such a relation, honourable to both, Government ought further to act on a suggestion made, or reiterated, by yourself in the Bengal Blue-book—that whenever the Governor-General may see fit, questions on Executive subjects may be put in the Legislative Council. If this were done, and if a better use were made of the Official Supplement to the *Gazette*, by publishing more official papers and occasional narratives of events and summaries of reasons for the policy of Government, every object at which a *Moniteur* is supposed to aim would be secured without creating greater dangers to Government.

"I use the word 'danger' advisedly. Whose policy is the *Moniteur* to express or defend? The Government of India, in its widest sense, consists of the Secretary of State in Council, the Governor-General in Council, Governors in Council, and Lieutenant-Governors without Councils. Especially since the Mysore Grant, published Blue-books and the proceedings of the Legislatures show that each of these bodies is occasionally, or in some cases frequently, not only in collision with the others, but at variance within itself. It is not for the public good that there should be no such difference of opinion. As a rule, we in India believe that, in disputed questions, the Governor-General is right and the Secretary of State wrong, and it seems to me to be one of the highest duties of the Governor-General to resist up to a certain point that encroachment of the Secretary of State on His Excellency's functions which Sir John Lawrence lately deprecated. The Governor-General does not always agree with his own Executive Council. Still less does the Government of India agree with Governments which behaved so scandalously as that of Bombay used to do during the mania, and that of Madras did before Sir C. Trevelyan was recalled. So with the Lieutenant-Governors. Take Bengal in the tea question, where the whole local community thought it in the right. Take the Punjab in the land question. Take the North-West in the days of Sir G. Edmonstone and Lord Canning. If the Government of India is to have a *Moniteur* it can hardly prevent the local Governments from establishing similar organs; or if it does, the officials will fight more effectually in the ordinary papers. The same remark is true of the relation of the

Government of India to the Secretary of State, and of the Governor-General to the colleagues who may differ from His Excellency. It would be impossible to avoid scandals under a system the tendency of which is to create them, as well as to drag those which are inevitable into the light of day for the public amusement or derision.

"I need only hint at the effect of a *Moniteur* on the mass of officials. In a country and under a Government where so many questions are personal, or are bound up with the exercise of patronage, there must be frequent heartburnings and many complications. Much better would it be to let the present state of things continue under which all these find vent in a natural way, and to encourage officials to write much more than they do in support of those measures of which they approve. It is my experience that the severest and the most valuable critics of Government are frequently its own servants or members.

"What would be the influence on the natives, even in a modified form? Where would be our prestige? In a crisis like that of 'Fifty-seven a *Moniteur* would not do half so effectually that which was done by the English Press. In ordinary times the utterances of a *Moniteur* would be subject to suspicion and misunderstanding. Natives would search for hidden meanings where none existed, and draw deductions the opposite of those intended.

"What would be the effect on the existing Press? All support of Government is valuable only in so far as it is honest and known by the public to be independent. Except in one or two cases—and even with them the tendency to be hostile would be irresistible—Government would not only in ordinary times, but in days of difficulty, convert the whole Press into an 'opposition' ever on the watch for mistakes, and the best Government as well as the best Editor in the world frequently makes mistakes.

Nor is this only a question of newspapers. Government would alienate the whole independent opinion of the country, whether official or non-official, or cause it to suspect policies and acts which otherwise would seem both intelligible and satisfactory.

"Nor is the difficulty only one as to what the *Moniteur* published. There are many subjects, and there are stages in the course of all subjects, of which it is true that public discussion would be premature. The silence of the *Moniteur* would in such cases ultimately be more misunderstood and misrepresented than its utterances.

"Finally, there is a practical question. Where is Government to get an editor or editors? If it knew one-tenth of the difficulty experienced by ordinary Indian Journals in this respect it would hesitate. The *Moniteur* must be perfect in all its arrangements, if it is not to prove a weakness. An official editor, if he is to be worth anything, must have a conscience like his independent brother, and the changes among officials in ordinary cases, no less than in the policies of successive Administrations and Governor-Generals, are only too frequent.

"Let me repeat my solution of the question which you proposed to me—such a relation between Government and a Journal as Lord Auckland described, for the more delicate questions or for questions at a delicate stage; such a change in the law as will empower the Governor-General to permit questions to be put in the Legislature on Executive subjects —this Mr. Wilson did frequently, I may remark; and a very considerable improvement in the official supplement to the *Gazette*.—Yours very truly, GEORGE SMITH."

INDEX

THE END